# Ocracokers

Alton Ballance

# Ocracokers

*To Tom & Susan —*

*I hope this will add to your appreciation of Ocracoke.*

*Alton Balla[nce]*

The University of North Carolina Press    Chapel Hill & London

Copyright © 1989 The University of North Carolina Press
All rights reserved

Library of Congress Cataloging-in-Publication Data
Ballance, Alton.
    Ocracokers / Alton Ballance.
        p.   cm.
    Includes index.
    ISBN 0-8078-1878-X (alk. paper). — ISBN 0-8078-4265-6 (pbk.:
alk. paper)
    1. Ocracoke Island (N.C.)—History. 2. Ocracoke Island (N.C.)—
Social life and customs. I. Title.
F262.H9B35   1989
975.6'184—dc20                                                        89-4886
                                                                          CIP

The paper in this book meets the guidelines for permanence
and durability of the Committee on Production Guidelines
for Book Longevity of the Council on Library Resources.

Manufactured in the United States of America
93  92  91  90  89     5  4  3  2  1

Design by April Leidig-Higgins

To the Ocracokers

especially two of them,

Lawrence and Vera Ballance,

whose love and support

over the years have

made this work possible

# Contents

# Preface

I grew up on Ocracoke during the 1960s and 1970s. My mother and father, Vera and Lawrence Ballance, were both born and raised on the island. Their parents were also born and raised here and spent their entire lives here. Like many other Ocracokers, I can also trace my ancestors on both sides of my family back to some of the island's first settlers.

In this book I won't try to explain the complex network of my genealogy. I generally accept the explanation my mother sometimes gives when there's any discussion about what side of the family this or that trait came from. "You've got some of the Williams, a little of the Gaskins, some of the Spencers, some of the Ballances, and a whole lot more."

This book is about Ocracoke and Ocracokers, past and present, and how both have adapted to the changes that have taken place within the last few years. I began writing it in the late 1970s when I was a student at the University of North Carolina at Chapel Hill. Although I've had many stops and starts which corresponded to other happenings in my life, the biggest challenge was trying to capture the "present" at Ocracoke during the island's most rapid period of change. Since I began work on the book, some people portrayed here have died or no longer do the things described. This difference doesn't bother me too much because the book is really about the past, about the people and events that have made Ocracoke what it is today. For all that might happen to the island in time to come, it will always have its past—a past full of rich history, some of it alive today.

Ocracoke, over the years, has been and continues to be one of those special places in the hearts and minds of many people who live and visit here. We have been the subject of many magazine and newspaper articles, most of which tout the place as a "unique fishing village by the sea." The more I read of such articles, the more I realized that much of the real story of Ocracoke was being left out. It seemed that most reporters were only scratching the surface in their portrayals of Ocracoke and Ocracokers. Left out were the many stories of ordinary people, their struggles, pain, and joy.

When I began writing, I only had to look next door and recall the many times I had been mullet fishing with Uriah and Sullivan Garrish, as well as remember other incidents from my childhood, for material to present Ocracoke as most Ocracokers know it.

Although our dialect and accent have been the subject of much interest over the last century or so, I won't try to explain them. Maybe our speech does have traces of Elizabethan English, as some historians claim. Other areas, such as isolated communities in the North Carolina mountains, also retain such speech patterns. Any community which has experienced few outside influences is likely to keep the speech of its first settlers.

Ocracoke place names also reveal much about the way Ocracokers have lived their lives for many years. No example is better than the name most Ocracokers give the body of water that cuts into the heart of the village, known to many people as Silver Lake, but known to those of us who use it almost daily as, simply, the Creek. The Creek it has always been and the Creek it will always be. The Creek.

And there are other simple names: Down Point, for the southern section of the village near the lighthouse; Around Creek, for the area along the Creek near the post office; and Down Beach, for the stretch between the village and the Hatteras ferry. Most are so simple that some people, upon hearing them for the first time, have trouble remembering them.

Since little is written here about dialect or accent, you'll have to hear it for yourself; listen and learn, and along the way pick up other fragments of Ocracoke's continuing history.

# Acknowledgments

Many people are to be thanked for all the help they have given me during the ten years I've taken to write *Ocracokers*. In addition to all the Ocracokers themselves, who gladly shared with me their lives and those of their families, I'd especially like to thank Martha Carowan, who kept saying, "You've got to finish it," and who provided needed encouragement and patience during the final months before publication. I'd like to thank David Perry of the UNC Press, who, in addition to being a great editor, taught me more about writing than anyone yet. I owe a special thank you to Mike, Myra, and Jenny Smith of Chapel Hill whose home has always been open to me. Since a major part of my life has involved Ocracoke School, either as a student or teacher, I'd like to recognize its importance by donating every cent I make from this book to the school. Lastly, I wish that Uriah and Sullivan could be here to see what all those great mulleting trips really meant to me.

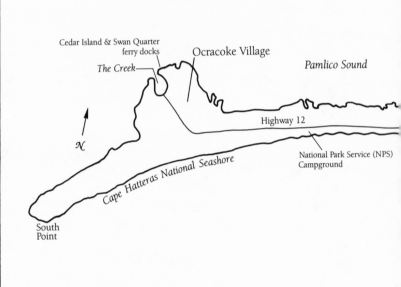

Cedar Island & Swan Quarter
ferry docks

Ocracoke Village

Pamlico Sound

*The Creek*

*N*

Highway 12

*Cape Hatteras National Seashore*

National Park Service (NPS)
Campground

South
Point

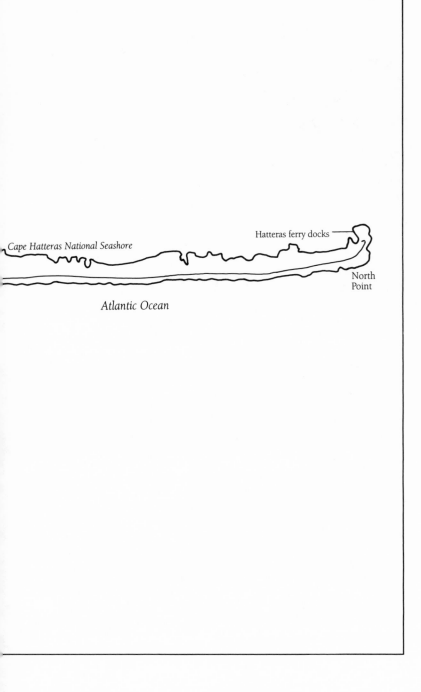

Cape Hatteras National Seashore

Hatteras ferry docks

North
Point

Atlantic Ocean

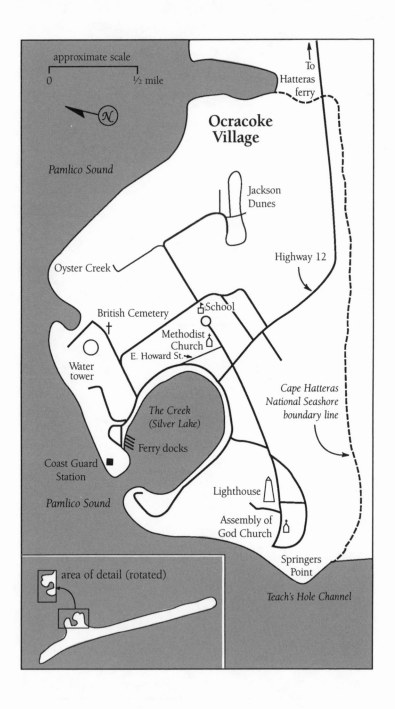

Part One        The Inlet, the Island, the Village

On a cold November afternoon I got in my boat and started for a ride. I wasn't going fishing, oystering, or hunting. I just wanted to be out on the water on such a beautiful afternoon. An old man on shore watched me as I got ready to leave. He wanted to know where I was going so late. I told him I was just going for a ride. As I left the shore, he kept staring at me, hands in his pockets. He stood there until I reached the mouth of the Creek, then he turned around and walked back toward his house.

The wind had been strong most of the week from the northeast, had lost strength throughout the day, and had finally died to a "slick ca'm" by late afternoon. I had about one hour of daylight left. The western sky had already turned a pale orange.

As I cleared the Creek, I scanned the horizon. Several boats were racing toward the village. When I passed them, the men slowed their motors and waved. They had been oystering.

The cold began to sting my face and hands as I increased the speed of the motor. I steered toward Beacon Island, located several miles west of Ocracoke and about one mile north of Portsmouth Island. Strings of cormorants flew swiftly along the waterline, and a large raft of redheads flared up miles away along the northwest horizon. Occasionally a nearby gull would interrupt its gliding and hover above a small disturbance in the water before settling down gently to investigate; then it would rise up, a tiny scrap of something in its beak, and fly off, leaving a radiating pattern of tiny waves on the otherwise smooth and undisturbed water.

My ride would take an egg-shaped course. After reaching Beacon Island, I would turn south into Blair Channel, follow it to Ocracoke Inlet, then take Teach's Hole Channel back to the village. The three main channels that branch from Ocracoke Inlet are Teach's Hole Channel, which runs northeast from the inlet toward Ocracoke Village; Blair Channel, which runs north from the inlet toward the mainland; and Wallace's Channel, which runs northwest from the inlet along Portsmouth Island.

The sun slipped below the horizon as I raced along Blair Channel. Except for the gentle breakers on the sandbars next to Ocracoke beach, the sea was flat and barely rippled in the faint breeze. Several trawlers dotted the eastern horizon. One was entering the inlet, traveling so close to the beach that a sudden turn to the right would send it crashing against the shore. Only a few months earlier the deep water of the inlet had been further to the southwest.

Inlets are in a constant state of change. They react daily to the natural forces of wind, waves, currents, and high-energy storms, all of which move the sands of the barrier islands, opening new inlets and closing others.

Like the inlet, the island itself has been changing for thousands of years. Part of the North Carolina Outer Banks, Ocracoke is one of a chain of islands that form a barrier (hence the name "barrier island") between the Atlantic Ocean and the sounds behind the islands. These barriers, geologists tell us, have been gradually moving toward the North Carolina mainland, while it too erodes.

According to Duke University marine geologist Orrin Pilkey, the geological formation of Ocracoke probably began about 17,000 years ago at the end of the last Ice Age. If an Ocracoke existed then, it was a barrier island approximately twenty-five miles offshore on the edge of the continental shelf, a broad, shallow shelf that extends from the shoreline to deep-sea depths. As the sea level rose, the island migrated landward to its present location.

"Judging from other islands," said Pilkey, "Ocracoke probably got to its present location around three or four thousand years ago. Some of the same sand that once existed when the island was out on the edge of the continental shelf is probably present on the island today."

Pilkey also believes that during its retreat toward the mainland, Ocracoke was not as wide as it is today. "All barrier islands are a product of rising sea level," he explains. "When the island began retreating across the continental shelf, it was a narrow sand island. As sea level rose more slowly, then the island began to widen to something like its present width."

Another marine geologist, East Carolina University's Stan Riggs, also recognizes that the barrier island part of Ocracoke has migrated to its present location. Riggs maintains, however, that Ocracoke Village is an old "chunk" of island, similar to Roanoke Island, that has existed in its present location longer than the barrier island which migrated up to it. When the beach finally reached what is now the village, it "bumped into it" and got "hung up," forming basically the present-day shape of Ocracoke.

This process also explains other features of the Banks. Capes have formed as migrating barrier islands bumped into chunks of old islands. "The Outer Banks town of Rodanthe has just come off Wimble Shoals where it was once hung up. There used to be a place called Cape Rodanthe. This is also being done at Hatteras and it's about to do it at Ocracoke," says Riggs.

Looking at a map of the Outer Banks, you can see evidence of Riggs's theory, especially at Cape Hatteras, where an ancient island is being wrapped by a migrating barrier island. Ocracoke Village, as well, is about to be wrapped by the same process. Riggs further theorizes that as Nags Head migrates toward the mainland, it could one day run into Roanoke Island, and thus another cape will form.

These geological changes have of course taken place over thousands of years, but for a good view of these processes at work, you have only to go to one of the Outer Banks inlets. There, deep channels and low sand islands form overnight, especially after storms, when vast quantities of water move in and out of the inlets. "Ocracoke Inlet is greatly affected by the sound behind it," says Pilkey. "It has a cross-section of water that adjusts to the volume of water that goes in and out. Although there's not much tide on a daily basis, when a storm occurs, even a minor one, then it really serves its function. It would have been very exciting to be at Ocracoke Inlet during Hurricane Gloria. It must have looked like some of the rapids in the Amazon."

According to Outer Banks historian David Stick, Ocracoke Inlet is perhaps the only inlet on the Outer Banks that has been open continuously since the first European explorers visited the North Carolina coast. Like other inlets, however, Ocracoke Inlet has always shifted. Sometimes the deep water is closer to Ocracoke, other times closer to Portsmouth. Moreover, the exact location of Ocracoke Inlet at the time of the first explorations is uncertain. Early maps indicate that Ocracoke may have been connected to Portsmouth Island, and together they formed Wokokon. On other maps Ocracoke appears to be joined to Hatteras Island and is referred to as Croatoan.

Wherever it was located, though, Wokokon Inlet was important in the early settlement of Ocracoke. The first visitors to North Carolina, and later the settlers in the Pamlico and Albemarle Sound area, needed a reliable entrance into the safer sound waters. Ocracoke Inlet and later the island itself were placed on the map for good.

Legend has it that Blackbeard the Pirate gave Ocracoke its name. In the early morning hours before his fatal encounter with Lieutenant Robert Maynard, Blackbeard, anxious for dawn to arrive, was supposed to have looked ashore near Ocracoke Village and bellowed "O Crow Cock! O Crow Cock!"

This makes a good story, but a more likely source for the name is the Indian name "Wokokon," which itself is thought to be a misspelling of "Woccon," a tribe that once lived near the Neuse River. The Woccons occasionally traveled to Ocracoke, but none actually settled on the Outer Banks. Like other coastal mainland tribes, the Woccons came to the Outer Banks to feast on seafood. The feasts usually took place during the warm months when a canoe trip along the Outer Banks was smoother and fish were more plentiful.

The Indians used crude nets and weirs to catch large quantities of fish, while smaller catches were made by spearing or clubbing the fish in shallow water. Spears were made of wood and often tipped with stingray stings or horseshoe crab tails.

Early colonists John Lawson and Thomas Harriot described the Indians and their fishing techniques. Harriot observed that the Indians fished with poles sharpened at one end, "shooting the poles into the fish after the manner as Irishmen cast darts, either as they are rowing in their boats or else as they are wading in the shallows for the purpose." Lawson wrote that the "youth and Indian boys go in the night, and one holding a light wood torch, the other has a bow and arrows, and the fire directing him to see the fish, he shoots them with the arrows; and thus they kill a great many of the smaller fry, and sometimes pretty large ones." Flounder and other fish are still speared today by similar methods.

Another possible theory for the origin of the word Wokokon comes from Professor James A. Geary. According to Geary, the word seems to derive from such Indian words as "waxkahikani," which means "enclosed place," "fort," or "stockade," or "wahkahikani," "wakahigan," and "waskahigan," which refer to "stronghold." If this theory is correct, then such a structure may once have stood on Ocracoke, suggesting at least a temporary Indian settlement.

The Hatteras Indians were the only tribe that lived permanently on the Outer Banks. Their villages were located in high wooded areas near Buxton on Hatteras Island, approximately twenty-five miles northeast of Ocracoke. Since several thickly wooded hammocks also existed on Ocracoke, Indians may have settled here for short periods. Unfortunately, very little evidence is available to support this connection.

One of the first European explorers to write about the North Carolina coast was Giovanni da Verrazano, an Italian navigator in the

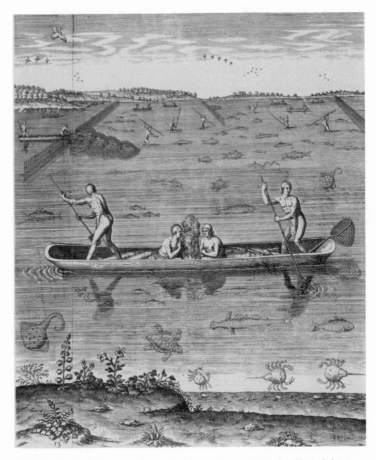

*Theodor de Bry engraving from a John White drawing of Indians fishing on the Outer Banks.*

service of the French. After exploring briefly the Cape Fear area in the spring of 1524, his expedition departed and sailed east, anchoring at a place further up the coast. Some historians think Verrazano was anchored in the Raleigh Bay area located between Cape Lookout and Cape Hatteras. If this is true, then Verrazano could well have been anchored off Wokokon. While at this anchorage, they sent a man ashore with "trifles" for the Indians, whom they saw on the beach burning large fires. The man, exhausted from his swim through the surf, was helped to the beach by the Indians.

They carried him by the fire, stripped him of his wet clothes, spread the garments to dry, and gave him some food. From the ship it appeared that the Indians were preparing to roast and eat him. When the man later revived, the Indians provided him with a canoe so he could return to the ship, where he reported the kind treatment he had received.

Not until sixty years later, when the Sir Walter Raleigh expeditions began, would the Outer Banks again gain the attention of Europeans. Ocracoke and the rest of the Outer Banks would play a major role in that story, which would lead to the settling of North America.

But history often evades us. As I raced along Teach's Hole Channel on that cold November afternoon, I tried to imagine what it must have been like to see Blackbeard's ship anchored in the channel, and beyond, in its original pristine state, Ocracoke.

I shifted my gaze from Teach's Hole to Springer's Point, and finally stopped to stare at the soft light atop the Ocracoke Lighthouse. Although most Ocracokers see the lighthouse many times every day, we seldom give it much thought. Yet, the tall, white structure, lighted at night, has towered over Ocracoke since long before any of us came into the world and will probably be there for some time to come. A friend once said, "When you sit right down and think about it, you can't help but be amazed that it's been there so long. It must have been a pretty sight way back when it didn't have a lot of electric lights surrounding it. You notice it a lot more when the power goes off."

Although the lighthouse still serves its original role, it belongs more to the past. Since it was built in 1823, many generations have depended on its steady light: the early sailors who used Ocracoke Inlet as a port of entry; the Navy men who fought in the surrounding waters during the Civil War and World War II; and the fishermen who, even today, work within its fourteen-mile range. The familiar light must have been a reassuring sight on a stormy night at sea, especially for those whose homes were spread on the same land.

As I approached Springer's Point, I swept my eyes along the roof-lines of the village several times. I slowed the motor and stared toward the Coast Guard Station. Something had interrupted my line of sight, something that towered above everything else, including the light-house. Silhouetted faintly against the growing darkness of the eastern sky was the new Ocracoke water tower. If the lighthouse belongs to the past, then the water tower belongs to the future, a future in which more water is needed for the thousands who are now visiting Ocracoke. Most people are now so used to seeing the new tower that they have taken it too for granted. Change is often difficult, but eventually it takes place, is absorbed, and becomes part of the past.

More change has taken place at Ocracoke in the last few decades than at any other time in its history. Even though parts of the old fishing village have made way for motels, restaurants, and shops, there are still remnants of the past: wooden, white-painted boats tied to stakes in the Creek; nets and other fishing gear cluttering front yards; and old people who watch a faster way of life, measuring its worth against days long past. And there are the children of the transition, myself included, who must balance the old ways and the new and go on living in the village beneath the lighthouse and the water tower.

When I reached Springer's Point, I turned off the motor. The boat drifted on, propelled by the last push of the motor and the incoming tide. The water is deep here and the current runs strong. This is Teach's Hole. I held my breath for a few seconds and stared at the lighthouse once again. When my eyes started to water, I allowed my focus to shift to Springer's Point, looming dark and silent before me. A great blue heron glided along the shoreline in front of it, raised itself quickly, and disappeared into the darkness back toward the inlet.

In 1584, sixty years after Verrazano's expedition along the North Carolina coast, Philip Amadas and Arthur Barlowe left England on an expedition outfitted by Sir Walter Raleigh to scout likely locations for colonization. While some historians claim that they entered Pamlico Sound at Wokokon Inlet and then sailed on to Roanoke Island, it seems certain, according to their measurements, that they entered at a place much closer to Roanoke Island known as Port Ferdinando. The glowing report they gave of the North Carolina coast prompted Raleigh to send a second expedition the following year.

In 1585 an expedition of seven vessels and six hundred men—half seamen and half soldiers and specialists—set out on the first attempt to establish an English colony in the New World. Sir Richard Grenville was general of the expedition, Simon Fernando, chief pilot, and Ralph Lane, lieutenant. After probing the North Carolina coast, the expedition arrived at Wokokon Inlet on June 26. Because of Fernando's carelessness, their flagship, the *Tiger*, ran aground in the inlet. Following a struggle to prevent the ship from breaking up, the *Tiger* was finally beached, but most of the provisions aboard were destroyed by salt water. This was a severe blow to the colonists and one of the first recorded shipwrecks on the North Carolina coast.

At the time of Grenville's arrival, Ocracoke was connected to part of Hatteras Island, and together they were known as Croatoan. While at Croatoan, Grenville was reunited with thirty-two men from his expedition whose ships had been scattered weeks before by a severe storm.

After battling the storm, the two ships had continued toward Roanoke Island, stopping at Croatoan to place a small party to wait for Grenville.

A few days later the missing ships returned to Croatoan. The *Tiger* was eventually caulked and refloated, and the entire expedition left Croatoan on July 11 to explore the mainland shores of Pamlico Sound.

Grenville soon returned to England, leaving Lane in charge of the expedition at Roanoke Island. Lane himself later returned to England, and in his report denounced the area, especially Wokokon Inlet, for being so treacherous and lacking reliable harbors.

After the failure of John White's colonists in 1587 to establish the first permanent English colony in the New World at Roanoke Island, known since as the Lost Colony because of its mysterious disappearance, England slowed in its attempts at settlement until the Jamestown colony in 1607. Very few, if any, people lived at Ocracoke during the time of the Jamestown settlement. Not until the early 1700s, when the North Carolina colonial assembly passed an act for the placing of pilots at Ocracoke, did people begin to settle on the island. But settlement was slow; most settlers preferred inland areas along the coastal plain. Besides, in the early 1700s Ocracoke had a reputation as a pirate hangout. It was the favorite spot of at least one pirate—Blackbeard.

Blackbeard's real name was Edward Teach (some records indicate Edward Drummond). While he is historically associated with Ocracoke, he actually spent little time here. He grew up in Bristol, England, served on ships of privateers, and, while operating out of the Bahama Islands in 1716, formed a friendship with Captain Benjamin Hornigold, a pirate of sizable reputation. Soon Hornigold allowed Blackbeard to take command of his own ship. Later Blackbeard acquired a larger French ship, piratically taken, and renamed it the *Queen Anne's Revenge*. He mounted forty guns on the ship and manned her with a crew of three hundred men.

Blackbeard eventually began to spend more time along the North Carolina coast, not only at Ocracoke but also Bath, on the North Carolina mainland. After wrecking the *Queen Anne's Revenge* at Beaufort Inlet and loading the cargo on another ship, the *Adventure*, Blackbeard sailed to Bath to receive a pardon issued by King George I. The pardon had been offered to pirates if they surrendered before a certain date.

Blackbeard was apparently well received in the homes of the wealthy as well as colonial government officials. He became friends with North Carolina Governor Charles Eden, from whom he had received his pardon, as well as such officials as Tobias Knight, who served as council member, secretary of the colony, collector of customs, and chief justice.

Although for a time Blackbeard appeared to settle in Bath, he soon returned to the high seas and the life of a pirate. On a trip to Bermuda, he and his crew captured a French merchant ship laden with sugar and cocoa. The ship and cargo were taken back to North Carolina, where Blackbeard reported to Governor Eden that he had found the ship out on the open sea and salvaged it. Some of the cargo, as was the custom of the time, was given to Governor Eden and Tobias Knight. Blackbeard later burned the ship, fearing, perhaps, its being recognized.

Shortly before Blackbeard's fatal battle with Lieutenant Robert Maynard, a group of other pirates joined him at Ocracoke for a feast and a short period of relaxation. Blackbeard probably anchored his ships in Teach's Hole Channel, coming ashore at a high, thickly wooded area of the island known today as Springer's Point. No evidence exists to support the belief that he had houses or other structures at Ocracoke or that he might have used other sections of the island. One old Ocracoke resident said that he once heard his father talk about a possible Blackbeard anchorage in a small cove northeast of Ocracoke Village. According to the story, which has been passed down from generation to generation, Blackbeard used to enter Pamlico Sound through an inlet just north of the Ocracoke Airstrip. Old maps indicate that an inlet once cut through this part of the island, even though it was not open very long (such temporary inlets existed all along the Outer Banks). The soundside location is still called Nigh Inlet, adding further credence to the story.

Blackbeard was supposed to have taken his ship through this inlet and hidden it in a small cove known locally as the Bay, which was more sheltered during the pirate's time. Poplar trees grew profusely around it, and, as the story goes, he often cut these trees and used them as a cover to conceal his ship. Two features of the Bay also existed that provided added security, both of which have since been claimed by erosion. One of these was a small peninsula located at the northernmost point of the village. At the end of this peninsula was a large hill called Mayo's Hill. Approximately one-quarter of a mile to the east were two hammocks called Negro Hammocks, so named because a black man was supposed to have been hanged there. Although these names were probably not in existence then, Blackbeard may well have taken advantage of the snug harbor between these two land features, especially if an inlet deep enough to accommodate his ship was close by. The North Carolina coast offered many such harborages, and pirates, of course, would be the most familiar with them.

Another reason that Blackbeard spent so much time in North Carolina was that the area was not a royal colony and the laws were not as strictly enforced as in Virginia, a royal colony to the north. News of Blackbeard's continued presence at Ocracoke, as well as of the other pirates on retreat, soon reached Governor Spotswood of Virginia. Spotswood considered the gathering of pirates a serious threat to trade and travel and began planning the capture of the leader, Blackbeard.

In the middle of November 1718 two sloops commanded by Lieutenant Robert Maynard arrived at Ocracoke Inlet. At dawn on the morning of November 22, Maynard weighed anchor and headed for Teach's Hole Channel, where he found Blackbeard and the *Adventure* with a smaller than usual crew. Maynard had twice the men.

In the battle that followed, many of Maynard's men were killed or injured. Finally, Blackbeard himself, after taking many gunshot wounds and cuts, was killed. He was beheaded and the corpse thrown overboard. The surviving members of his crew were taken to Virginia, with the head of Blackbeard hanging from the bowsprit.

According to legend, Blackbeard was so strong that when his body was thrown overboard it swam around the boat several times before it sank. Legend also has it that his ghost still wanders along the North Carolina coast looking for its head. But Ocracokers generally haven't taken much interest in Blackbeard. One old woman told me, "I don't believe all that mess about Blackbeard." Another man said, "Why do you reckon people want to build up somebody like him, somebody who robbed and killed. Been anybody decent and he'd be forgotten by now."

Three years before Blackbeard's death, the colonial assembly, recognizing the need to improve trade and navigation along the North Carolina coast, passed an act for "settling and maintaining Pilots at Roanoke and Ocacock Inlett." The act called for locating at least one pilot and two assistants at Ocracoke. The pilot's responsibility was to see that all vessels entering the inlet reached the deeper sound waters safely. He was required to keep a good boat capable of getting through rough water, and if he could not reach a ship requiring piloting, he was to provide proper signals so the captain of the ship could find the channel for himself. The pilot was to be paid a certain fee for his services. If he failed to respond when called on, he would be suspended. If he were responsible for any misfortune befalling a ship, he would be liable for all damages.

Although the act was passed and the need for establishing pilots was urgent, it was not until the 1730s that pilots actually began settling on Ocracoke. Traffic through the inlet, especially after the death of Blackbeard in 1718, continued even before the pilots began to settle there. Much of the traffic was smuggling. The nearest collection district for duties was in Bath, some thirty miles across Pamlico

Sound. Ships often unloaded most of their cargo at Ocracoke before going across the sound to pay the import duties. The off-loaded cargo, meanwhile, was transferred onto smaller vessels that proceeded directly to various ports along the sound and rivers.

One documented instance of smuggling involved a ship loaded with French wines, brandy, tea, woolens, and other dutiable commodities which entered Ocracoke Inlet and transferred its cargo to smaller ships, which in turn delivered it to merchants in Virginia, thereby avoiding the duty in that colony. New England skippers were the main smugglers, exporting North Carolina tobacco without paying duty and charging North Carolina and Virginia traders unreasonable rates for British commodities shipped conveniently to their more accessible ports.

North Carolina Governor George Burrington (1724–25, 1731–34) was well aware of the loss to the colony from such practices. In July 1736 he urged the home government in England to establish a customs house at Ocracoke, a location which appeared to have many advantages. Besides two reliable channels, Burrington identified a harbor at the south end of the island where ships could be careened and plenty of wood and fresh water were available. He also described a high spot of land where a suitable fort could be built to protect shipping within the inlet. Burrington added that "Ocacock Island is an airy and healthy place abounding with excellent Fish and wild Fowl," and he predicted that if a port were established, "a Town will soon be built which will become in a little time a place of great commerce." He also speculated that large numbers of Negroes could be brought directly from Guiana to North Carolina, thereby avoiding the duties charged by Virginia and South Carolina, where they were usually bought.

Governor Burrington's attempts to encourage trade through Ocracoke Inlet and to set up a port there resulted in little action at first. Not until the Spanish started plundering around Ocracoke Inlet was serious consideration given to the matter. The Spanish had arrived on the North Carolina coast in 1741 during the War of Jenkins's Ear and again in 1747 (with minor attacks within this span of time) from St. Augustine, Florida, with several small sloops and barcalonjos full of armed men, mostly mulattoes and Negroes. During the 1741 action, they landed on Ocracoke, erected a small tent town, slaughtered numbers of hogs and cattle, killed several inhabitants, and monitored the movements of ships near Ocracoke Inlet, plundering them whenever possible.

Angered by the actions of the Spanish and the threat of continued attacks, the people of coastal North Carolina demanded greater protection. Several forts were proposed for the area, including a large one at Ocracoke Inlet to be called Fort Granville. Construction of this fort began several years later in 1756, and a town was begun at the same time on Portsmouth Island.

An event in late August 1750 furthered the establishment of the fort and town at Portsmouth. A 500-ton Spanish ship called the *Nuestra Senora de Guadalupe*, after losing her masts and rudders during a storm in the Gulf Stream, was forced into Ocracoke Inlet. She carried a valuable cargo worth one million pieces of eight and an additional four hundred thousand pieces of eight in coin money. The commander of the *Nuestra Senora de Guadalupe*, Don Juan Manuel de Bonilla, failed to report his circumstances to the governor of North Carolina, thereby endangering the ship and crew.

The people of Ocracoke, referred to at this time as "Bankers: being a people so called from their inhabiting near the banks of the seashoar," were prepared to plunder the ship, thinking their actions a just reward for the losses and injuries recently received from the Spanish. The Spaniards remained on Ocracoke for almost forty days before reporting to any official of the province. They traded freely with vessels that passed near Ocracoke Inlet and unloaded and reloaded the ship several times, breaking the Laws of Trade.

Realizing the threat to the Spaniards, and a possible injury to the delicate relations between the two countries, who had only recently been in a state of war, Governor Gabriel Johnston had a member of his council dispatched to investigate the matter. Finding the situation perilous, the council member reported back to the governor immediately. Governor Johnston then sent a British warship to Ocracoke to protect the Spanish ship and crew. Since the Spanish had broken the Laws of Trade, customs officers at Ocracoke claimed that the ship and cargo were seizable. When the governor refused their request, they sought the surveyor general of the customs for the American colonies, who was at that time in Virginia, and he approved their proposal. Governor Johnston had the ship seized, however, and he agreed to Captain Bonilla's request that the *Scorpion*, a British warship, transport the cargo, almost half of which was lost to a mutinous crew, to Europe.

Commerce through Ocracoke Inlet continued to grow. More pilots and their families began to settle in the village, identified on one map as "Pilot Town." In 1766 an act was passed for the setting aside of twenty acres of land "in the most proper part of the island" for the benefit of the pilots of Ocracoke. The land was to be purchased from the proprietor of the island. Up until this act of distribution, Ocracoke had been owned by several inhabitants at different times. The pilots who lived there were mere squatters.

Shortly after the death of Blackbeard, John Lovick had received the island as a grant from the Lords Proprietors. In 1733 Richard Sanderson acquired Ocracoke, which was transferred to his son Richard shortly thereafter. None of these three owners lived on the island, but they allowed livestock to be kept there. With the sale of the island, the livestock was sold as well. The fourth owner, who bought the island from the younger Richard Sanderson in 1759, was William Howard. He lived there until his death in 1795, deeding all of his Ocracoke land to his son, Wallace Howard. In addition to the purchase approved by the assembly, much of the island had been sold by William Howard and his son to various families on the island. Thus began the legal parceling of land that continues today.

Up until 1770, Ocracoke was part of no county, and the people who lived on the island therefore paid no taxes. They were referred to as "lawless bankers." In that year, however, Ocracoke was annexed to

Carteret County, thereby subjecting the inhabitants to the same "Duties, taxes, Impositions, and entitled to the same Privileges, Benefits, and Advantages, as the other Inhabitants of the said County of Carteret." (Ocracoke remained in Carteret County until 1845, when it was moved to Hyde County where it remains today.)

The occupation of piloting developed steadily, and more pilots located on both Ocracoke and Portsmouth. Among these early settlers were a number of Negroes, free men as well as slaves. They evidently realized that the only way to survive in this area was to do what the others did—piloting. This put them in direct competition with the "legal" pilots (pilots who were qualified and held licenses). Soon the Negroes began piloting vessels from Ocracoke Inlet to New Bern, Bath, and Edenton. The legal pilots, many of whom were the first settlers on Ocracoke, sent a petition to Governor Josiah Martin, complaining of the actions of these illegal pilots. Governor Martin supported their petition and the illegal practices slackened.

The Ocracoke pilots played an important role in the American Revolution. Their involvement began in grand style on the afternoon of April 14, 1776. The *Polly*, a schooner loaded with Indian corn and staves, had left Edenton and stopped at Ocracoke Inlet before proceeding on to the island of Madeira off the coast of Africa. At four o'clock on that afternoon, an armed British sloop, the *Lilly*, under the command of John Goodrich and outfitted by the British for the purpose of seizing vessels at and around Ocracoke Inlet, entered the inlet, came up alongside the *Polly*, and ordered her master, Silas Henry, on board. Henry, as well as James Buchanan, half-owner of the vessel, obeyed the command and boarded the *Lilly*, carrying with them the ship's papers. Goodrich informed them that the *Polly* was being seized as a prize.

Later that evening, another British vessel, the *Fincastle*, under the command of Lieutenant John Wright, entered Ocracoke Inlet, came alongside the *Polly*, still anchored inside the inlet but without her master, and seized her for a second time. Armed men from the *Fincastle* went on board the *Polly*, plundered her of all livestock, disarmed the men, and left guards and a prizemaster to guard the ship.

Several days later the *Fincastle* sailed out of Ocracoke Inlet, leaving the *Lilly* and the *Polly* with slim crews. With the *Fincastle* out of the way, the pilots of Ocracoke, armed and in five whale boats, boarded the *Lilly*, took Captain Goodrich and his crew prisoner, and then retook the *Polly*. The *Lilly* and the *Polly* were then taken to New Bern and sold at a public auction. Two-thirds of the proceeds went to the owners and one-third to the captors, the pilots of Ocracoke. Soon after this event, the Ocracokers captured another ship and her cargo and men.

Such efforts by the Ocracoke pilots notwithstanding, the defenseless state of the coast was a matter of concern for colonial authorities. A special committee appointed by the General Assembly to look into this situation observed that the sea coast from the Virginia line to the South Carolina line was totally defenseless. They also pointed out, strategically, that since the estates of people who lived on the Outer Banks consisted of livestock—cattle, sheep, and hogs—and since these open areas were exposed to ravages by vessels, the crews of which would need fresh provisions, it would be in the interest of the American cause to protect the coast. Five independent companies were therefore raised to protect the coast, with one company stationed at Ocracoke Inlet. The captains of the companies were encouraged to seize any enemy ships that ventured near.

Captain James Anderson soon informed the Council of Safety that his company at Ocracoke was formed and ready to meet any opposition. Several armed vessels were also placed in service and took turns guarding Ocracoke Inlet, among these the *King Tammany*, the *General Washington*, and the *Pennsylvania Farmer*. For added protection, two row galleys were later provided by Virginia, which depended on trade through Ocracoke Inlet after its ports were blockaded.

Ocracoke Inlet was well protected throughout the winter of 1776–77, but this state of armament slackened during the early spring. The three armed vessels protecting the inlet were sent to the West Indies, leaving the nearby waters unprotected until the completion of the two row galleys and their placement at Ocracoke in May.

For a while, trade through Ocracoke Inlet was checked by British ships cruising nearby. Further complications arose when the company at Ocracoke was disbanded, their boats sold, and the arms stored away, leaving the area once more practically defenseless. To add to these problems, John Shepard, commander of the *Diamond*, a vessel stranded at Ocracoke, accused "some of the inhabitants at or near Ocracoke" of swindling goods from his ship. He petitioned the General Assembly, and a reward was offered for information leading to the people who "unlawfully possesed themselves of a large quantity of goods."

The British soon began to ignore Ocracoke Inlet, a move which enabled the Americans, in early 1778, to use the inlet as a major route for supplying General George Washington and his army at Valley Forge. Although residing in New York, Josiah Martin, who still claimed to be royal governor of North Carolina, pointed out the importance of Ocracoke Inlet in a letter to Lord Germain in London. He wrote that "the comtemptibel port of Ocracock has become a great channel of supply to the rebels, while the more considerable ports have been watched by the King's ships. They have received through it very considerable importation."

Before the arrival of the two row galleys from Virginia, the British scored a quick victory by taking advantage of Ocracoke's defenseless state. In early April 1778, an English privateer from St. Augustine anchored at the bar in Ocracoke Inlet and waited for the Ocracoke pilots. The pilots recognized the vessel since it had lately been at Ocracoke, but they were unaware of its alliance with the British. The captain of the privateer held the pilots at gunpoint and threatened their lives if they did not pilot the ship over the bar and into the channel, where a French ship and brig were anchored.

After the British ship was brought through the inlet by the pilots, its crew proceeded to plunder the two vessels of their valuable cargo of tobacco and salt, both of which were in great demand, and then sailed out the inlet, taking the two vessels with them. Once again a plea was made to keep a sufficient force at Ocracoke Inlet to protect trade so necessary to the colonies.

A month later the row galley *Caswell*, with 145 men under the command of Captain Willis Wilson, was finally placed at Ocracoke Inlet. This force evidently restrained the British, since Captain Wilson soon reported that the place was "not at all infested with British crusizers." Several cruisers were nearby, according to Wilson, but they were "not disposed to venture in."

Although the British ships were not an immediate threat, the Ocracoke pilots decided to stir up trouble themselves. In a May 20, 1778, letter to Governor Caswell, the first governor of the state of North Carolina, Captain Wilson complained of the problem of acquiring a pilot from Ocracoke to pilot a French ship and brig. "I went ashore to get a pilot to go off to the French ship, but could not prevail on one to go. The officer is still on board, and under the greatest anxiety for his ship, which I fear will be cast away or taken. I have not a pilot to the Cashwell, or I would compel him to go off. This is not the first instance by many of the rascality of those men; every merchantman coming to this place experiences it, and it's clearly evident to me that they wish every vessel cast away, as they may plunder them."

The pilots were actually refusing to provide their services at the low official rates, in an action resembling a modern-day strike. Captain Wilson soon reported this to Governor Caswell. "The Pilots of Ocracoke have finally stopped bringing in or carrying out vessels having entered into an association to that purpose, the reasons they give me for this extraordinary step is, that having no branches, they are liable to a penalty for taking charge of any vessel, and that they will not take branches because the Legislature have rated their pilotage at too low a price, being all in a class. I fear our trade will be hurt by the infamy of these people."

In the meantime the British had once again begun cruising off the North Carolina coast. Captains McFarling, Neale, and Goodrich, in three separate privateers, seized several vessels near Ocracoke Inlet.

To add to the problem, the row galley *Caswell*, which had been so effective in checking the British at the inlet, was soon out of service. According to Thomas Jefferson, the row galley was "sunck at her station, that her bottom is eaten out, and her original Form such that she could not be hove down to be refitted." The *Caswell* had lasted approximately one year. This left Ocracoke Inlet, once again, almost defenseless.

Although the protection of the inlet was left in the hands of the Ocracoke pilots, they were almost drafted for service elsewhere. Adam Gaskil, however, petitioned the North Carolina Council of State, asking that his company of men, mostly pilots, be exempt from military duty. They were needed, he said, on the Outer Banks to prevent attacks from enemy privateers. The council refused to exempt the pilots, but did allow them to remain at Ocracoke to protect trade there, perhaps considering their effectiveness in the taking of several enemy vessels at the inlet earlier in the war.

In November 1779 the assembly established the Ocracoke Militia Company, which was composed of twenty-five inhabitants whose main responsibility was to protect the inlet. This company held together through the remainder of the war, guarding their territory with a tenaciousness composed of loyalty to colony and love for their island home.

At the close of the Revolution, approximately seventy-five people were living on Ocracoke. This estimate is based on the 1790 census, the first official United States census. At that time only the head of each family was listed, and there were twenty-five family heads living on both Ocracoke and Portsmouth islands, which was included along with Ocracoke. They were Jesse Bragg, Joseph Brag (the census taker, as well as the people themselves, often added or deleted letters from names; the names are copied as they appear on old documents and lists), Henry Garrish, Adam Gaskins, John Gaskins, Sarah Gaskins, Thomas Gaskins, Cornelius Howard, George Howard, William Howard, Sr., William Howard, Jr., Francis Jackson, Francis Neale, John Neale, William Neale, Henry Salter, Thomas Scarborough, William

Scarborough, James Scott, James Stiron, Mary Stiron, William Stiron, John Williams, Joseph Williams, and William Williams.

In 1795 Jonathan Price wrote an article entitled "A Description of Occacock Inlet." Although written for the benefit of the pilots and ship captains who navigated in and around Ocracoke Inlet, a small section of the article was devoted to describing Ocracoke Village. Price noted that about thirty family heads lived there and that they were all pilots. One resident had reached "his ninetieth year" and did not "appear to feel any of the infirmities of age." Since he is also described as one of the "original proprietors," the man was likely to be William Howard, Sr., the fourth owner of Ocracoke.

Price described Ocracoke Village as a peninsula, with a length of three miles and a width of two and one-half miles. His description was based on the village once being separated from the rest of the island by a shallow inlet located about one mile northeast of the present Ocracoke Airstrip and later called Nigh Inlet. The inlet was gradually filled up, according to Price, by a "heap of sand," joining the village to the rest of the island. He also noted that the "green trees" that covered the peninsula were "strikingly distinguishing" from the "sandy bank" that stretched east of the village.

Concerning the village itself, Price wrote that "small live oak and cedar grow abundantly over it, and it contains several swamps and rich marshes, which might be cultivated to great advantage; but its inhabitants, depending on another element for their support, suffer the earth to remain in its natural state." The inhabitants, of course, were more interested in piloting, an occupation that involved more Ocracokers as the inlet continued to be one of the few ports of entry in the state. According to Price, "It is the only one which admits vessels of any burden, bound to any of the ports of entry or delivery of the State of North Carolina, excepting those on Cape-Fear river and those of Beaufort and Swannsborough."

As the War of 1812 neared, Ocracoke's population had increased to more than 200 residents, rising steadily from 137 in 1800 to 209 in 1810.

The pilots of Ocracoke saw little action during the War of 1812. As the war began, they expected to see British blockades and an increase of activity similar to the Revolutionary War. Not until July 12, 1813, however, did the British appear off Ocracoke. Early that morning a sizable fleet of British ships, including nine war vessels, anchored just offshore. The British soon deployed about twenty barges, each manned by forty men. The barges entered the inlet and began attacking a revenue cutter and two American privateers, the *Anaconda* and the *Atlas*. The two privateers were captured and the revenue cutter was forced to retreat to the safer sound waters.

The British spent five days at Ocracoke and Portsmouth, collected hundreds of cattle and sheep, and then sailed away, leaving the impression that their blockade remained in effect. They did not return.

Very few people living on Ocracoke today are able to recall anything about the early pilots or their experiences. Several remember snatches of conversation from old people who used to talk extensively of the past, of families, ancestry, and particular events in their small world of history. I did find one old couple who managed to save an ancestor's pilot's branch, or license, and who remembered their fathers talking about piloting and sailing on schooners themselves. The couple, Captain Billy Scarborough and his wife, Dell Garrish Scarborough, shared with me what they knew about the subject.

I went to visit them on a cold January afternoon in 1980. At the time both Billy and Dell were suffering from illnesses that eventually claimed their lives, Billy in 1982 and Dell in 1983. As Billy and I drew our chairs closer to the oil heater, Dell joined us, handing me an old, yellowed document that licensed her great-grandfather, Christopher O'Neal, Jr., to "act as a Pilot for the Bar of Occacock, and the several ports of Bath, Roanoke, Currituck, and Beaufort." His branch was issued by the Commissioners of the Navigation of Port Roanoke on July 30, 1826. "My grandfather, Christopher O'Neal, Jr., managed to save this old license along with his father's will and a record that he used to keep of the people who boarded with him, mostly ship captains who came through Ocracoke Inlet. There were also some old

*This Pilot's Branch, or license, issued in 1826, qualified Christopher O'Neal, Jr., to pilot ships through Ocracoke Inlet.*

receipts for slaves and several other documents. He kept all this stuff in a small trunk that belonged to some of his father's ancestors way back.

"When we were all growing up, I remember seeing the trunk stored away in Papa's room, but we never messed with it. So one night during the Second World War, I told my brother Sullivan that I was going to go and look in that trunk to see what had been locked up in there all those years. We must have gotten a bushel basket of stuff that was packed away in there. Some of the things were hard to read and falling apart so we throwed 'em away. I guess we throwed away things that might have been of interest, but at the time we didn't think anybody could use 'em."

During the decade that Christopher O'Neal, Sr., received his pilot's branch, Ocracoke's population had again risen steadily, from 344 residents in 1820 to 490 in 1830. This pattern continued with increases to 531 residents in 1840 and 536 in 1850, although the latter date saw an increase of only five people in ten years. Factors that may have contributed to this leveling off include westward expansion, the establishment of other ports along the Eastern seaboard, and an ample supply of pilots. In 1850 there were thirty-six pilots listed at Ocracoke.

With the approach of the Civil War, Ocracoke's population had leveled off and begun to decline. In the early stages of the war, Confederate officials were very concerned about protecting the Outer Banks, especially the inlets, which were important supply routes for the Confederacy. Ocracoke Inlet was protected by a fort called Fort Ocracoke, or Fort Morgan, which was built on Beacon Island, located about one mile inside the inlet.

Federal troops attacked Confederate positions on the Outer Banks early in the war, in 1861. Much of the action took place at Fort Hatteras on the southwestern end of Hatteras Island. When Fort Hatteras fell, Fort Morgan was abandoned. Realizing the importance of Ocracoke Inlet, the Federal forces took steps to hinder any further trade. Several schooners loaded with stone were sunk in the inlet, blocking it for the rest of the war.

Any period of history yields a certain amount of folklore. Perhaps one of the most interesting stories relating to Ocracoke and the Civil War concerns my great-great-grandfather, Captain Horatio Williams, and his two-masted schooner, the *Paragon*.

As the story goes, Captain Horatio and the crew of the *Paragon* were

*My great-great-grandfather Captain Horatio Williams stands at the wheel of his ship, the* Paragon, *late 1800s.*

anchored in Charleston Harbor at the outbreak of the Civil War. Before the first shot was fired, Horatio was told that he could not leave the harbor, that a Yankee fleet was on the way and the *Paragon* might be needed. Though loyal to the Confederacy, Horatio was determined that neither side would use the *Paragon*. After the fighting had begun, Horatio eased the *Paragon* out of Charleston Harbor under the cover of darkness and a gathering fog. Although Horatio headed north to Ocracoke, his plan was to pass the island and head for the Roanoke River. The crew was confused and wondered why they had gone so far past what they thought to be their original destination.

He planned to sail the ship far up the Roanoke River, sink her in the fresh water, and bury the sails on shore. Everything went according to plan, and the *Paragon* remained there until eighteen months after the war. Horatio then raised her with barrels as pontoons, and hand pumps when the deck finally reached the surface. Since she was sunk in fresh water and built of red cedar, the *Paragon* was still in excellent shape. The sails were dug up, and Horatio readied her for the trip back to Ocracoke. Before long the *Paragon* and her master, Captain Horatio Williams, were once again sailing the trade routes.

The Civil War appeared to have had an effect on Ocracoke's population. In the 1870 census the number of residents had declined to 368. The next two decades, however, saw gradual increases, to 400 residents in 1880 and 466 in 1890.

Coastal trading, interrupted somewhat during the Civil War, began to prosper once again. More Ocracoke men began to set sail on schooners, many of which made regular trips to the West Indies. Dell Scarborough's father, Uriah Wahab Garrish, Sr., sailed on these schooners. She recalled with pleasure the times when her father used to talk about his sailing experiences. "I believe that Papa made around seven or eight trips to the West Indies on those schooners. He sailed on two-, three-, and four-masters. Probably the earliest trip he took was when he was seventeen years old. He even spent his seventeenth birthday on Puerto Rico. It always fascinated us to sit around and hear him talk about such places. I remember hearing him tell us that on one trip he and the captain went ashore on one of those islands. On one side of the island cold water ran down the hills and on the other side hot water ran. They went on the hot water side and even boiled several eggs to eat that they had brought for their lunch."

During one of his sailing experiences, Mr. Ri, as he was called, witnessed one of the most catastrophic events in history. They had traded on the island of Martinique in the French West Indies in early May of 1902 and were anchored several miles offshore before returning to Ocracoke. Suddenly Mount Pelee, an active volcanic mountain 4,583 feet high, erupted and produced a glowing avalanche that destroyed the town of Saint-Pierre, killing nearly 30,000 people. Two escaped death, one of those a prisoner. The force of the eruption was so strong that hot ashes spread all over the ship and the men had to bail water on the deck to keep her from burning.

Captain Billy Scarborough added, "I had nothing but respect for the men who used to sail on those schooners. I can remember when some of 'em used to go all the way down to the West Indies to trade lumber and different cargo from North Carolina for molasses and such stuff that they had to offer. I didn't particularly care to sail with them because they had it so rough all the time. You see, take bad weather and they would still have to stay on deck and steer the ship. And there was always the man who had to climb up in the masts to take care of the sails. I believe your grandfather Elisha used to sail with some of 'em on the *Cora*."

My grandfather did sail on the *Cora*. I heard him talk about his West Indies experiences many times before he died. The *Cora* was a two-masted schooner about seventy-five feet long with a fourteen-foot bow. When he was nineteen years old, he shipped out to sea on his first trip to the West Indian islands of St. Christopher (St. Kitts) and Martinique. The ship carried a load of wooden shingles. Three days from Ocracoke they ran into gale force winds that forced seas to twenty feet, washing part of the cargo on deck overboard. They battled the storm three days before everything settled down. The remaining trip took seventeen days. Upon arriving at the islands, the ship was greeted by numbers of small native children in long canoes. Crewmen from the *Cora* would toss coins overboard in fifteen to twenty feet of clear water and the children would dive and come up with the pieces every time. In exchange for their cargo of wooden shingles, they received fifty barrels of molasses. The return trip to

Ocracoke took only eleven days, aided by favorable trade winds (named for this reason) and nice weather.

As I got ready to leave, I asked Billy if he remembered when some of us used to play in the woods near his house. We often crossed his yard to get to a path that led to the shore. He never seemed to mind and always greeted us with a smile and wave. Did he remember those times? "Yeah, that I do remember 'em. You see, when I was younger I used to go in the same woods with your great-grandfather, Mr. Mark Gaskins, to chop wood for the winter. You could always learn a lot being with some of the old ones."

On October 9, 1837, one of the worst maritime disasters ever to take place on the North Carolina coast occurred at Ocracoke. Ninety-one people perished as the steam-packet *Home* ran aground and went to pieces in the heavy surf six miles northeast of Ocracoke Village.

The ill-fated voyage was only the third for the *Home*, a 550-ton vessel built at a cost of $115,000. At the time, she was considered the finest steam-packet in operation, with a 198-foot keel, 22-foot beam, and overall length of 220 feet. Although designed for river travel, the *Home* began with two trips from New York to Charleston, the latter trip achieved in sixty-four hours. No other steam-packet or ship had made a quicker passage.

As the *Home* left New York Harbor at four o'clock on the afternoon of Saturday, October 7, 1837, expectations were high for breaking the record set on the previous voyage. Much of the information about the trip from New York, as well as of the actual destruction of the vessel, comes from Captain Carleton White, who survived the incident along with nineteen other crew members and twenty passengers.

By noon the next day the wind had shifted from a light southwesterly breeze to a hard northeaster. Little did the passengers and crew of the *Home* realize that a hurricane, referred to as "Racer's Storm," was on its way to the North Carolina coast. Between seven and eight o'clock that evening the wind had increased, and heavy seas had caused the feeder pipe of the forward boiler to open at the joint, letting more water into the hold. The boiler was shut down, but was put back into operation four hours later when the chief engineer reported that he was able to repair the feeder pipe.

As the *Home* continued on a course toward Charleston, the wind increased to gale force. The second engineer falsely reported that the boilers had given out, and Captain White ordered the jib and foresail set with the intention of beaching the vessel. When he learned the true condition of the boilers, and that the troublesome feeder pipe had once again been repaired, Captain White had the foresail taken in and the course resumed.

As they passed Wimble Shoals, located off the present Outer Banks villages of Rodanthe, Waves, and Salvo, the ship was shaken by "the shock of three heavy rollers on our larboard beam, which stove in our gangway, several of the larboard stateroom windows, and one of the dining-room windows." One of the passengers, Captain Salter of Portsmouth, New Hampshire, tried to persuade Captain White to begin looking for a place to beach the *Home*, but the captain refused, ordering the vessel to be held offshore.

Between two and three o'clock on Monday afternoon, the chief engineer reported that the boat was leaking badly. Captain White and two passengers, Captains Salter and Hill, went below to find the leak. Although they did not find the leak, Captain Salter observed that "the boat was ceiled with nothing but thin, common pine plank, whereas she should have been ceiled throughout with seven inch oak timber, champered down to the edges." The vessel continued to take on water, and even the passengers were employed in bailing at this point.

As the *Home* approached Diamond Shoals, off Cape Hatteras, Captain White made the decision to go around the shoals rather than through the inside: "My reason for this conclusion was, that if, in an attempt to pass inside, with such a heavy sea and thick weather, the vessel should strike, probably every life would be lost." After rounding the shoals, the *Home* was placed on a course "for the purpose of getting under the lee of the shoals." Captain White then went to his room to get some rest, but he soon returned to the wheelhouse. By eight o'clock that evening he had learned that the furnace fires had been put out by the water which had continued to leak into the vessel and wrote that "all hope was now abandoned of making a harbor under the lee of Hatteras; and our only alternative was to run her on shore, for the purpose of saving our lives."

At about ten o'clock the *Home* struck on an outer reef, sluing her bow to the north, and exposing the deck to the heavy seas. Passengers rushed to the inshore side of the vessel, seeking protection from the pounding surf. The lifeboats had been prepared earlier, but Captain White refused to get in one, fearing that no one would be saved in them. One boat had already been lowered and upset. Another larger one was lowered and brought alongside the *Home*. Many passengers and both mates got in this boat, and several clung to the gunwales. They managed to get only ten yards from the wreck before upsetting.

According to Captain White, "Most of the passengers, who had placed themselves along the guards, had, by this time, been washed off; their shrieks and cries, during this time, were appalling and heart-rending beyond description." B. B. Hussey, a passenger who survived, gave the following account of the wreck:

> Now commenced the most heart-rending scene. Wives cling-ing to husbands,—children to parents,—and women, who were without protectors, seeking aid from the arm of the stranger; all awaiting the results of a moment which would bring with it either life or death. Though an intense feeling of anxiety must, at this time, have filled every breast, yet not a shriek was heard, nor was there any extraordinary exclamation of excitement or alarm. A slight agitation was, however, apparent in the general circle. Some few hurried from one part of the boat to another, as if seeking a place of greater safety; yet most, and particularly those who had the melancholy charge of wives and children, remained quiet and calm observers of the scene before them.
>
> One mother sustained the noble character which, in all ages, has distinguished maternal affection. Her infant was in her arms,

pressed close to her bosom, as if the whisperings of hope in-
spired the devoted woman with a belief that the feebel protection
of a mother's love would shield her child from the conflict of
warring elements. But for a moment did this dream of hope last;
a wave wrested the infant from her grasp, and plunged it into the
foaming waters! A convulsive shriek proclaimed the agony of the
bereaved mother, and ere the relentless surge had hidden her
lost one forever, she sprang amongst the breakers and perished!

Captain White tied a piece of rope to a small ladder, took the other
end around his hand, and waited for the vessel to break up. Turning
to the chief engineer, he said, "Mr. Hunt, we little thought this would
be our fate when we left New York."

Thinking that the remaining place of safety was the topgallant
forecastle, Captain White joined the others there as the main deck
began breaking up. For some time a passenger, Mr. Lovegreen, was on
the gallows frame, tolling the bell. One passenger later recalled that
the bell "sounded, indeed, like the funeral knell over the departed
dead."

Soon the forecastle broke loose and floated toward shore, carrying
Captain White and six others with it. They reached the beach safely
and proceeded toward the Ocracoke Lighthouse. After going some
distance, they realized that the lighthouse was further than they had
first believed. Captain White and one of the crew returned to the surf
to assist those who washed ashore, while the others continued toward
the lighthouse.

B. B. Hussey was part of the small group that eventually reached
Ocracoke Village. He later reported that the "inhabitants of the island,
generally, treated us with great kindness; and so far as their circumstances would allow, assisted in properly disposing of the numerous
bodies thrown upon the shore." Most of these bodies were buried in
the sand dunes not far from where they washed ashore.

Hussey also reported quite extensively on the fate of the Reverend
and Mrs. Cowles. As the *Home* started to go to pieces, another passen-

ger heard Reverend Cowles say, "He that trusts in Jesus is safe, even amid the perils of the sea." The Reverend and Mrs. Cowles were then seen to go forward, arms around each other, in calm expectation. When the vessel struck, the first breaker "swept them together to their watery grave."

Hussey noted that "we have the melancholy satisfaction of adding, that the body of Mrs. C. was found the morning after the fatal disaster, carried to the residence of Mr. William Howard, there shrouded by the humane hands of Mrs. H. and other ladies,—whose tender and feeling conduct deserves the highest praise of the community, as it has evoked the blessing of many bleeding hearts,—and thence removed to an adjoining place of sepulture, and decently interred, with a board, bearing her name, to mark the spot."

After spending three days on Ocracoke, the survivors of the *Home* returned, some to New York, others to Charleston.

In a detailed journal written after the wreck, authorities speculated on the cause of the wreck as well as the seaworthiness of the vessel: "The cause of this terrible disaster was the unseaworthiness of the vessel. However well she might have performed her accustomed trips on a calm river, she never should have ventured outside of Sandy Hook; being totally unfit for ocean navigation, so unfaithfully was she built.

"She went to pieces in less than an hour; and all agree that the speed of her dissolution indicated a weakness and rottenness of constitution entirely unfit for the service on which she had been sent."

For all the 131 passengers and crew on board the *Home*, the ship carried only two life preservers. Congress soon passed a law requiring a life preserver for each person on board, as well as the Steamboat Act, which subjected vessels to safety laws and inspections.

Shipwrecks have been an important part of Ocracoke's history. Although many wrecks were never documented, we do know that at least forty vessels have been lost here, along with 122 lives known lost. Aside from newspaper accounts and reports given by survivors, such as that of Captain White of the *Home*, little information exists about these wrecks.

Another captain who witnessed the destruction of his vessel and the loss of lives at Ocracoke was Captain Hand of the sloop *Henry*. The *Henry* was en route from New York to Charleston when it ran aground off Ocracoke on December 10, 1819. Captain Hand survived the wreck and provided a written account of the incident—in this case a letter written from Ocracoke, reprinted here from the January 15, 1820, *Norfolk Beacon and Portsmouth Advertiser*:

I have a melancholy affair to relate. I am the only one living of the crew and passengers of the sloop *Henry*. We left New York on Monday, 30th November. On Wednesday following experienced a heavy gale, but received no damage, only split our jib, which after the gale, was unbent and repaired. On Friday afternoon following, took the wind from the southward, blowing fresh. Saturday morning made Cape Lookout lighthouse, hove about and stood off, wind canting in from the southeast, and the gale and sea increasing so fast that we were obliged to heave to.

Lay to until 5 o'clock p.m., then began to shoal water fast, and blowing, instead of a gale, a perfect hurricane. We set the head of the foresail to try to get offshore, but to no use, it blowing away in an instant; likewise the jib. We then lay to under the balance of the mainsail until we got in 10 and 9 fathoms water, when the sea began to break and board us, which knocked us on our beam ends, carried away our quarter, and swept the deck. She righted, and in about five minutes capsized again, which took off our mainsail. We were then left to the mercy of the wind and waves, which were continually raking us fore and aft. With much exertion we got her before the wind and sea, and in a few minutes after run her ashore on the south beach of Ocracoke Bar, four miles from land.

She struck about 10 o'clock at night, bilged in a few minutes, and got on her beam ends, every sea making a fair breach over her. At 12 o'clock her deck blew up and washed away altogether, and broke in two near the hatchway. The bow part turned bottom up, the stern part righted. Mr. Kinley (passenger) and Wm. Bartlett (seaman) washed off. The remainder of us got on the taffil rail, and that all under water. About 2 o'clock a.m., Mr. Campbell (the other passenger) and Wm. Shoemaker (cook) expired and dropped from the wreck. About 4 o'clock, Jesse Hand (seaman) became so chilled that he washed off. At daylight, Mr. Hawley (mate) died, and fell from along side of me into his watery grave, which I expected every moment would be my own lot. But thro' the tender mercy of God, I survived on the wreck 24 hours alone.

On Monday morning, about 2 o'clock, the stern broke away and I went with it. At sunrise I was taken off, so much mangled and bruised that few persons thought I could survive. I, however, am gaining, having received the kindest treatment, and every possible care from the inhabitants. My chest has been picked up, but it had been opened, and all my clothes of value taken out. I am here almost naked and shall try to get home as soon as I am able.

The vessel and cargo are a total loss. The fragments have drifted into Albemarle Sound. I have heard of some barrels being picked up some distance from the sound, but the heads all out. I have noted a protest, and shall have it extended according to law. I wish this published. It is the first of my being able to write. There is no way of conveying letters from this place except by water.

The bodies of Wm. Bartlett and Jesse Hand have been picked up and decently buried.

Early Ocracoke residents realized the tragedy involved for shipwrecked survivors, and often they were called upon to provide much-needed shelter and care for those who had washed ashore. At the

*Shipwreck of the* Nomis *in 1935. Ocracoke residents built a rough dock out to the vessel in order to salvage it. (Courtesy of Larry Williams)*

same time, they were well aware of the benefits to be had every time a ship came ashore, especially one that went to pieces, sending forth its cargo to the beach. Such gifts from the sea were quickly scavenged and put to use.

Shipwrecks have yielded such freight as lumber, clothing, fruits and vegetables, and other items of general cargo. Although many wrecks had little to offer, those that did, especially larger vessels loaded with valuable cargoes, were protected by the laws of vendue and supervised by a wreck commissioner.

Sullivan Garrish, who was present at a number of wrecks, recalled the procedure. "Whenever there was a shipwreck, different ones around here would go down to the beach and start making piles of stuff that drifted ashore. If the stuff was worth anything, a wreck commissioner would come down to auction the stuff off. You had to bid on it, and people sometimes bidded on each other's pile.

"In the case of lumber, they often had a job getting it back to the village. Sometimes they used a horse and cart and other times they lugged it to the sound side, put it in their boats, and sailed it up to the village."

Many ships that wrecked were loaded with lumber, a product of the North Carolina mainland traded along the East Coast as well as the West Indies. Some Ocracoke houses still standing today were built with this salvaged lumber, along with wood from the ships themselves.

Several wrecks have given up unusual cargoes. One was the *Cibao*, a Norwegian vessel known locally as the "old banana ship," which ran ashore near Hatteras Inlet. Most of its cargo of green and red bananas had to be tossed overboard before the vessel could be refloated.

My grandfather and several other Ocracokers collected bunches of these bananas and sold them in Washington, North Carolina. My father, who was a small boy at the time of this wreck, recalls, "Most people managed to get bunches of these bananas. Papa got a couple of bunches for us and tied 'em up in the rafters of our house. We used to sneak up there all hours of the night and eat 'em. A lot of 'em were green, and we stayed cramped a lot."

Another vessel carrying a load of general cargo wrecked off Ocracoke and yielded up a large quantity of shoes. Since the shoe boxes were torn apart by the surf, individual shoes of various sizes washed ashore. But shoes were hard to get in those days, and so many Ocracokers made do with pairs of different sizes or even wore two left or two right shoes.

Like the hundreds of ships lost elsewhere along the North Carolina coast, most of the wrecks at Ocracoke occurred during stormy weather. Ships were driven ashore by strong winds and heavy seas, quite often aided by a crew intent upon saving lives and property. Sailors were well aware of the treacherous waters off the Outer Banks. Such shoals as Frying Pan Shoals off Cape Fear, Lookout Shoals off Cape Lookout, Diamond Shoals off Cape Hatteras, and Wimble Shoals off present-day Salvo, Waves, and Rodanthe, reach out to hinder vessels as they ply the north-south coastwise routes. Many ships were lost on, or trying to avoid, these shoals.

Early mariners lacked the modern navigational equipment available today. Relying on compasses, sextants, and the various lighthouses positioned along the coast, they navigated the waters off the Outer Banks with great care to avoid the watery grave that had claimed so many ships. On stormy nights at sea, especially in the dead of winter when the icy water and air made things worse, the soft twinkle of the Ocracoke Lighthouse must have been a welcome and reassuring sight.

The first lighthouse at Ocracoke Inlet was located on Shell Castle Island, just inside the inlet. It was authorized by Congress in 1794, and bids for the project were published in the *North Carolina Gazette* one year later. The lighthouse was completed in 1798, but was soon rendered useless due to the shifting channel. A light vessel authorized by Congress in 1820 was also a failure, and so steps were begun to put into operation the present lighthouse.

The land where the Ocracoke Lighthouse would later stand was deeded to North Carolina in 1790 by several Ocracoke property owners. The state later transferred ownership to the federal government, since lighthouse construction was their responsibility. Another tract donated to the state for the same purpose was also given to the federal government.

In 1822 Congress appropriated $20,000 for a lighthouse to be built on Ocracoke Island. One year later the lighthouse, along with a one-story keeper's dwelling, was erected by Noah Porter of Massachusetts at a cost of $11,359.55.

Since the lighthouse's initial construction in 1823, gradual improvements have been made to the lighting fixture and overall structure. In 1854 a Fresnel lens replaced the old reflecting apparatus, but it was removed in 1862 during the Civil War. One year later the lights were again put into operation. A second story was added to the keeper's quarters in 1897, and by 1899 new modern lamps were installed.

The same structure built in 1823 is still in use today, making it the oldest lighthouse in operation on the North Carolina coast. The

8,000-candlepower electric light can be seen fourteen miles at sea. While the lighthouse is the responsibility of the Coast Guard, the keeper's quarters and grounds are maintained by the National Park Service. Because the structure is fragile, especially the brick walls and the inside spiral stairway attached to them, the lighthouse is not open to the public. Visitors are allowed to view the inside during guided tours by the National Park Service.

In addition to the lighthouse, several lifesaving stations were built at Ocracoke. The first one was erected in 1883 and was called the Hatteras Inlet Lifesaving Station, or Cedar Hammock Station. (Some sources indicate that this station was actually the Gull Shoal Station.) The second was built in Ocracoke Village during 1904.

The Ocracoke Village Station was put into operation in response to the increasing number of shipwrecks at Ocracoke toward the end of the 1800s. The closest lifesaving station to Ocracoke Village was the Portsmouth Island Lifesaving Station, built in 1894. The crew of this station often had difficulty getting across Ocracoke Inlet when a vessel needed assistance off Ocracoke Beach. The next nearest station was the Hatteras Inlet Station, located about thirteen miles northeast of Ocracoke Village. The wreck of the *Richard S. Spofford* in 1894 pointed up the need for a station at Ocracoke.

The *Spofford* was a 488-ton vessel en route from Boston to Darien, Georgia, with a load of stone ballast in the hold. As the vessel passed Cape Hatteras, Captain Roger Hawes decided to sail closer to the beach, especially since strong winds were prevailing and he wanted to stay away from the Gulf Stream and its northbound current. He held the *Spofford* on a course parallel to Ocracoke Beach, intent upon reaching the lee of Cape Lookout and anchoring there until the wind died down.

Since Captain Hawes thought they were sailing in plenty of water, the centerboard of the three-masted schooner was down twenty feet below the surface. In the early morning hours only two days after Christmas, the *Spofford* struck the shoals close to Ocracoke Inlet, wedging in the sand and exposing herself to the full force of the sea.

*This 1934 picture is of the first life-saving station built in Ocracoke Village. Constructed in 1904, the station was torn down shortly after the present Coast Guard Station was built in 1939–40. (Courtesy of National Park Service, Cape Hatteras National Seashore)*

She then drifted closer to shore and lodged on the inner bar just outside the inlet.

The crew remained on the ship well into the next day. Although a group of people from Ocracoke Village gathered on the beach, without proper equipment they could make little attempt to rescue the stranded crew. The Portsmouth lifesaving crew made an attempt to organize a rescue, but their efforts were unsuccessful, mainly because their station had just been built and they lacked equipment and organization. The keeper of the Portsmouth Station did manage to get a message to the crew at the Hatteras Inlet Station, and they finally arrived later that night. By that time, five of the crew had made it to shore in a capsized yawl and were pulled from the surf by the people on the beach. Captain Hawes, the steward, and another crewman remained on the *Spofford* until dawn the next morning. While the captain and the remaining crewman were taken off by the breeches buoy, the steward had died, and his body had been lashed to the rigging. It was later recovered.

An investigation soon followed the wreck of the *Spofford*. In a March 1895 letter to the general superintendent of the Lifesaving Service, the assistant inspector for the First and Second Districts argued for another lifesaving station at the southern end of Ocracoke. The inspector complained that the Hatteras Inlet Lifesaving Station, which was located at the northern end of Ocracoke, was too far to render immediate assistance to vessels stranded near the village. "There is always the possibility of a wreck occurring in that locality, that might not be known for days to the crew of this station." The inspector also explained that the Portsmouth Lifesaving Station, which was the nearest to the southern end of Ocracoke, was of little use when weather conditions prevented the lifesaving crew from crossing the inlet.

The inspector reasoned further that the number of wrecks at Ocracoke was increasing. "During the past few seasons, quite a large percentage of the wrecks within the Sixth Life-Saving District, have occurred upon or in the vicinity of Ocracoke Island. The cases of actual assistance required appear to be on the increase. It is claimed that many of these disasters are caused by the masters, of vessels coming from the southward, mistaking Ocracoke Light for Hatteras Light. Thinking they have cleared the dangerous Diamond Shoals, they keep off to the Northward, and as a natural result, often bring up on Ocracoke Beach."

His recommendation was to establish "an additional Life-Saving Station upon Ocracoke Island, at or near a point eight or nine miles Southwest of the Ocracoke Station."

Until the lifesaving station in Ocracoke Village was constructed, some ten years later, rescues continued from the Hatteras Inlet Station and the Portsmouth Station. The keeper of the Hatteras Inlet Station was James W. Howard. He was appointed to this position in 1883 at a salary of seven hundred dollars a year. In addition to the keeper, approximately twenty-five surfmen also manned the station. Because they were present at the station only part-time, the surfmen were paid a salary of fifty dollars per year. Like other Ocracoke men, they spent the rest of the year fishing or sailing on schooners. Their service at the station was needed most during the fall and winter months.

"They were tough men," said an Ocracoke man who, as a boy, knew some of the crew who manned the stations. "They had to be tough to go out and mess in that cold surf in the middle of the winter. They didn't have all the stuff to work with like the Coast Guard has today."

The "stuff" they had to work with included lifeboats, surf boats, and life rafts, each of which were employed under different circumstances depending on weather conditions. These boats were placed on carts and drawn by horses or mules, sometimes as much as ten miles from the station to a wreck site. Wreck reports, kept by the keeper of the station, are filled with brief descriptions of the difficulty of moving rescue equipment through the soft sand. Phrases like "the men are all wore out" or "the mules wouldn't go any further in the soft sand" are frequent in the reports.

Other rescue equipment included a Lyle gun, used to shoot lines out to stranded vessels, and life-cars and breeches buoys. The life-car, which had a capacity of three to five persons, was made of corrugated iron with a convex deck, locking hatch, and two lifting rings. It was moved along a line running from shore to the ship in distress. The breeches buoy consisted of sturdy breeches attached at the waist to a ring buoy that is suspended from a pulley running along a rope from ship to shore or from ship to ship.

A typical wreck report included such information as the name and type of vessel, number of passengers and crew, the kind of cargo, details relating to the weather and the rescue itself, the amount of damage and number of lives lost, and other particulars worth noting.

As the end of the nineteenth century approached, the number of shipwrecks off Ocracoke continued to increase. The second most disastrous shipwreck at Ocracoke, in terms of lives lost, occurred on December 24, 1899, when the 2,265-ton schooner-rigged steel steamer *Ariosto* ran aground about three miles southwest of the Hatteras Inlet Station.

The *Ariosto* had left Galveston, Texas, a few weeks earlier bound for

*Although now used as a cistern, this small craft was once employed as a life car, which was used in rescues. The rings on top of the life car supported a rope along which the vessel was moved. (Photograph by Ann Ehringhaus)*

Hamburg, Germany, with a load of wheat, cotton, lumber, and cottonseed valued at one and a half million dollars. The ship had been scheduled to stop in Norfolk to take on coal for the trip across the Atlantic. In the early morning hours on Christmas Eve, the *Ariosto* struck the shoals about one-half mile off Ocracoke Beach. A strong southwest wind had pushed up rough seas. Apparently the navigator had mistaken Ocracoke Light for Hatteras Light and had placed the ship on a more northerly course. As Captain R. R. Baines was roused from his bunk, his first impression was that they were aground on Diamond Shoals off Cape Hatteras.

While plans were being made to abandon ship, several flares were fired. They were soon answered by flares from the Hatteras Inlet Station. Although this was a signal from the station that help was on the way, twenty-six men crammed into two boats and cast loose from the *Ariosto*. The two boats soon capsized, and only two men managed to swim back to the ship. Three others reached shore, one of these holding on to a line that had been fired out to the vessel. The line had fallen across his shoulders as he struggled to stay afloat. The remaining twenty-one crewmen perished in the rough surf. Although the lifesavers from the Hatteras Inlet Station had difficulty moving their beach carts, eventually Captain Baines and the five crewmen left aboard the *Ariosto* were brought to shore.

The tiny settlement of Cedar Hammock, located near the Hatteras Inlet Station, housed the families of the lifesavers. Although their Christmas celebration had been interrupted by the wreck of the *Ariosto*, the lifesavers and their families nevertheless came together to care for the surviving crew and to help bury the bodies that washed ashore over the next few days.

Among other notable shipwrecks that have taken place at Ocracoke, the wreck of the *George W. Wells* on September 3, 1913, was perhaps one of the most exciting. The six-masted schooner was the largest sailing vessel ever to wreck on the North Carolina coast, as well as one of the largest sailing ships ever built.

The 2,970-ton ship, with a total of twenty-eight sails, was en route from Boston to Fernandina, Florida, when she ran into hurricane-force winds off Ocracoke. She soon lost her sails and came ashore six miles southwest of the Hatteras Inlet Station.

When their horses refused to drag the heavy rescue equipment over the tide-swept beach, the determined lifesavers from the Hatteras Station proceeded to hitch themselves to the carts and drag the heavy equipment six miles along the mucky beach. In the strong winds, seven shots were fired out to the vessel before one reached it. This line broke, however. Next the captain tied a line from the ship to an empty oil barrel and set it adrift toward Ocracoke Beach. Before it could reach the beach, though, a crazed crewman cut it loose from the vessel. A second line tied to a small boat eventually reached shore.

With the breeches buoy finally set up, the crew and passengers started to abandon ship. In addition to the fifteen crewmen, Captain Joseph H. York, his two-hundred-and-fifty-pound wife, two other women, and two children were taken ashore. Along with the captain came his St. Bernard dog.

Although some of the residents of Ocracoke managed to salvage some of the lumber from the vessel, she was later set on fire—a sad end for one of the greatest sailing vessels ever built.

Even in the twentieth century, ships continued to wreck at Ocracoke. Although no other lives were lost after the wreck of the *Ariosto*, much valuable cargo was destroyed or later salvaged by the people of Ocracoke. The old lifesaving station gave way to the present Coast Guard Station, which was built in 1940.

With modern navigational equipment and improved weather forecasting, fewer wrecks occur today. Most of these are fishing vessels, caught offshore during rough weather. Several years ago a small fishing boat got out of the channel that leads into Hatteras Inlet, floundered in the breakers, and was finally cast ashore on Ocracoke Beach, where it lodged in the sand at the high-water mark. Although several attempts were made to refloat it, the grip of the sand was too strong, and the boat was eventually pounded to pieces by the breakers.

# Part Two                    The Ocracokers

For many years Ocracoke has been known as a small fishing village. Even today travel literature about the island continues to promote this "quaint" fishing village atmosphere.

Although Ocracoke's major economic activity is now tourism, both commercial and sport fishing contribute greatly to the economy. A few residents still rely on commercial fishing for full-time employment, while many others supplement their incomes by fishing part-time. Sport fishing, a major attraction for the many tourists who visit the island, employs some residents as full- or part-time guides.

Several fish houses operate throughout the year, buying and selling thousands of pounds of bluefish, mackerel, trout, croaker, spot, mullet, flounder, shrimp, and crab.

When I was growing up in the 1960s and 1970s, the commercial fishing industry at Ocracoke was not very prosperous. Only one or two markets were in operation (at one point there was none), and these had been open but a few years. Few fishermen were willing to invest in equipment, fearing that the market would close at any time. Tourism was not as developed as it is today, nor did the ferry division provide as many jobs. Therefore many Ocracokers had to leave the island to find steady employment.

By the beginning of the 1980s, more reliable fish markets were buying year around and offering good prices for crabs, fish, and other seafood. A number of Ocracokers who had left the island or tried other local employment soon found it profitable to fish full-time.

Others who were employed by the state or held some other job fished part-time. Reliable fish house or not, though, several fishermen remained faithful to the occupation. To them fishing was a way of life; the pursuing, catching, and selling of fish was so much a part of their lives that they kept at it and they wouldn't have thought of doing anything else. Two such fishermen were Uriah and Sullivan Garrish, brothers, who fished the waters off Ocracoke from their youth until they were well into their eighties.

Of all the different kinds of fish to be caught and the various methods of catching them, the favorite for Uriah and Sullivan was catching mullets. Found all over the world, the striped jumping mullet is bluish gray or greenish on top—greenish, according to Sullivan, if they have just come from the cleaner ocean waters—silvery gray on the sides, and white underneath. The stripes are formed by scales with dark centers. Although mullets average one to two feet long, Uriah once caught thirteen mullets that weighed as much as fifteen pounds each and were approximately two feet long.

Mullets are caught with gill nets. The diamond-shaped netting acts as a fence which prevents fish from swimming through. If the size of the netting, or "meshes," isn't too large or small, the fish will become entangled, or "meshed," by the gills as they try to free themselves.

At the top and bottom the netting is tied to ropes. Corks spaced approximately a yard apart along the top line float the net, while the bottom line is spaced with leads which sink the netting toward the bottom. At the two ends of the net the cork and lead lines are fastened to a staff, which keeps the net spread open and provides a means of pulling the net through the water.

Although an average gill net may be between thirty and seventy-five yards long, mullet nets are much longer, usually between two and three hundred yards. The net is placed in the stern of a skiff, which is normally manned by a crew of two men who use long oars to pole the skiff through the water. A standard mullet crew includes two skiffs, a net to each skiff.

At Ocracoke, mullets are caught along the many sand reefs and sloughs of Pamlico Sound that run the length of the island within a mile of shore. When a school of mullets is spotted, a staff from each net is tied together and pitched overboard. Since most mullets are caught in shallow water, the fishermen then pole their skiffs in semicircles, eventually meeting to close the circle after all the nets have been set. The nets are then pulled together, forcing the fish to mesh.

This whole process is really quite simple—simple, that is, when there are plenty of mullets and you don't have to look over every grass lump and into every slough to find them. When you're out there on those other days, though, scouring the reefs, and even the whirl of a stingray seems promising, then it takes a real mullet man to catch them. "There's an art to this mulleting," explains Sullivan. "A lot of ones that go out don't know this. They think you can just set a net a catch 'em. They don't know the art of it."

I first went out with Uriah and Sullivan when I was ten years old. My first mulleting trip will always be remembered as one of the most exciting days of my life. Growing up next door to Uriah Garrish, I had heard him, Sullivan, and other fishermen talk extensively about catches they had made, some recent, others long before. Although I had set nets within a hundred yards of shore, often wading to check them, I had longed to fish the sand reefs far from shore with Uriah and Sullivan. After that first trip, I began to go with them more often. My job was to hold the staffs together after they had been thrown overboard and to help pick out the meshed fish. My cousin Bobby, who is one year older than I and bigger and stronger, got to help Uriah pole his skiff. Sullivan had Zina Williams in the skiff with him. When Zina died, I took his place.

I started fishing with them again in the late seventies. At the time no one else would go with them and I felt they were a little discouraged. The thought of a summer without Uriah and Sullivan mulleting didn't seem right; they were a regular part of the season. And so, right out of college, I launched into a wonderful year of fishing with them, learning about the art of mulleting.

On a warm September morning Uriah woke me up, calling from

*Uriah Garrish, 1980.*

below my bedroom window, "Get up! Purty morning. We got to get going. Get a set early and come back in." I quickly dressed in my old fishing clothes, stained with salt and mullet blood from the day before, and joined them in my backyard. Sullivan had walked to Uriah's house. Sometimes he waits for me to pick him up, but this particular morning he seemed anxious and ready to go. He had called

Uriah twice to discuss the weather conditions and where we should go to look for mullets.

"This is the purtiest morning I've ever seen," said Uriah, encouraging us with one of his customary superlatives. The sun had risen in a clear sky and a light wind was breezing from the west. "You couldn't ask for a better morning to catch 'em," he added.

We walked to the edge of the Creek and waded to the boats, which were tied to stakes about thirty feet from shore. As the sun began to clear the tops of some oak trees along the eastern shore of the Creek, its golden rays were tinting the water, marsh, trees, and buildings along the southwest shore. "If you had your camera now you'd get a pretty picture," said Sullivan.

Of the three boats in our small mulleting fleet, the largest is called the *Rex*, named for Rex Beach, a New York author who used to take hunting trips to Ocracoke in the early 1900s. Uriah and Sullivan's father, Uriah Wahab Garrish, Sr., served as his hunting guide. The *Rex* was constructed from material belonging to a boat that Rex Beach once owned. The seventy-five-year-old boat is eighteen feet long and about five feet at the widest. It is usually painted once a year, the bottom and waterline with copper paint and the rest white. "You'd see a lot of fish if you could see all that she's held," said Sullivan.

They've used the *Rex* most of their lives, attaching to it many memories of good catches, rough weather, and even bullets hitting the side of the boat. "Nobody was meaning to shoot at us," recalled Sullivan. "It was just a bunch of men on shore shooting at livestock. There used to be a lot of cattle, sheep, goats, and hogs roaming all over the island. They were eatin' up all the vegetation and the government eventually made everybody get rid of 'em. It was a lot harder to ship 'em off the island so everybody started killing 'em. I guess they were shooting at 'em as they stood along the edge of the water."

"We thought for sure we were gonners," added Uriah. "We had to get right down in the *Rex*. I reckon she's the only thing that saved us."

Then there is the *Henry*, a small fifteen-foot skiff that once belonged to Henry Piggot of Portsmouth Island, a black man who used to pole out every day in this same skiff to meet the mailboat on its way from Atlantic to Ocracoke. The *Henry* is a perfect mullet skiff: small, light, and easy to sheer when setting after mullets. This last characteristic is especially important in a mullet skiff when you're trying to pole in a semi-circle. The *Henry* also has low sides, a slight rise in the stern, and a narrow width—perfect for one fisherman to handle.

The third skiff is simply called the "other skiff." It is about sixteen feet long and wider than the *Henry*—and will therefore carry more mullets, but it leaks like a basket. Uriah and Sullivan have tried several times to patch it, but haven't succeeded. They often talk of towing it to one of the creeks at the north end of the island and leaving it there to rot.

Mounted on the stern of the *Rex* is a fifteen-horsepower Evinrude outboard motor. They bought it soon after their previous motor, a twenty-five horsepower, was stolen. The theft occurred during the winter when they were fishing for puppy drum and the *Rex* was being kept under one of the bridges on Highway 12 about six miles northeast of the village. Also stolen the same night was an outboard motor belonging to Charlie Williams, who is blind. Only weeks after this incident, someone also stole their two large mullet nets, totalling their losses to well over one thousand dollars. "You'll never be able to leave your stuff in them creeks down below anymore," said Uriah. "Not the way things are today."

They are both pleased with the performance the fifteen-horsepower motor has given. "She's all the power we need," said Uriah. "We haven't had one minute's trouble out of her." They both agree that "she's good on gas mileage."

We would need fuel for the day's trip, so after untying the boats and securing the two skiffs astern the *Rex*, we headed for a local store to buy gas, oil, and a few things for lunch. Several men had gathered at the gas pumps as we reached the dock. I pumped the gas in our tank while Uriah went to get beer and crackers. "You know right well why he's so anxious to get to the store," said Sullivan, referring to Uriah's

*Sullivan Garrish stands in the bow of the* Rex *during the summer of 1980 as Uriah steers out of Hammock Creek.*

taste for beer. "This boat wouldn't hold what he could drink in one day."

As Uriah returned from the store, one of the men on the dock said, "Sullivan, what's he got in that bag?" Sullivan grunted and shook his head. They all laughed, looking at each other then at Uriah. "You boys have got a purty day for 'em," observed another man. "You want to put it to 'em." We waved and mumbled a few words at them as Uriah started the motor and steered toward the mouth of the Creek.

As we rounded the rock breakwater that protects the Coast Guard Station property, Uriah increased the speed of the motor. At full speed, towing two skiffs, the *Rex* will move along at perhaps five knots. This is plenty fast for them. They remember when a dependable five knots would have been quite welcome. "When we were growing up," recalled Sullivan, "everybody sailed. You didn't use the three boats like you do now. You just had the two mullet skiffs and they had the sails right on 'em. You could make pretty good time if you had a good souwester. Sometimes it only took about forty minutes to get down offshore of the park service campground. When it was c'am, though, you had to row over to the reef and pole the rest of the way. This took two or three hours.

"Even when we started to use motors, we didn't tow the skiffs that far. The old ones would only use the motor to get across the deep water. When they reached the reef, they'd anchor and shove the rest of the day. They claimed that the noise of the motor would run the mullets off a shoal. They were right, too."

Since they have always been used to slow speeds while traveling on the water, Uriah and Sullivan are very uncomfortable when they get in a boat with a high-horsepower motor. They especially don't like to go fast when it's rough, even though the newer fiberglass boats can withstand the pounding. They'd rather run slowly and have plenty of time to study the areas they're passing. Besides, the big motors are loud and sometimes you could find yourself in the middle of a school of mullets before you had had a chance to see them from a distance. By that time it would be too late; they'd already be heading for the deep water.

Uriah and Sullivan had already discussed where we should go to look for mullets—today we were headed for a place called Six Mile Hammock Reef. Most of the shoals, reefs, sloughs, creeks, and channels have names, some of them two hundred years old. They are simple names, derived from the names of persons (Johnson Brown

Shoal, Clark's Reef, John Gaskins Creek), animals (Hog Shoal, Terrapin Shoal, Stingray Point), or something similar in appearance to the feature being named.

Uriah always steers the boat. I have never seen Sullivan steering. He usually stands toward the bow, holding on to the painter and scanning the water for any sign of mullets. Neither has ever worn glasses.

Uriah is of medium height, Sullivan about six inches shorter. Both have a stoop. Their skin is dark and wrinkled on their faces, necks, arms, and hands. On this particular day they were also dressed alike. They would wait until we were about ready to set the nets before changing into their mullet pants. In addition to an old pair of stained pants, each wore a pair of cheap tennis shoes, a short-sleeve shirt, and a cap. On the front of Sullivan's cap was written "Jack's Store," while Uriah's advertised "Tradewinds." Sullivan was wearing a pair of large sunglasses. "I don't understand how he can see through those old big glasses," said Uriah.

After twenty minutes of running, we arrived at a place called the Western End of the Reef, actually the inshore edge of Howard's Reef. Uriah slowed the motor as we approached a sandy shoal that juts out toward the deep water one hundred feet from the regular contour of the reef. We are attentive for a moment, our eyes examining every inch of the shoal. "That's a good place for 'em," said Sullivan. "I have caught 'em there. Keep your eyes peeled. You might see one jump here in a minute."

One of the characteristics of the striped mullet, or "jumping mullet," is that it will often break the surface of the water and jump several feet in the air. A jumping mullet may mean there's a school below. During the cooler spring and fall months mullets don't jump that often. In the summer, however, it's not uncommon to see three or four jump at one time, especially in the warm shallow water when the sun's rays are dancing off the surface.

Having examined the shoaly point, we continued north toward Six Mile Hammock Reef, hugging the edge of Howard's Reef and looking ahead for signs. "You got good eyes," said Sullivan to me, "look over toward the back of the reef and see if you can see one jump." After several minutes of intense scanning, I saw a small one barely break the surface. I yelled the discovery to Uriah, who slowed the motor. We looked over the area for a few minutes, then abandoned the prospect. Their minds were set on Six Mile Hammock Reef.

In his 1795 article titled "A Description of Occacock Inlet," Jonathan Price mentions Six Mile Hammock. The location is approximately six miles northeast of Ocracoke Inlet and just to the northwest of the Ocracoke Campground. Large live oaks, several centuries old, stand on this high section of the island. The reef just offshore of Six Mile Hammock is, appropriately, Six Mile Hammock Reef.

Sometimes we leave the boats in a creek near the hammock. All along Highway 12 creeks cut into the island from Pamlico Sound, and we sometimes use these if we happen to be fishing in the area. With the aid of an old truck, it takes less time to reach the good mullet shoals. When we are fishing from the village, much of the day is spent getting to and from the shoals.

Although early Ocracoke fishermen kept their boats and nets in the Creek, they also fished from the various creeks and bays northeast of the village. Since travel was slow, the fishermen constructed small fishing camps to house themselves for short periods of time. In the early years when lumber was scarce, the fishermen used any material they could find. "Back before I came along," recalled Sullivan, "Poppie used to tell that the old timers made their camps out of black needle rushes. They'd build some kind of frame, usually A-frame so the water would run off, then tie a bunch of rushes to it. They didn't leak either. They did most of their cooking outside. If it rained they had to get right close to the door or cook inside. In that case they'd have to cut a small opening in the ceiling to let the smoke out.

"Later on they started building the camps out of wood. They'd sleep about four or five people. They didn't have much in the way of furniture, maybe an old table, a couple of rough chairs, and a few bunks. I remember that sometimes we'd get seaweed that had washed

*This 1950s picture shows old cotton nets drying on a makeshift rack. In the background is a fisherman's small net house located along the northeast edge of the village. (Courtesy of Margueritte Boos)*

up on shore and dried to use for our beds. It always made them a lot softer."

Fishing from the camps was mostly a seasonal activity. During the spring, summer, and on into the fall, groups of men from the village would adjust their occupations, if they happened to be employed in something other than fishing, to spend time at the camps. This often included members of the lifesaving crews who were required to take off most of the summer months. Those who owned the camps invited others to join them and work in their particular crew.

When Uriah and Sullivan were growing up, they often spent time at the fishing camps. Along with their brother Mace, they had to help their father support the family. The sisters, Dell, Frances, Lucy, and Ellen, were left to maintain the household. Their mother, Ellen Garrish, died when they were children. "We'd go down to the camps," recalled Sullivan, "Poppie, Uriah, Mace, and myself on a Monday morning and stay to Saturday. Sometimes we'd take a horse and cart, go in our boats, or even walk.

"Our camp was about eight or ten miles from the village—right good walk when you think about it with cars and all today. We didn't mind the trip too much back then; guess we did it without thinking about it too much. Besides, you had to do it.

"Anyway, after we got down there and got situated, we'd start out about daylight most mornings and go out and fish for mullets. A lot of the time we didn't fish during the day because it was too hot and the mullets wouldn't keep by the time you could get back to the village with the catch. We cleaned and salted a lot of 'em. Most of the time you went out fishing of the night when it was cool. Not many people fish for mullets at night nowadays. You could really put it to 'em if you had a purty night. Many the time we fished all day and went right back out that night.

"Me and Uriah used to play tricks on Poppie. We'd be out there in the middle of the night, around one or two o'clock in the morning, and we wanted to come in. We were tired and disgusted because we hadn't caught nothing and we wanted to go to sleep. If we did see a sign we kept right quiet, hoping that Poppie would give up. Finally he'd say, 'Well, I want to try one more place.' He was waiting for the tide to make right, you see, and then we'd shove all over the reef to check on these places. We'd go to the place he had in mind and the mullets would be there. This would happen plenty of times. After we loaded both boats, he would say, 'Now see, if we hadn't come here to this last place we wouldn't have caught these.'"

After an hour of running, we finally reached Six Mile Hammock Reef. As we approached the edge, Uriah slowed the motor. The bottom along the edge of the reef is covered with eelgrass and other marine vegetation. We try to avoid setting the nets along the edge because the grass gets caught and weighs down the net. Our eyes focused on the white sandy bottom, approximately one hundred yards further up on the reef and already illuminated by the bright sunlight.

The propeller began hitting the bottom, chopping and churning grass, mud, and sand. "Cut her off," yelled Sullivan. Uriah didn't hear him. "Cut her off, Uriah! You're gonna tear her up and run everything off here in the bargain." Uriah stopped the motor, allowing us to drift slowly with the tide and wind. Without the steady drone of the motor, the natural sounds of wind and water seemed amplified. The tide was low, but would soon be flowing. "Sullivan, ain't this tide soaking up?" asked Uriah.

"I don't know about that," answered Sullivan. "I reckon it is."

"If you find 'em, they'll be up there on that white by Charlie's box," added Uriah. "Where's that stake?"

"There it is right there," I said, pointing to a short stake about two feet above the water, marking the location of a sink box used for hunting ducks and geese.

I stood on the bow, scanning along the edge of the white shoal. Further northwest, on across the reef perhaps two hundred yards, the shoal was dry. In places this dry lump of land was covered with seagulls and pelicans. Several gulls took to the air and flew toward us, perhaps expecting that our presence would mean food. "There's one jump, right there," I said. "About half-a-net's-length to the right of Charlie's box there on the edge."

"That's where they are, on that edge," said Sullivan, quickly. "You can be sure there're some there. Uriah, how about let's anchor the boat here and shove up there in the skiffs and see if we can't get a set."

"Let's hold on here a minute till we find out for sure where they're jumping," answered Uriah. He is always cautious and a bit skeptical of Sullivan's optimism and enthusiasm. "He's messed us up so much," Uriah often says, "always wanting to set before we know for sure where the mullets are."

Uriah had the oar and was shoving the *Rex* slowly in the direction where I had seen the mullet jump. "How do you expect me to see anything with you standing up there," Sullivan said to me. I pretended not to hear him and continued my close watch along the edge of the reef. "You got to get down from there," he added. "They'll see you up there like that. They can see a long ways." I sat down on the bow while Sullivan readied the anchor.

Uriah saw a mullet jump. "That settles it," said Sullivan. "There must be some up there if he saw one. What size are they?"

"About inch and a half," I said. We describe the mullets based on the size of the net mesh that would fit perfectly around the head of the fish. While many people refer to the size of nets by the stretch of the mesh, we always identify them by half of this. So a three-inch stretch mesh would be "inch and a half."

Sullivan eased the anchor overboard. They both changed into their old pants, stained with salt, mullet blood, and jellyfish parts.

"Get your skiff, Buddy," Uriah said to me. He then placed the Playmate cooler in his and Sullivan's skiff. Our lunch was in a small canvas bag and I took this in my skiff. We shoved away from the *Rex* and were ready to go "try 'em."

"Take her right easy now boys," said Sullivan. "Don't make no noise, be right easy."

By the time we got close to the white sandy bottom, the sun was up high enough to reveal the shape of the reef. Our eyes were fixed on the slight grassy bend, sometimes called a "bite," that bowed into the white. The depth of the water there is slightly deeper than on the white shoal, and it was there that I had seen the mullet jump. "They've got to be in that bite that kinda works up in there," said Sullivan.

"That's the only place they can go with the tide like this, unless they're way up there on the white with their backs out." Several more jumped. We were within twenty yards of the edge. "I believe we can reach them mullets," said Sullivan eagerly. "Come on, Uriah, let's try 'em here."

"Hold on, Sullivan, let's find out where they're jumping," said Uriah.

"Where they're jumping? I know where they're jumping. Right here. I don't expect you to see anything, never have." According to some people who know them well, one of the things that keeps Uriah and Sullivan going is that they argue with each other so much when they're out mulleting.

We shoved closer. "They're here by this water," observed Sullivan. "This water's getting thicker all the time." When mullets are feeding in an area, especially a sizable school, they often stir up the bottom sediments, giving the water a brown, milky appearance.

"Time to be gettin' ready to set here," said Sullivan. "If you're gonna do anything now's the time before they drop off here. Go ahead and get yeh net ready." I walked to the stern of the *Henry*, removed the canvas covering from my net, cleared the staff that would go overboard, then reached over and did the same for their net.

"There's another one," I said. Sullivan had one leg overboard and the other in the boat as he grabbed the staff from their net. After getting out of the boat, he called for mine. I pitched him my staff and started poling at the rate of one shove every three seconds.

Looking to the bottom, I could tell that mullets were feeding here. I came into a patch of thick, mullet-stirred water when half of my net was over the stern. As I started to turn and head up on the white shoal, Uriah yelled across the water to me. "Turn this way! Come this way!" Several mullets hit my net as I turned toward him.

"They're hitting your net there!" yelled Sullivan.

As I met Uriah, he said, slightly short of breath, "I think we took some of 'em in. Did you see anything?"

"Yeah, some hit my net." Uriah and I stood talking for a moment about the prospects of the set. Sullivan was muttering to himself about seeing a lot run on the bottom. He called to us: "They're whirling in here."

Uriah anchored the two skiffs. I tied the two staffs together and began dragging the nets toward Sullivan. Ebb tide was still running a little and that gave me an easier pull. "You better go down there and help him," said Uriah. "He can't do much against this tide." Sullivan, in the meantime, was pulling his end of the nets toward us, stopping occasionally to look around for mullets. When I reached the other end of the net, he appeared a little shortwinded and relaxed the strain on the net. "Some in here, I believe," he said. I grabbed the staffs and started pulling, my body inclined toward the water at a 45-degree angle. "Slack up on her when they go to her," Sullivan said. "Gotta watch that you don't drag her off the bottom."

We had set part of the nets on grassy bottom. Since it's easier to draw the nets together on sandy bottom, Sullivan and I began pulling the staffs toward Uriah. "I better go around and clear the net," said Sullivan. "This grass might have rolled her up. You work that way toward Uriah."

After pulling the nets for about ten minutes, I stopped to rest for a few seconds, then continued. Gradually the distance between Uriah and me narrowed and we soon met. The two nets were then separated. Sullivan and I would draw one net together, Uriah the other. This process is called "backing the net up." It limits the space available for the mullets to run, forcing them to mesh. Many mullets hit the net before the nets are backed up, thrashing their tails through the water and air in an attempt to break loose. All this thrashing around produces tiny geysers of water, and to Uriah and Sullivan this is one of the prettiest sights imaginable.

After another twenty minutes of pulling on the lines, they were finally brought together, forcing the last fish to mesh. Uriah finished shortly after we did. I went to get the *Henry*. My estimate was that we had caught about 150 pounds.

Sullivan had the staffs untied and was smiling as I came up to him.

A good catch of mullets in the small skiff we called the Henry. The approximately two hundred yards of net runs out over the stern when the boat is poled with a long oar.

To take in the net, I stood overboard, handling the lead line and taking out the fish as they came along. He stood on the stern thwart and pulled the cork line, piling the net on the platform in the stern. Our conversation was limited to short statements which were usually followed by long pauses. After all, the mullets might hear us. "Regular summertime mullets," said Sullivan.

"Yeah."

"I don't know what Uriah got in his net."

"He got a few."

"He ought to got some. His net is just right for these mullets."

"I believe this tide's starting to flow."

"Ought to be flowing on a shoal. Get another set here in a minute."

Uriah still had some net out when we finished. "Uriah's a good hand at taking fish out by hisself," observed Sullivan. "I never could do nothing taking a net in like that. I reckon I'd better go over there and help him." I stayed in the boat, packed the mullets under the stern thwart, placed a soaked burlap bag over them, then bailed out the bloody water. There was a tiny sore spot on each of my hands where a spine on the dorsal fin of the mullet had pierced them. Very seldom do you take mullets from a net without getting stuck at least once.

This catch of mullets was the smaller "summertime class," ranging in length from ten to fourteen inches and weighing approximately a pound or a pound and a quarter each. Uriah and Sullivan were just lifting the staff into the boat as I came up to them. "Well, did you put it to 'em?" I said.

"Oh, got a few," answered Uriah. He had about 50 pounds. We had about 150 pounds. It was a "right good little set."

By the time we began poling back to the *Rex*, the wind had strengthened a little and "backened up" from the west to a more southwesterly direction. "She'll probably blow this evening," said Sullivan. He judged the time to be approximately ten-thirty. We didn't wear watches. None of us owned one. Sullivan usually judged the time correctly, however, by looking up at the sun then down at the reflection on the water. I seconded his guess after spotting the ten o'clock Ocracoke–Cedar Island ferry heading west after leaving Big Foot Slough Channel.

"Well, I reckon we ought to get something to eat," said Sullivan.

"Eat. That's all the crowd of you study," I said, jokingly.

"Might as well," added Uriah, "and get it over with."

We reached the *Rex* and tied the skiffs to the stern while we ate.

After lunch we pulled the anchor and began shoving the *Rex* with the two skiffs in tow toward the edge of the reef slightly west of where we had just set the nets. The tide was starting to flow, and they were sure that some mullets would be moving up on the shoal. I had seen several jump all along the edge, and this gave them more encouragement.

After poling for several minutes we decided to anchor and lay there until the mullets moved up on the reef. Sullivan was eager to set again, attracted more by the assurance of a clean set on sandy bottom than the possibility of a good catch.

"We don't want to make nary faux-pas," said Uriah, as we boarded the skiffs to investigate the few I had seen jump. When Sullivan finally saw one only a few yards from the boat, he said, hurriedly, "Gimme here, gimme here" and the staffs were pitched to him. I followed the edge along as Uriah headed toward the white.

When Uriah and I had at last come together, he asked, "Did you see anything?"

"Not a thing."

"I didn't neither. He's always in such a hurry all the time." He then shouted across the water, asking Sullivan if he had seen anything. Sullivan yelled back that he had seen some run and reckoned that there must be at least a few in the nets.

We pulled the nets together as before. The flowing tide made it easier to drag them up on the reef. After the nets were separated and the two staffs from the ends of each net pulled across to the other side, we decided to boat them. "I don't see no need of backing her up," said Uriah. "Nothing in here to amount to anything."

The nets in the boat, we shoved back to the *Rex*. We had each caught about a dozen. "I think they were some in there," said Sullivan, trying to justify his decision to set. Most times his enthusiasm pays off. Then he reminds us that "you wouldn't have caught these hadn't been for me."

Uriah started the motor and steered west along the edge of the white, sandy shoal, keeping about fifty yards away so we wouldn't run off any mullets. The flowing tide also made it easier to run through the shallow water. Several times the propeller bumped across a grass lump. Sullivan shot a quick glance at Uriah then at the motor.

"Let's go to the head of Six Mile Hammock Reef Channel," yelled Sullivan toward Uriah, who nodded his approval.

When Uriah reached the deep water he steered northwest, knifing the *Rex* toward the back of the reef. He then stopped the motor and Sullivan eased the anchor overboard. "They could be over there on the back with this flowing tide," said Sullivan.

Uriah spit a mouthful of tobacco juice in the water, watched the tide carry it away from the boat, and said, "What about there in Eastern Bite?"

"They could be in there," answered Sullivan.

"Getting hot now," I said, with a slight tone of discouragement as I spotted the twelve-thirty Ocracoke–Swan Quarter ferry heading toward the mainland. They said nothing. Many mornings we have gone out, set the nets immediately, caught all we wanted, and been back in before noon. After we had set the nets the second time, I knew that it was going to be a long day. They were not satisfied. Regardless of the heat and how they might be feeling physically, they were not going ashore with 200 pounds of mullet. This was the source of their endurance. Sullivan had once said, "Different ones have asked me how Uriah and myself can get out here and do such works at our age. I tell 'em if you got anything you like to do you gotta keep at it. There were plenty of mornings we went out when we didn't feel like going." We had been out four days straight, and they wanted to finish the week with a good catch.

I got overboard with a clam rake and started raking a patch of sandy bottom surrounded by eelgrass. "There used to be some clams here," said Sullivan. He says that about every place I rake. After five minutes of intense raking, I banged the rake back into the boat. "Don't make too much racket," warned Sullivan.

Sullivan thought he saw a mullet jump about a net's length toward the back of the reef. Attempts to measure distances on the water are often deceiving, and that's one reason why we measure by our net's length. Having seen them strung out in the water many times, we have a clearer idea of that distance than of feet or yards. When one jumps close to the boat, however, Uriah usually says, "There's one like to jump in the boat."

We decided to leave the *Rex* and pole in the direction Sullivan thought he had seen one. The water was shallow in this area, white bottom with broken patches of eelgrass. The tide carried us easily. I still poled, keeping a boat's length ahead of them. "Not too fast," Sullivan warned several times. Although they shoved occasionally to sheer the boat in the right direction, they let the tide do most of the work. I saw one jump and did not tell them. It was far from the place we were heading and would have involved a much further shove.

My face was stiff with salt and splotches of mullet blood baked by sun and wind. "I gotta feeling there might be some in that Eastern Bite there by Jakie's blind," said Uriah. Eastern Bite begins west of Six Mile Hammock Reef Channel and covers an area about as big as two football fields. Most of the reef there is covered with eelgrass, but there is plenty of white shoal toward the back of the reef similar to the white on Six Mile Hammock Reef. Where Uriah had the "feeling" the mullets would be was a distance of about two hundred yards from the edge of the channel.

The light was no longer soft as it had been earlier in the morning. As the glare reflected off the tiny waves, I wished for my sunglasses. The wind had increased to about ten knots. "You can look up at them jacks there in the sky," observed Uriah, pointing to several patches of clouds, "and tell that it's going to blow."

"Yeah, she'll pull the stopper out this evening," added Sullivan.

Farther north along the distant edge of the white, about one hundred yards from the blind, I saw two big mullets leap high into the air then land on their sides with a splash that even Uriah could have seen. I told Sullivan this and added that they might be scattered. I had emphasized the word "scattered," which means the mullets are not schooled together and chances of a good set are not likely. With a slight tone of impatience, Sullivan said, "If you fellars don't want to set, we'll go in."

Uriah saw one jump. We finally agreed to pole closer toward the blind to investigate. If we didn't see anything after a few minutes we would go in.

The two o'clock Ocracoke–Cedar Island ferry was now on its way through Big Foot Slough Channel. Uriah drew a deep breath and let it out slowly.

I kept my eye on the spot where the two big ones had jumped. I saw several more. "That must be a big school of mullets," I finally announced.

"Where at?" asked Uriah.

"On the other side of that blind about a net's length. They've been jumping out of the water three and four at a time."

"What size are they?" said Sullivan.

"Big size."

"If anybody else is willing to try 'em, I am," said Sullivan.

Both Uriah and Sullivan finally saw the mullets I had been talking about. As we poled nearer to them, Sullivan said, "This water's getting thicker all the time. They're here by this water. We'd better lash the staffs together this time so I can help Uriah."

A big mullet jumped out of the water, barely cleared the surface, then landed on its side with the tail slightly bent. "There's one jump in his crook," said Sullivan hurriedly, referring to a mullet which had curved its body as it came out of the water. "Just as good a sign as you want." He then pitched the staffs overboard as we began poling away from each other. Mullets hit the nets as soon as they went over the sterns. We then encircled an area with more white bottom.

At last we came together and stood for a moment, looking around at the bottom. Several dozen mullets raced toward us. Some hit the net within a foot of the staffs. Most turned and followed along my net, looking for an escape. "Buddy, we got 'em this time," said Uriah.

"They hit mine and Uriah's net as soon as we put off," added Sullivan.

As we pulled the nets together for the last time, quite a few mullets could be seen lying idly in small holes on the bottom. This is unusual since mullets are such an active fish when trapped. I stepped into several of the holes and stirred the sand with my foot. Most of the mullets then ran into the net, but some remained in the hole.

These were bigger mullets, inch and three quarters and two inch (approximately a foot and a half long). "These big ones won't go to the net either," said Uriah, "not till you make 'em." As the nets were pulled together, mullets began bumping into our legs. They had stirred up the bottom sediments so that it was difficult to see where we were walking. A large brown object glided past my foot and headed toward Sullivan. "There's one of them ole big stingrays in here," I said.

"You better watch out for them," Uriah warned. He has been stung three times. A stingray is a flatfish and has a whiplike tail with a venomous spine (the sting). Some stingrays have several stings. Normally a trip to a doctor or even a hospital is necessary so that penicillin can be administered to counter the poison.

Uriah was stung before drugs and doctors were so accessible to the island. "The first time I got stung was the worst," he recalled. "We were fishing down on the eastern end of the Legged Lumps, and when the stingray stuck me he rammed it right through my heelstring and it came out the other side. He didn't leave it in me. Anyway, your Uncle William brought me home in the old *Kingfisher*. There was a doctor here for a while, and he took one of these small swabs and put Mercurochrome on it and pulled it through the hole on a string. Somebody gave me a fifth of liquor to kill the pain. He told me not to drink it, and he took the bottle and wouldn't let nobody in the room with me. Sometime later that evening after I woke up, he was there drunker than a bat. He had drinked all my liquor. I was laid up a month before I could walk. The other two times weren't too bad. I only missed a couple of days of fishing."

Sullivan has been stung once. This occurred in the 1960s near the same spot where Uriah had been stung so badly. Bobby and I were fishing with them then. My clearest memory of the incident was Uriah taking Sullivan's heel to his mouth and trying to suck out some of the poison. Sullivan didn't see a doctor for several days (there was no resident doctor at the time). His foot became infected and he was finally hospitalized for a week. The doctor told him if he had waited for several more days that he would have probably lost his foot to gangrene.

I managed to get the stingray out of the net. I have seen them far inshore, almost to the bank, big as the hood of a small car. There is always the chance of being stung while walking around in a net, especially if the water is cloudy. The best way to move about is to shuffle your feet slowly across the bottom. If you bump one they usually run. If you step on one and it happens to whip its tail just right, you get stung.

Mullets continued to hit our nets. Uriah had finished pulling his net together and was walking toward the skiffs. The corks and lines of his net wiggled and bobbed in the water, and mullet heads and tails stuck into the air. A space about the size of a car remained open. "Ain't you gonna back that part up?" I asked.

"Got enough of 'em."

Uriah pulled the anchor of the *Henry* and sent the skiff toward us. As we began to take up the net, he shouted across the water, "You fellars get your net up and then come here and help me with mine."

The white undersides of mullets were showing all along our net. Many were too big to mesh. Most drowned as the three-inch mesh stretch choked the head and prevented the gill covering from opening and closing, which is necessary to send the needed supply of water to the gills. "We put it to 'em this time, didn't we," I said to Sullivan.

*Standing in my boat, Sullivan hands me a staff of a mullet net while Uriah looks on. In the background is Fowler O'Neal's boat, which we used in the hunting trip in the following chapter. (Photograph by Ann Ehringhaus)*

"Don't know all of what you would have got hadn't been for this bottom."

"Few crabs in here too."

"Where's that stick? Have you got that stick?"

When crabs get stuck in the net, you often have to break their claws to get them out. Sometimes you have to smash the entire crab to pieces.

Along with the nuisance of blue crabs, countless jellyfish were everywhere. "The tourists call 'em jellyfish," said Sullivan. "If they felt 'em as much as we do, they wouldn't think they were jelly." Locally they are called "stinging nettles" or "sea nettles." Our legs and arms were burning. The irritation lasts for several minutes and then is gone. They are especially painful, however, when a tiny fragment of the tentacles breaks apart from the fish and lands on your eyeball. I cursed them being in the net. Sullivan said, "Everything is put here for a purpose, I reckon." A crab bit my finger as I was trying without much success to free it from the net. I grabbed the stick and smashed the crab into tiny pieces of shell and crab guts, muttering a string of invectives. Sullivan responded by calling me "Ole" Horatio. That was Horatio Williams, my great-great-grandfather, who used to captain a schooner and sometimes cuss at the wind. Sullivan recalled, "They always said that one time when he was out sailing, the wind died out and left him in the middle of the sound. He ripped and rared till finally he took a silver dollar and nailed it on the deck and dared God Almighty to make it blow. The wind shifted and near about blew the sails and masts off. He was supposed to have said that he only asked for a dollar's worth of wind."

The four o'clock Ocracoke–Cedar Island ferry was on its way toward Cedar Island when we finished our net and walked over to help Uriah. With Sullivan helping him lay the net back in the skiff and me wading along in front of them picking out mullets, we had Uriah's net in the skiff within fifteen minutes. Our estimates were that we had about 400 pounds in the *Henry* and that Uriah had about 300 pounds in his skiff. "You can't beat this set," said Sullivan.

"Have you had enough of it for today?" I asked Uriah.

"All I want of it for one day."

We poled back to the *Rex* and began the slow trip up the channel against the souwester that had increased to twenty knots. The tide had also started to ebb, making it that much rougher as the wind bucked it. We kept constant watch on the skiffs, especially the *Henry*, afraid that the waves might break over the gunwales and fill them with water.

We were getting soaked. Sullivan put on an oilskin jacket. Uriah held one in front of him and draped a burlap bag over his legs. Sullivan sat on the stern thwart facing Uriah and shielding him from much of the spray. I straddled the bow and let the water splash over me. We all three had a beer.

By five o'clock we had at last rounded the entrance to the Creek. Water was dripping off our noses. We were tired but happy. It was Friday and we had not caught this many mullets in at least a month.

My father, Uriah's wife Maude, their son Bobby, and his wife and little girl were standing on the bulkhead as we passed on our way to the fish house. The owner of the fish house, several employees, and two local men (one who had wished us well that morning) were standing on the dock. "You boys have had a washing out there today, haven't you," said the owner.

"Uriah, they're purty mullets," said one of the local men.

"Purtiest I ever saw," said the other man.

"Get you a mess of 'em," said Uriah. They each took six.

By five-thirty we had the mullets unloaded and were securing the boats. As we walked up out of the water, Maude asked, "Where in the world have you all been at all this time?"

"Look at how wet they are," added Bobby's wife.

"We thought you might have got broke down," said my father.

"Fishing," said Uriah. "Fishing."

"Well, what did you get?" asked Bobby. Uriah took the wet sales ticket from his shirt pocket, looked at it, put it back in his pants pocket, and said, "Six hundred and ninety-three pound."

When I was growing up on Ocracoke, most of my free time was spent fishing, playing basketball, or hunting. While the busy summers were filled with mulleting, swimming, and getting to know some of the summer people, the lonely winters were passed playing basketball and hunting birds, ducks, and geese.

Like other Ocracoke boys, my interest in hunting began when I was given my first BB gun. In addition to shooting at makeshift targets, we also tramped all over the village in search of birds, especially robins and cedar waxwings. Although the idea now seems a little atrocious, we actually killed and ate scores of these two birds.

Eventually we outgrew BB guns and began to take an interest in shotguns. Most of the boys had been hunting with their fathers, and they were eager for their sixteenth birthday, which meant a hunting license and gun of their own. My father didn't hunt, but I sometimes got to go hunting with Fowler O'Neal and his son Bobby. Bobby and I spent many hours together, not only mulleting but also hunting birds, ducks, and geese. Many mornings and afternoons we would scout the creeks and shorelines of the village for any ducks and geese that might have strayed inshore.

Bobby was the hunter. I soon found out that he hunted not because it was the thing for an Ocracoke boy to do but because he loved it. To him hunting was a serious activity, a constant search for something to shoot, something that would eventually wind up on the supper table. Often he would get up early and go out by himself. Most of the time he wouldn't tell me or anybody else what he had killed. His father had taught him not to "blab" his kill to anyone, and I soon realized that he would rather hunt alone.

We still took many hunting trips together, and I think that the most memorable one occurred on a cold December afternoon long before we were old enough to get our hunting licenses. We left our houses soon after school and began the long walk to the shoreline along the northeast part of the village, our pockets stuffed with hard Christmas candy. Since we had only two hours of daylight left, we both had the feeling that we wouldn't get the chance to kill anything. Besides, we were armed only with BB guns.

As we neared the shoreline, we slowed our gait, readying our guns should any black ducks fly up out of the marsh. The evening sun had colored the marsh grass a dull red by the time we reached the shoreline. When we found nothing there, we picked up our pace and headed for the creeks, trying to cover our normal track before dark. The cold northeast wind stung our faces and hands and watered our eyes.

We searched several creeks, spotting ducks here and there, but we were unable to get close enough for a shot. Far out over the water, toward Howard's Reef, strings of geese, brant, and redheads dotted the horizon. Bobby remarked that it would have been a good day hunting out on the reefs, and he was sure that if he had been over there he would have killed something.

As it got later, we decided to give up the hunt and head back home. We weren't terribly disappointed, for we often came back empty-handed on these after-school trips.

I think we both saw it at the same time, sticking straight up through the marsh grass, the long black stalk of a neck, curving slightly toward the top, the head, and the black interrupted with a white patch resembling a bandage wrapped under the chin, and just beyond the white patch the brown-black eye that stared straight at us, not in surprise, but watchful as if it had been looking at us for some time.

We froze in our tracks, not knowing what to do next, and surprised that a goose would be this close to shore. Soon, though, it dawned on us that we could actually kill and take home one of the most prized of water birds. While we studied all this, the goose decided that it would be best if he tried to make his escape. As the bird scampered across the almost dry shoal, sometimes swimming, sometimes walking, and sometimes trying to fly, we soon realized why it was in so close, alone. It had a broken wing.

We stood on the shoreline, helplessly watching the goose as it drifted out toward the channel but still in very shallow water. If we had only had a shotgun we could have killed it the moment we saw it. Our BB guns were not powerful enough to stop it. It was then that Bobby said that he was going to get that goose if it was the last thing he did. He pulled off his shoes and socks and ran out into the ice cold water, occasionally shooting at the fleeing goose. He kept getting closer and finally got within a few yards, shooting it in the breast with his BB gun. The shots slowed the goose long enough for Bobby to run up to it and grab it by the neck. From the shoreline I could see the goose offering some resistance, but then it was all over. With several rotations around his head, Bobby broke the bird's neck, then threw it down forcefully in the water where it floated motionlessly. He then picked up the goose by the neck, slung it over his shoulders, and began walking proudly back to the shore as if the cold water didn't bother him at all.

By the time we left the shoreline, it was getting dark. We headed on across an empty field of dredge spoil where dove occasionally flew up out of the short weeds. Bobby held the goose's neck with one hand and his BB gun with the other. We both had our mouths stuffed with Christmas candy.

When we reached Bobby's house, his father came out, took one look at the goose, and knew that it was poor, too poor to eat. He scolded us for killing something so disabled and explained that the goose had been shot in the wing and had gone inshore where it might have had a chance for survival in the quieter inshore environment. He said it seemed like a poor injured goose couldn't even die in peace for us, and that we might spend our evenings better if we played basketball in the backyard.

We were both disappointed that the excitement of our prize kill had been shattered, and we knew that if we wanted to get a "good" goose, we would have to go hunting with Fowler out on the reefs in his blind.

Fowler O'Neal is a stocky man of medium height with a full head of ash-colored hair. He retired on disability from the North Carolina Department of Transportation, Ferry Division, where he worked as a quartermaster on one of the Ocracoke–Cedar Island ferries.

His retirement came about after two heart attacks, the first while he was fishing shad nets several miles offshore in Pamlico Sound. He says that he's lucky to be alive, especially after that day so far out on the water, alone, when he had to steer the boat almost an hour in rough winter water with increasing pains running throughout his chest and arms. After his retirement, Fowler was able to spend more time doing the things he enjoys the most: fishing gill nets and hunting.

I've never been much of a hunter. Although it is difficult to believe, given my early interest in the sport, when I finally got old enough to buy my hunting license, I had lost interest in hunting. I go out with Fowler occasionally, but only to observe.

We went out one morning when conditions were promising. "You couldn't ask for a better hunting day," said Fowler. After a week of clear, warm weather—perfect for tourists but lousy for hunting—the wind had shifted from the southwest to the northwest, increasing steadily throughout the night to approximately twenty knots, and the sky had thickened to a heavy gray overcast.

Early that morning we left the Creek in Fowler's boat, a sharp-looking skiff, powered by a twenty-five-horsepower Evinrude outboard motor. Bobby called the skiff the "shark" because of its slender appearance and the way it shot through the water when the power was increased.

I sat near the stern as Fowler steered from the bow with a stick connected with cables that ran to the stern and the motor. The waves slapped against the port side of the boat and cold spray pelted us as

*Fowler O'Neal, 1989. (Photograph by Ann Ehringhaus)*

we headed toward Howard's Reef. Bobby had told me that his father's blind was located "on the back edge of Eastern Bite" and added that I wouldn't mistake it for any other blind, since it was the tallest blind on the reef. I knew exactly which blind was his. We often fished for mullets there during the warmer seasons.

After the cold trip across the channel, Fowler slowed the motor as we approached a short stake that stuck out of the water along the edge of the reef. We would tie the boat to this stake and wade to the blind, located almost a quarter of a mile away on the back edge of the reef.

When the boat had been secured to the stake and the anchor thrown overboard, we tightened the straps on our waders and began walking toward the blind. I offered to take some of the gear, but Fowler insisted on taking all of it. Slung over his shoulders and dangling from his arms were two decoys, one a goose, the other a duck, an oilskin coat, a twelve-gauge shotgun, and a small "starfoam" cooler containing binoculars, several boxes of shotgun shells, and a lunch consisting of sandwiches, crackers, Pepsi, and candy.

Near the boat the water was waist deep, but as we walked up on the reef further it shallowed to our knees. The strong northwester had spread an unusually high tide, and tiny white caps slapped up against our boots as we walked. The winter reef looked cold, gray, and lifeless, and felt quite a bit different from the way I remembered it from my summer mulleting expeditions.

We continued wading, talking about a variety of subjects and at times turning our heads to look back over our shoulders to measure the distance we had traveled. Most of the time we looked down into the milky gray water, which allowed only a dim view of the reef bottom.

As we approached the blind, I could see that Bobby had been right when he said it was the tallest blind on the reef. While the others measured about nine feet from the waterline to the top of the blind, Fowler's measured at least twelve feet. It was more like a small watch-tower than a duck blind.

The legs of the blind were six-inch round creosote poles, each buried with a slight inward tilt for greater stability and support. Barnacles, oysters, and other aquatic growth covered the underwater portions of the legs. Nailed between two poles were four two-by-fours used as a ladder. The climb seemed rather steep to me, especially for a man who had heart trouble. While I was pondering over this potential hazard, Fowler began to climb up the ladder, pulling himself up with one hand and holding the gun and the cooler with the other. When he reached the entrance of the blind, he set aside the gear near the door, entered the blind, and began tossing the decoys down into the water.

Bobby had told me, "Wait till you see his stand of decoys." The collection of decoys, which included geese, brant, and ducks, looked like a pretty sick bunch of birds. Out of the whole flock of about twenty-five, maybe two could pass for attractive decoys. Several of the geese had their heads broken or shot off. The neck of one was plugged with a crooked stick, painted black with the bill turned toward the tail. A number of the others had been repainted with colors resembling the original blacks, grays, browns, and whites. There were also two styrofoam crab pot buoys, each with a blade of plywood wedged in the top to resemble the tail feathers.

When Fowler had thrown the last decoy from the blind, he climbed back down the ladder to spread them in an arc several yards northwest of the blind. Each of the decoys was strung with about two yards of eighth-inch nylon cord, one end tied to the decoy and the other to a small lead anchor.

I climbed up the ladder and stood in front of the door. Fowler shouted from below that I should get in the blind and sit down. I pulled aside the small door and entered. The blind itself was a patchwork structure made from second-use, nail-ridden two-by-fours and pieces of plywood salvaged from scrap lumber piles and other dilapidated blinds. The two-by-fours served as the framework onto which the plywood was nailed. The entire house was four feet square and about five feet high. Fowler again yelled for me to make myself comfortable on the seat, a two-by-six placed on braces at either end of the blind.

It had been nearly eight years since I had been in a blind, and the last time had been with Fowler and Bobby. When friends asked me to go hunting with them or encouraged me to get my hunting license, I often considered accepting their invitations, but the thought of sitting for hours in a cold, drafty blind made the whole idea less inviting.

*These hunters are hunting from a sink box, which is a structure fixed below the surface of the water. Since the tops of the boxes are level with the water, the hunters are better hidden from approaching birds. (Courtesy of Elizabeth Howard)*

It had been a long cold walk from the boat, and as I positioned myself on the seat, I felt more comfortable and just a little excited and expectant. Looking up, I noticed the one-inch peep crack that had been left along the sides of the blind which allowed hunters a strategic view, half of the water, half of the horizon. We would spend a great amount of time looking through this crack.

Standing up, I found the top edge of the blind level with my shoulders. It sure was an excellent view, and I could see why Fowler was proud of his towering structure. In the water below he spaced the last decoy, then started to wade back toward the blind. "That's a stand for you, ain't it," he said, referring to the flock of decoys that rode the small waves with firm inanimate resistance. As he approached the blind, I could hear him laughing, amused at his decoys.

I sat back down and slipped over to the left to make room for Fowler as he entered the blind. He slid the door back in place and pulled off his oilskin coat. Before sitting down, he picked up his shotgun and unsheathed it from its plastic insulated case. He then rummaged through the cooler until he came out with a handful of shotgun shells. He placed one shell in the chamber of the gun, gave the pump handle a quick slick-slack, and then inserted two more shells. After putting the gun in a corner, Fowler sat down, repositioning himself several times before getting comfortable.

"I've got two blinds here on this reef," he said. "I reckon they've been here for fifteen years or more. Of course I've rebuilt 'em year after year when they've needed it, but I've been using the same location for a good while. This blind is a sturdy one. I don't expect she'll go anywhere. Sometimes the blinds get torn up during hard blows, hurricanes and such as that, but you've got to come out during the first of the season anyway to check on 'em and rebuild 'em if they need it.

"One job that most people don't like is cleaning up all the mess from seagulls and pelicans. They sit along the top edge of the blind and mess in it and then the sun bakes it right into the wood. I fix 'em. What I do is take and hammer a bunch of little headless nails along the edge after I leave the blind when the season's over. They don't take to sitting around too much then."

The wall facing us was partially constructed from an old sign that Fowler had found washed up along the shore. The faded letters had once been part of a sign advertising cottages for rent. "I have another blind back there along the inside edge of the reef," he continued, pointing his thumb over his left shoulder. "I hunt there sometimes when the weather's mild. It seems that on the mild days the fowl tend to fly along the inside edge. When it's bad and blowing like today, it's better along the back edge of the reef near the sound. That's why we came here, because I think that some fowl might be following this back edge down."

We continued talking, all the while scanning the horizon through the crack. Fowler took out his binoculars and spotted a large flock of geese about a half mile north, only several hundred yards from another hunter's blind. At the time no one occupied it. We sat almost nervously, anticipating something flying within range.

Occasionally we spotted dark objects that upon closer inspection proved to be cormorants. It always seemed that there were thousands upon thousands of these water birds, flying in endless strings, the first to arrive, the last to leave. Even though the birds are fish eaters, some Ocracokers eat them. One resident said, "Take the breast and fry it and there's nothing better. Just as good as any steak." From a distance they often fool even the best hunter into thinking that a goose or duck is on the way.

I got into the habit of whispering "what's that" when I spotted anything that threatened to fly into range. Eventually we both began to whisper, thinking that even over the howl of the northwester the ducks and geese might hear us if we talked too loudly.

We had been sitting there no more than an hour when I spotted the white flash of color on several pintails. They appeared suddenly overhead and just to the north of the blind. Fowler was looking far over to his right at a large flock of geese. I blurted out several what's thats and he responded with several wheres. Before I could say anything else, he had sensed the location of the pintails and jumped up quickly to his feet, pulling the gun to his shoulder and firing three quick shots at the ducks. For all his quickness on the draw, though, he had missed. The pintails were out of range by the time the shots were fired. "If I had seen them a few seconds earlier we might have a pair of sprigtail now," said Fowler, referring to the pintails by a name local hunters use.

The noise of the shot resounding through the blind and the sharp smell of gunpowder gave the feeling that something momentarily powerful had taken place. At least there had been a shot, and this gave us hope that more fowl would fly our way. Fowler took up his binoculars again and looked at the large flock of geese. "Boy, I'd like to get a shot at them," he said. "I know there'll be some sprigtail around today, maybe some other ducks, but I don't know so much about that flock of geese. You see, you've got a problem when you're out here hunting by yourself. It's better if different ones are hunting all along the reef and inshore. That way they keep 'em runned up and flying around, and there's a better chance of getting some good shots."

Settling down again after the first shots of the day, Fowler continued, commenting on the present hunting season. "I believe there have been more fowl flying around the first part of this season than since I was a boy. For a while there was flock after flock of sprigtail, widgeons, and even a good sign of brant and geese. You can't kill brant this particular season, even though there are a lot of 'em around here. They're pretty dumb birds and easy to kill. I reckon that's one of the reasons, but I think it has more to do with their migration patterns and the fact that the people who are setting the laws want to try to build up their numbers."

Although the waterfowl today are fewer in number and the daily limits are becoming more restrictive, there was a time when a reasonable income could be made from killing and selling ducks and geese. Thurston Gaskill, Sr., who has spent most of his life in the fishing and hunting guide business, well remembers the market hunting times before Congress passed the Migratory Bird Act during the 1917–18 hunting season. This act outlawed the killing of large numbers of ducks and geese.

"In my early years as a boy," recalled Thurston, "I remember that my father used to depend on market hunting for part of his living. Along with other men of the island, he used to go out on the reefs, most of the time over near Beacon Island and Portsmouth Island, and kill numbers of geese and ducks.

"Sometimes they used rolling blinds. They were something on the order of the regular duck blinds, but they had rollers on the bottom so you could roll the whole blind up to a flock of fowl. It was not uncommon for him to shoot five to seven hundred shells per week.

Back in those days they had plenty to shoot at, however, and their kill would often be in the hundreds.

"They would come back in the village, usually with the boat loaded, then sell the birds to Captain Will Willis, or some other merchant operating at that time, who would in turn transport them to New Bern or Morehead City. They packed the fowl in flour barrels, and I believe they were paid by the barrel. My father used to make as high as one hundred dollars per day, and of course that was good money in those days.

"Perhaps my clearest memory of my boyhood times was during the winter of 1917–1918. My father, myself, and another man were hunting over on Beacon Island and staying in the camp that my father had built there. We were stranded inside this camp when part of Pamlico Sound froze over. It was just impossible to run a boat through the ice. The mailboat tried, but had to turn around and go back. We had plenty of canned food and meat to eat and enough firewood to last us, so we weren't really bad off. The main problem was that we couldn't go anywhere, therefore we couldn't make any money. We had killed 325 geese, brant, and ducks, and stacked them inside till no more could fit there. When the ice finally gave way, we headed home and sold the entire lot of birds for one hundred dollars.

"It wasn't long before people began to realize that too many ducks and geese were being killed and that there would soon have to be a limit set. The winter of 1917–1918 was the last winter that you could kill and sell migratory fowl. That put an end to the market hunting. The first limit was eight geese, eight brant, and twenty-five ducks per day. Compare that to the one goose and several ducks that you're allowed today and you'll get an idea of how the limit has gradually decreased each year."

Even though the end of market hunting eliminated a source of revenue and angered the hunters, they were aware that such freedom with the trigger couldn't last. Several men had already begun practicing another way of making a living during the winter: serving as a hunting guide. "During the market hunting times," continued Thur-

*Captain Ike F. O'Neal (standing second from left), in his two-masted schooner,* Relief, *1918. This hunting party had killed 106 geese, brant, and ducks. (Courtesy of Danny Garrish)*

ston, "my father and other men of the island also took hunters out and served as a guide for them. He had this camp built over on the southern end of Beacon Island and used to take hunters over there to stay periods of time.

"You see, Beacon Island was mostly man-made. During the Civil War they built it up to around fifteen feet above water so they could put a fort there. After the fort was destroyed, my father built a camp at the foot of the hill. Some of his customers from up north had financed the building of it. The actual structure was one of those knock-down, prefabricated buildings about thirty feet long and twenty-six feet wide. It was lined inside with a heavy red paper, something that always stands out in my mind when I think back on the time of my boyhood. It was also laid out in rooms and had a fireplace in one corner and later on they added a kitchen on the west end of it.

"My father seemed to make the adjustment from market hunting to hunting parties pretty easily. Serving as a hunting guide was a more dependable income.

"After I got out of the Navy, I started to build up a fishing and hunting guide business myself. For a while hunting wasn't so good because of the disappearance of the eelgrass. I believe it covered about a ten-year period. Anyway, this was prime food for the waterfowl and they simply migrated where the grass could be found. Some of the grass eventually came back and hunting also improved.

"I don't take out hunting parties like I used to. My son Bill does some. There are also a few other people who do it around here. They haven't been at it as long as I have, but they have their blinds in some pretty good places. They do all right. The seasons differ. Sometimes you'll have a good one, sometimes a bad one."

My grandfather Elisha Ballance recalled when geese were so plentiful that their honking would keep people awake all night. He also said that on several occasions he shot geese on moonlit nights from his backyard.

A February 10, 1887, article from the *Weekly Record* of Beaufort states, "Messrs. Dan Williams and Ben Neil while patroling the beach at Ocracoke during a stormy night last week, were compelled to lie down to escape injury from a tremendous flock of geese making their way down the banks. In the meantime, Mr. Williams, while lying on his back, caught four of the geese alive. This story seems almost incredible, but it is nevertheless true."

In addition to Canadian geese, brant, pintail, and widgeon that Fowler had seen during the season, other waterfowl frequent the Ocracoke area. These include redheads, called by many the best eating duck, which appear at times in flocks so large and dense that from a distance they resemble a dark cloud moving swiftly in an undulating pattern along the horizon; canvasbacks, a close cousin of the redhead and sometimes found mixing with it, but mostly found in pairs; common, red-breasted, and hooded mergansers, locally called the "fisherman duck" and eaten less often than other waterfowl due to their sometimes fishy taste; black ducks, good eating, hard to shoot because of their alertness, but still visible in pairs throughout the hunting season and on into the spring and summer when they lay their eggs in the marshes along the soundside of the island; ruddy ducks, small, less prized ducks that frequent the ponds and creeks of the island, usually individually or in pairs; buffleheads, probably the smallest duck hunted, though often ignored, seen in small flocks or pairs; greater and lesser scaup, locally called the "blackhead," mostly found in pairs on the reefs of Pamlico Sound; and blue and green winged teal, small ducks that fly in tight flocks on the reefs, though they are sometimes found in ponds and creeks. Other waterfowl that occasionally show up include mallards, gadwalls, wood ducks, common goldeneyes, and shovelers.

As the morning flew by—and time did fly, not miserably creep along as I had thought it would—it appeared that the thick cloud cover of early morning might break. Far out in the northwest over the middle of Pamlico Sound, long reddish cracks lined the horizon.

Fowler and I turned to watch several boats speeding up the channel toward us. One boat was a small wooden craft and the other was a new twenty-foot fiberglass Pioneer with a 55-horsepower motor. While we talked and scanned the horizon through the crack, the two boats pulled up to the edge of the reef not far from Fowler's boat, and the hunters got out and began walking to their blinds. The man in the wooden boat was older. He continued wading until he reached a stake stuck in the middle of the reef. He then tied his skiff there and walked several hundred yards to his blind. The fiberglass boat held two younger men. They tied their boat to a stake along the inside edge of the reef. Their blind was also along that side of the reef and close to Fowler's other blind.

Fowler soon spotted several more pintail. His head moved continuously from side to side and up and down to keep sight of the fast-moving ducks. I kept still and could feel his body get tense, see his hand tighten its grip on the pump handle as the third finger on his right hand pushed in the safety of the gun.

Within the next moment a pair of quite different sounds that often occur together could be heard: the airy sound of wings beating and the whistlelike call of the pintail, followed by the sudden booming of three quick shots from a gun. But once again the ducks had flared upward at the crucial moment, over the blind, out of range, and Fowler had missed. Sinking down on the seat, Fowler said, "Talk about a bum shot. That's all you can call it, a bum shot. You don't want to tell Bobby about that one."

I told him it seemed to me that the pintail had never gotten close enough, that they were out of shot range. He laughed and said, "Yeah, bum shot."

The cloud cover had loosened gradually, pushing to the southeast in thin white patches of vapor. Through these clouds clear blue sky could be seen. As much as we both hoped against it, the day was going to turn out to be beautiful after all.

The harsh sound of a jet, probably out of Cherry Point Marine Corps Air Station some sixty miles away, broke through the ordinary sounds of wind and lapping water. Fowler and I watched the jet as it raced by, flying on a course that included the reef. "These jets help you out sometimes," he said. "It scares the fowl and they fly up and move around."

As he predicted, a large flock of geese perhaps a mile and a half inshore taking advantage of the big tides that made feeding along the marshbank profitable, rose up and began to fly, slowly and majestically, in our direction. About half of the flock soon settled back down, while the other half suddenly veered to the left and continued on a southward course, flying along the edge of the island. We both strained to keep sight of them in the glare of the bright new sun reflecting off the water. Trailing behind them were four that refused to follow the larger flock and instead headed directly toward the reef and more or less toward us. We continued watching, attentive to the direction of their flight path. When they began flying parallel to the inside edge of the reef, only a hundred yards or so from Fowler's boat and very near his other blind, it was time for him to take out his goose call. He blew out several loud honks, hoping that the geese would hear it and turn our way.

The geese soon halted their sluggish flapping and began gliding on a descending slant until they splashed into the shallow water. "Look at that, won't you," Fowler said. "Now there's something pretty, especially when they start falling like that." The geese had fallen only yards from the other blind on the inside edge of the reef. "This weather's starting to clear now," he continued, "and the wind seems to be falling out some. If we were there in that other blind we'd have a goose by now."

But we weren't in the other blind and all we could do was watch. At first it appeared there might be a chance of the geese drifting toward us, but it wasn't long before they saw the larger flock about four hundred yards to the south that we had spotted earlier. As the four geese started to swim toward the others, Fowler said, "You got a problem, you know, when different people are not scattered all along the reef hunting."

While we waited, the cloudy morning had broken away and developed into a beautiful, almost cloudless afternoon. For the first time that day we stood up and revealed ourselves without reason, perhaps a little discouraged about not killing anything but perhaps more discouraged about the weather changing for the better, or worse. We both felt a little uneasy with our heads and shoulders exposed, and when I pointed out several flying objects along the back of the reef, we sank down on the seat and followed their movements through the crack. As they came closer, passing directly in front of us but far out of range, Fowler said, "Cornables." This is how many Ocracokers pronounce cormorant. He laughed at this and added, "About the only thing we'll get today will be a sunburn."

During the next half hour we talked, ate sandwiches and candy, and occasionally checked on the other hunters in the blinds to the north and east of us. They had not even fired their guns. It was now about two o'clock and Fowler asked if I was tired and said that anytime I wanted to go that he would be ready.

I think we both saw them, but still I said, "What's that," pointing north at another group of ducks. From a distance we both could tell that they weren't pintail. Nothing appeared white on these ducks and they were flying slower. But they were headed directly for the blind.

Fowler readied his gun. "Boy, talk about pretty," he whispered. "Ain't that something pretty. They're headed right this way."

For the next half minute the ducks continued our way. As they got closer, Fowler identified them as widgeons. From one moment to the next they had disappeared from our crack view and flashed visible in the open sky over the blind. They were high and I thought that Fowler didn't have much of a chance at hitting any of them. While I was thinking this, he jumped up and fired three times. I then stood up alongside him to see if he had hit any. About four or five fluffy white feathers glided downward gently.

"I hit one of 'em," he said excitedly. There were three of them and two had flown ahead of the third. It was the third one that had been hit. "Watch him fall, watch him fall," said Fowler quickly. Just as he had said, the widgeon began a downward glide, almost as if it were settling down to rest or feed. It didn't seem to me that the duck had been wounded bad enough to fall.

Fowler didn't waste any time getting out of the blind and scrambling down the ladder. The widgeon had fallen about 200 yards westward. Fowler would have a good walk, and it was quite possible that the duck might get up and fly again or simply swim away.

The widgeon stayed within several yards of where it had fallen, however, and Fowler gained on it fast, trudging through the cold water like a marine during a beach landing. The two other widgeons circled back, almost as if to check on their wounded companion. I yelled to Fowler and tried to point them out, but he did not hear. All his concentration was focused on the downed bird, ready to react should it try to escape. The two other widgeons then flared off toward the back of the reef and were gone, leaving their triplet to the mercy of the approaching hunter. By then Fowler was within shot range but he refused to shoot. He was trying to get close enough to grab the duck, and several times he came close, but it flew out of range. He didn't want to risk tearing up the body with another shot.

The little dodge game continued another several minutes before the duck gradually gave up. Fowler finally got close enough so that his shadow cast down over the doomed duck. He then reached down and grasped the flapping creature by the neck. With six or seven rotations the neck was wrung.

Fowler began walking back toward the blind, taking his time, obviously pleased with his first kill of the day. When he reached the blind, he stood in front of the ladder before climbing up and threw the widgeon through the door. It banged lightly against a wall and lay limp on the floor. Aside from a few ruffled feathers, nothing showed that it had been shot. This widgeon was a hen, mostly brown with speckles of black and white.

Climbing the ladder, Fowler was laughing again. "Yeah, you want to be sure to tell Bobby about that shot. You want to tell him that you've seen a lot of shots in your day but nothing to match this one. Be sure to tell him how far away he fell from here after I hit him. I had no idea that they were close enough. Why, some of the sprigtail that I missed a while ago were a lot closer than that. Let him have it, anyways."

Fowler was restless after this shot. Perhaps he now considered the day successful after killing something. Bobby had said that his limit was one duck per day.

The restlessness turned to mild foolery as he stood up and began picking the duck. The wind had backened up from the northwest to a more westerly direction, and that would cause the feathers to drift downwind toward the young hunters in the blind along the inside edge of the reef. "I want to let Terry know that I got something," he said. Within a few minutes there was a line of feathers adrift on the water toward their blind. Two heads appeared over the top of the blind, looked our way for several seconds, then disappeared.

The older man in the other blind was out and had started collecting his decoys. He had not fired his gun. Except for a line of white clouds on the eastern horizon, the whole sky was clear and blue. We stood up, more relaxed and less concerned about being seen. With our arms resting on the top edge of the blind we looked around us. There were a few ducks flying around here and there, but it really didn't seem to matter much. After a few moments of silence, Fowler spoke, this time with a more serious tone. "You know, it's peaceful out here. I've been doing this stuff ever since I was a boy. I love it, though, and I reckon I've been out here more lately since I retired than I have in years. It's pretty some out here. You get your peace of mind, you know. It's good just to get away from home. Yeah, good to get out of the house with all the phones ringing, television, record players, and all that mess that we didn't have when I was growing up. Things have changed around home a lot, but as long as I can get out here I think I'll be alright."

After a few moments of silence, as if he had made up his mind right then, Fowler said, "Well, let's get out of here. We could stay longer and maybe get another shot but I don't think that it'll be worth it." He told me to stay in the blind and he would toss up the decoys.

When he had collected the decoys, dragging them along behind him by their nylon cords, he came up to the blind. All I could think of was that he looked like some kind of wild bird himself, towing his young chicks behind him.

The flock all stored away and the blind door pulled by, we left and waded back toward the boat. The whole reef looked different now, almost like summer. Fowler had no doubt that the weatherman was going to be right in his forecast for a beautiful weekend. That didn't matter too much to him. He would still go out, even if he had to sit in the blind all day and watch the reef as the day passed before him.

For many years only one black family has lived at Ocracoke. They are the Bryants, descendants of Harkus and Winnie Blount, who came to the island after the Civil War. Harkus and Winnie had two children, Elsie Jane and Anna Laura Blount. Anna Laura and her husband lived at Ocracoke for a short period of time and then moved to Belhaven. Elsie Jane met and married Leonard Bryant of Engelhard and New Bern, and they decided to remain at Ocracoke and make it their home.

Jane and Leonard Bryant had nine children, five boys and four girls. Of the nine children, only three have made Ocracoke their permanent home. They are Musa Bryant, Mildred Bryant, and Julius Bryant. Musa and Mildred live together in an old house near the Island Inn, and Julius lives alone in a nearby trailer. None of the three married.

Mildred has been a friend of our family for many years. Her grandmother and mother were close to my grandmother. Having spent many hours with me on her knee, she often tells people that I'm "one of her babies."

Since she has always had a good memory of past events, I asked her one day if she would tell me about her family and what it was like growing up on Ocracoke.

I went to visit her on a cold February evening. At the time Musa was not living with her and the house was without the numerous renovations that have since taken place. After walking up to the backdoor that evening, I stood on the steps and knocked several times. I waited for a few minutes, thinking that it would take her that long to get up if she happened to be resting. I then opened the door and called her name but received no answer. Finally, I settled down on the steps to wait for her; I knew that she couldn't be far, since the shiny new padlock that locks the outside door was missing.

After sitting on the steps for about fifteen minutes, I still saw no sign of her. I continued to wait, listening to the ever-present sound of the ocean's waves crashing on the beach and absorbing the feeling of peace among all the junk, trees, and approaching darkness.

A few stars began to appear through the bare branches of the white poplars. One of these was Rigel, part of the constellation Orion, which had begun its westward sweep over us.

The afternoon lengthened into evening as I waited. Then, to the left of Mildred's house a door suddenly opened and I could hear the low tones of two people talking. Within a few minutes the sounds of twigs snapping and feet dragging over dead leaves indicated that she was returning home. She was mumbling to herself as she found her way along the dark path.

Clad in a white overcoat, she finally appeared around a clump of red myrtles. I stood and knocked on the door so I wouldn't frighten her. "Here I am," she called out.

"I thought you were a ghost coming through there like that," I said.

Mildred is a large woman of medium height. "She's shaped just like Winnie," said one old woman who knew her grandmother. She took her time approaching the house, complaining along the way of a foot ailment. I told her that I had been waiting on the steps for nearly an hour. This worried her, and she said that I should have gone inside where it was warm.

We entered the house, passed through the dark kitchen, and stopped in the living room. I sat down in a chair as she returned to the kitchen for a few minutes. The living room is small and the ceiling is low. Against one wall stands an oil heater, which had recently replaced two small kerosene stoves. On one side of the heater is a rocking chair and on the other side is a china closet. The room is cluttered about

*Mildred Bryant, 1989.*

with clothes chests, suitcases, stacks of blankets, small stands, and a medium-sized couch.

She came back into the living room, stood for a moment looking around at all the "mess," shook her head, then pulled a sliding door by and entered her bedroom. I got up and went into the bedroom, sat down on the edge of a chair filled with towels and sheets, and listened to her talk about the house. "This ole house ain't much, but it's mine," she began, staring up at the high ceiling. "I bought it in 1949. It used to set about a hundred yards down the road toward the lighthouse. Pa always said that it was about as old as I am, so I reckon they built it around 1910.

"The government used to own it. They had it for a boathouse when the old lifesaving service was in operation. You see, they had two of these houses. One was located over where the Coast Guard Station is now, and the other was where it used to be down the road before I had it moved. This was the boathouse for the boats that they used in the ocean. The beach used to come up almost to my backyard then. They kept two boats on carts, and they had these big government horses to drag the things down to the beach.

"You see that big doorlike thing," she continued, pointing up to a wall of the house. "Well, that was the door where the boats went through." The big door she was referring to and another like it at the opposite end of the house are shingled over on the outside, but on the inside they still look like doors. There is even a long rod on one side of the door that runs from floor to ceiling and served as a lock.

The ceiling is high and pitched, the rafters visible, and the wood is dark heart-pine. With the exception of the living room, which has paneled walls and a low ceiling, the rest of the house is unfinished on the inside, relatively untouched since the days when the surf boats were stored there.

"Let's go in here," she said, indicating the living room. I took a seat on the floor and listened to her complain about how "junked up" the room was. Though she spent several minutes trying to persuade me into a chair, I told her I was comfortable and remained on the floor.

After hanging up my coat and pulling by the sliding door to the bedroom, she returned to her chair. She joked about her mind being bad and about how old and crazy she was, then settled down for the first time that evening and began the long story about herself, her family, and how they came to settle at Ocracoke.

"My grandmother was a slave. A lot of people around here think she was a slave here, but she wasn't. She was a slave in a place called Blount's Creek, about twenty miles south of 'Little' Washington, North Carolina.

"She never did seem to want to talk about the times when she lived there. The only thing that she ever told me was about a little boy she had named Joe. She had him during the slavery-time, but when he got old enough, they come and took him away from her and she never did see him again.

"It wudn't long after this happened with Joe that she met my grandfather. They called him Harkus Blount. Some called him Hark. I don't remember him. He died before I came along. I reckon they got married over there before they decided to come here to the island. I remember her telling me that after the slaves were freed, they walked from Blount's Creek, on across the old bridge that used to be there to Washington, then took the steamboat to Ocracoke. In them days that how folks got back and forth from here to there, by taking the steamboat."

Though never in great numbers, slaves once lived and labored at Ocracoke. The 1790 census, which covered both Ocracoke and Portsmouth islands, listed a population of thirty-one slaves. The 1800 census, which applied only to Ocracoke, listed sixteen slaves; the 1810 census, thirty-nine; and the 1820 census, fifty-seven. The largest slaveholder was William Howard, Jr., who held ten. The 104 slaves listed on the 1850 census was perhaps the largest number ever kept at Ocracoke.

Although most slaves appear to have been well treated, there were exceptions. One Ocracoke master used to send his slaves to tong oysters on even the coldest days. He then made them pick out the tiny oyster crabs with their bare, numb, and often bleeding hands. If they had done something he disliked, or if they didn't catch enough oysters to please him, he would sometimes cut open their hands and cake the wounds with salt.

According to Mildred, my grandmother once told her that after slavery was abolished, all the Ocracoke slaves left the island together

*Winnie Blount, grandmother to Mildred Bryant.*

late one night. Most supposedly settled around Washington, North Carolina. She also said that my great-grandfather, who owned several slaves, spent months trying to find one of his. After a number of trips, he did find her and gave her money to "help her along."

While the Ocracoke slaves left the island for the mainland, Winnie and Harkus Blount left the mainland for Ocracoke. Although her grandmother never told Mildred exactly why they came here, she did mention that her owner used to visit Ocracoke occasionally.

"Grandma always said that when they first come here that everybody treated 'em alright. My grandfather was a boat builder and a carpenter—and a good one so I've heard. While he was doing this, my grandmother used to help different ones in their housework.

"They lived in a small house in the backyard of a woman that my grandmother used to work for. I believe it was located where the Harbor View Guest House is now. Then they managed to buy a little house over on the shoreside where the ole Pamlico Inn used to be. They eventually tore that down and rebuilt it on this land.

"I'm not exactly sure how they got ahold of the land. I think that somebody gave my grandfather a small piece. Later my grandmother managed to buy twenty-five acres. Land was cheap then. Besides, a lot of this was marsh.

"Anyway, they rebuilt and we always called the place the 'Old Homestead.' It was made out of rough lumber. There was one big room and another smaller room that they used for a bedroom. They had a loft upstairs, and after my brothers came along, some of them used to sleep up there.

"They had the kitchen apart from the rest of the house like a lot of the older houses around here at the time. When the Old Homestead was first built, they cooked and heated with a fireplace. Later on they got a woodstove from Portsmouth Island, and it was supposed to have been the second one ever to be on Ocracoke.

"I remember she used to have one big table for all of us to sit at and plenty of straight-back, shuck-bottomed chairs. She made 'em herself and used to do it for other people. She got the shucks from her garden. She always had a good garden and grew plenty of stuff.

"You see, in them days everybody was just alike. Nobody had anything, so one person would give to the other if they needed something, and they would help each other with this or that. I've heard tell that when different ones around would kill a cow or pig, they'd usually let other people know about it and let them have some.

My grandma used to have cattle, sheep, and pigs herself and would walk clear down toward the beach where people let their cattle and stuff go to check on 'em.

"I've heard your Grandmother Brittie tell that one day her and some other women were walking down the path by Grandma's house, a-going somewhere, and Grandma called 'em in there. She had cooked a pig and stewed certain parts of it. She had a nice white tablecloth spread over the table and wanted 'em to sit down and eat. They did, and while they were eatin', my mother and aunt, they were just children then, were a-standing on the outside of the table a-looking at 'em. My grandmother saw this and raised on 'em. 'What's the matter with you all,' she said. 'Don't you know it ain't nice to stare white folks in the face while they eatin.'"

Soon after Winnie and Harkus got settled in their new house, Mildred's mother, Elsie Jane, and her Aunt Anna Laura were born. When Jane was only ten years old, however, Harkus died, leaving them to "do the best they could."

Shortly after Harkus's death, Winnie went to work at the Doxsee Clam Factory, which was located along the western shore of the Creek and remained in operation from the late 1800s to about 1917. Like most other women who worked there, she picked clams from their shells or labeled cans.

"The ole Doxsee Clam Factory was where my mother met my father. His name was Leonard Randolff Bryant. He was born in Engelhard and raised in New Bern. He came over here to the island to work for the Doxsees, helping with the loading and the unloading of the boats that carried the clams.

"Well, I reckon, as they always say, 'It was love at first sight.' Wurn't too long after he started coming here that they got married and built a little place over where my grandmother lived.

"He was a carpenter. That was his tool box there," she added, pointing to a rough-looking chest lying by the oil heater. "He also worked on the water like the rest of the men, and my mother she would do housework for different people around.

"My mother had to give up this doing housework when all of us come along. There were nine of us, five boys and four girls. Let's see, there was Artis, Lewis." She paused here a moment, staring straight ahead at the wall, trying to recount on her fingers all her brothers and sisters in the order of their birth. "Artis, Lewis, Musa, Mildred, Mamie, Anna Laura, Jiffery, Julius, and John Thomas. Ma also had two set of twins after I was born. Both sets were born dead, stillborn they called 'em.

"My only aunt on my mother's side of the family also had a house built over near the Old Homestead. Her and her husband didn't live in it but only a short period of time. They had a little boy, but one evening he fell off the back porch when there wurn't nobody around and fell into the water barrel and drowned. After this my aunt was never satisfied here. They moved off and went to Belhaven to live."

In addition to working at the Doxsee Clam Factory, Winnie also cured and sold yaupon leaves, which were used to make tea. As a child, Mildred sometimes helped her grandmother pick and cure the yaupon leaves. "When I was a little girl," she recalled, "she used to take me with her in the fall of the year, and we'd go all over the island and pick yaupon. Sometimes we'd break off the branches and take 'em home and then pick the leaves off. When we got the leaves home, she had a bench that she used to chop the leaves on, and she chopped 'em real fine.

"Then she had an old flour barrel buried in the ground that she used for the curing of the leaves. She'd take and put some heated rocks in the bottom of the barrel, then put in a layer of yaupon leaves, then some more rocks, then some more leaves until it was filled up. On top of all of this she then sprinkled some water and covered the barrel up so nothing could get inside. The steam would cook the leaves.

"Seemed to me that it took nearly a month to cure. Anyway, whenever she felt that it had cooked, she would dig it out. You'd have to dig it, too, because it looked just like molasses after it had been cooked. After she dug it all out, she'd take and put it in a place where the wind would blow through and dry it. The leaves were then packed in burlap bags and shipped to Washington on the ole *Annie Wahab*."

One of Winnie's last jobs was working at the Pamlico Inn, an establishment operated at the time by Bill Gaskill. According to Mildred, "The boarders were all crazy about her and everybody called her Aunt Winnie." Her employment there lasted until she suffered a stroke. "She was dressing chickens one day," said Mildred, "and one of these ole wild cats that used to hang around there jumped up on the table and took off with one of the chickens and ran underneath the house with it. Grandma she took out after him and crawled under there to get the chicken. He had crawled way up under the middle part of the house, but she managed to reach him. She got the chicken back, but she had a stroke. She had to stop working after this, and I reckon it wurn't three years 'fore she died.

"She came in the Old Homestead one day, closed the door with her back, and started sliding down on her knees, a-saying that she was sick. We put her to bed and she stayed there for seventeen days before she died.

"The whole time she was sick she kept calling for my oldest brother, Artis. He left the island around 1916 and went to Philadelphia to work on the dredges. About the time of the Second World War, he joined the merchant marines. The only time he ever came back home was for one night when the ship he was on got torpedoed offshore here during the war. He was with the survivors they brought in. After the war he moved back to Philadelphia. We never did hear much from him. His wife would write Ma a few lines now and then. He's dead now.

"Anyway, as Grandma gradually got worse, some of the older women of the island would come over and help tend to her. There was no doctor here then. One evening there were four of 'em here and they stayed till supper-time. Then they had to go home and fix for their menfolk 'cause they'd be coming in from fishing. Grandma died shortly after they left.

"By the time the women got back, they already knew that she had died. The word travels that fast. So, they came back and shrouded her. They'd wash 'em and dress 'em, stuff like that. At the time, the caskets were made right here on Ocracoke. Some of the men would build them, and the women folk would line the inside. They'd use white lining for the inside and put a narrow black strip down the outside.

"They buried her the next day around two o'clock. One thing about Grandma was that nobody knew how old she was. She didn't know herself, but it didn't seem to matter to her too much one way or the other."

When Mildred was growing up, she never went to school like the other Ocracoke children. According to her, two schools existed on the island at that time. One was a private "pay school runned by this lady called Miss Sarah" and the other was the public school, which was located in the downstairs section of the present Island Inn. Although a note was sent to her father, informing him to send them to school, he refused. "I think that some of the people might have bucked against it," she recalled. "I didn't think about it too much because I was so busy working in the home. I probably wouldn't have gone anyway.

"None of us really went to school here. The first six of us didn't go here at all. Musa and Lewis went for a couple of years in Philadelphia when they left the island for a while. Anna Laura left when she was fourteen and went to Washington, North Carolina, and I believe she had about three years of schooling. The last of us, Jiffery, Julius, and John Thomas, were taught evenings after school when the other children had gone home. Mamie worked for a woman here on the island, and I think she taught her some. As for me and Artis, we never got any schooling.

"About the only education I ever got was when I hung around with the other girls after school. They'd have to get their spelling up before they could play. If I hung around them, I had to spell just like they did.

"Everybody always treated us all right when we were growing up. They didn't seem to mind because we were colored. We played along with the other children. I remember evenings after school we used to play cat. This was a game something like baseball. You'd make the ball from pieces of string bound together with old shoe leather and the bat from a stick. The girls and boys didn't play together.

"When I look back on the times when we were all growing up, I always thought that if I had ever had any children, and they were into as much as we were, I reckon I'd of mommucked 'em to death 'fore now. When the first four of us had grown big enough, didn't seem like there wurn't a night go by that we didn't get a licking for something. My father had four little stools for us to sit on of the night, and whenever we had done something wrong, he call us in and sit us down, look each one of us in the eye, and ask who did it. He'd always find out, then he'd take the strap and tear us up. I believe I still got that ole strap around here somewhere in all this junk.

"I reckon one of the greatest lickings we ever got was the time he caught us stealing one of his boats. He used to have two or three little rowboats, and every once in a while he'd take and pull 'em up when they got water sobbed. One day he had pulled one of 'em up on the shore and told us that we'd better not mess with it. We just did let him get out of sight before we launched her and took off toward the middle of the Creek and started having the best time, a-splashing water and carrying on. We felt like he might be somewhere nearby, but we didn't let it bother us. Well, we played till we got tired then come on in. Who should we meet on the path on the way home but Leonard Randolff Bryant. We knew what we were in for. He took the strap and tore us up. But what good did that do? Next day we were into something else.

"I guess there were times when we had right much fun without being in a lot of trouble. We used to go swimming like the rest of the children. We used to swim out sort of in front of the Island Inn in a place called the Gut. It's filled in now with the stuff they dredged out of the Creek during the war. And we used to swim in the Creek too. Wurn't deep like it is now. We'd always go of the night, for we were afraid for anybody to see us in the daytime.

"Just about every Sunday in the summer some of us would take off and go to the beach. We'd always go of the evening when there'd only be a few people around. We'd never go swimming, but we would wade and walk around here and there.

"I'll never forget one evening me, Ma, and Musa walked across there. It was a purty evening, so we walked down not far from where the airstrip is now to a little building that the Coast Guard used to have up in the sand dunes. That's when they used to patrol the beach with horses and keep watch that way. People used to change in that building.

"So we started wading and having just the best time. It gradually got darker and Ma started to walk home and called for us to come on. But we were wading and kept waiting for the big wave to come, wurn't satisfied with the smaller ones, kept waiting and waiting for the big one. Well, just as Ma was a-going over the sand dunes, this ole big wave comes a-rolling up on the beach and goes clear past our knees and knocks us down. When it went back out, it was all we could do to keep from being pulled out it was so strong. I held on to Musa and started hollering for Ma, but she was on over the hill by then. We finally got up on our feet and waded up toward the sand dunes. When we got out of the water, we ran and ran till we caught up with Ma. I always thought that God sent that breaker to drive us home."

Along with caring for members of her family, Mildred began to make a living for herself by working for various people around the island. "One of the first paying jobs I ever remember having was working for a woman from Washington named Miss Nunlee who had a small cottage on the shoreside near where the ole Pamlico Inn used to be. Her husband was a big tobacco man over there and they used to take their vacations down here.

"She came to Ocracoke when she was pregnant one time so the baby could be born on the island. She had a woman to help her, and after the baby was born, the woman left and I went down there to do the cleaning and washing. I was only about fourteen at the time. She paid me eight dollars a week and I bought some clothes with that.

"At the time there were only a few cottages on the shoreside that people from off the island owned. Most of them seemed to be from Washington. Sometimes they'd bring colored folks with 'em to tend the younguns and do the cleaning and stuff like that. We used to go over to the beach on a Sunday with 'em sometimes.

"After I worked for Miss Nunlee, I went to work for a woman from the island called Miss Hilda. She paid me two dollars a week. I bought me some more clothes with that, but had to give most of it to Ma 'cause she was sick at the time.

"Then I worked for this one couple called the Logans till the man's wife accused me of stealing her diamond. She was Spanish and talked sort of funny. They had a little boy. He wore mini-blouses, and she used to wash 'em herself. She'd starch 'em so that they could've stood up and walked off.

"Anyway, she comes in one day crying, a-saying that I had stole her ring. I told her that I didn't steal the ring. I didn't even know what in the world a diamond ring was then. I told her that I had been looking at the things, that they were pretty things, but that I did not steal the ring.

"Well, her husband and different ones around here tried to make her believe that I didn't steal it. She wouldn't listen to 'em and went on a-cussing me and saying that she had colored folks to work for her before and that they had took stuff off of her.

"The days went on, and one day as I was folding the little boy's mini-blouse, the ring fell out. I went and gave it to her and told her that she probably pulled it off her finger when she was taking the blouse off. Well, she wouldn't believe me and said that I was holding it to get money. Her husband gave me five dollars for finding it. I stopped working for them after that.

"Miss Logan she finally came to her senses and tried to make up with me. She'd pass me on the road and wave and call my name, but I'd keep right on with my nose stuck straight up in the air and pretend like I didn't even notice her.

"When I was thirty-six years old, I went to work for a man named Carleton Kelly. I didn't want to go at first, for I was afraid of what people would say. It was the first time I'd ever worked for a single man. I went anyway and didn't let it bother me too much.

"He had a big house on East Howard Street. I stayed there and kept house for him even after I bought the old boathouse. My mother used to work for his mother. I worked for him for fourteen years.

"Pa lived in the boathouse till he died in 1960. I had it fixed up a little more and moved in for good myself. At about this time Ma was staying with my brother John Thomas. He lived in Elkin, North Carolina. He was married, but didn't have any children so Ma went to live with him. She died up there in 1964 and that's where she's buried. I didn't like this too much. I wanted her buried here."

She had talked at least three hours, and I could tell that she was getting tired. As I got ready to leave, she added, "I can't say that I really enjoy life. All I've got is a house full of junk to sit around and laugh at."

She was still laughing that deep-bellied laugh of hers as I approached the kitchen door. Standing on the steps listening to her talk, half to herself, half to me, I could tell right away that the air had gotten much chillier. The sky was clear and a crescent of a new moon hung over the roof. Orion was well above the trees and Jupiter and Mars had followed, visible through a small opening above the path that leads to Julius's trailer. "They're the brightest stars I've ever seen," she said. "I see 'em every once in a while when I come home late of the night."

I told her good night and walked on around the corner of the house, leaving her there staring at the planets and talking to herself.

**E**ast Howard Street. Ocracokers say it's about the only place left in the village that resembles "the way things used look around here." When the village roads were paved during the 1950s, East Howard Street was left unpaved. Although cars used to get stuck in the soft sand, today they rarely get stuck. Steady traffic has pressed the sand and dust hard, forming two ruts that wind past old houses, tiny graveyards, ancient live oaks, towering pines, and twisted cedars. Fences are so close to the sandy lane that you can reach out and touch some of them as you drive through.

A walk through East Howard Street is a more pleasant experience. The street is perhaps a quarter mile long; there are two main entrances: one east of the post office, the other next to the United Methodist Church. As you take the entrance next to the church, you realize that you have in fact "entered" the street. Live oaks, some of them centuries old, cedars, and yaupons grow close to the ruts and stretch their limbs out over the street, giving it a canopied appearance. This is especially noticeable at night and after snowfalls. Many people say it's one of the darkest places on the island. When I was growing up, I walked through East Howard Street to get to school, which is located near the Methodist Church. Like other kids, when the walk was at night, I often found myself taking the rut farthest from the graveyards.

Fifteen cemeteries are scattered along East Howard Street. Most of these contain only a few graves; the smallest is surrounded by a fence

*A huge live oak, located in front of the Methodist parsonage, stretches over East Howard Street. The sandy road is said by many to be one of the few places left that resembles the old Ocracoke. (Photograph by Ann Ehringhaus)*

which borders only one grave. There are wooden picket fences—some painted, others not—chicken-wire fences, and concrete block fences. Since most of the cemeteries are on the north side of the street, with tombstones only a few feet from the street's ruts, it's not uncommon to see people walking on the south-side rut at night.

East Howard Street was once called the "Main Road" or "Back Road." Another passage that ran along the Creek was called the "Front Road" or "Creekside Road." This was actually a foot path, and parts of it were blocked by wharves where freight was brought from the Creek to shore.

The street is Howard land. Stacy Howard, who gave the street its name, once nailed a small East Howard Street sign to a large live

oak in front of his house. At one time mostly Howards lived on
East Howard Street, including Wheeler and Tressie O'Neal Howard,
Homer and Aliph O'Neal Howard, Coleman and Ann Williams How-
ard, George and Mary Francis Gaskill Howard, Jim and Zilphia
Grey Howard, Hatton and Chloan O'Neal Howard, Tom Wallace and
Bessie Williams Howard, Sarah Emmaline Howard and Simon Gar-
rish, and Stacy and Elizabeth Ballance Howard. Some of their descen-
dants live there today.

Several of the approximately twenty houses on East Howard Street
are close to a century old. One of them belongs to Elsie and Irvin
Garrish. Elsie, who is my aunt on my father's side of the family, has
spent most of her life as a nurse. Even after her retirement from
nursing, she has remained active in the island's health care, serving on
local health boards and caring for the sick and injured when called
upon. Her husband, Irvin, is a retired ferry captain and former Hyde
County commissioner, the first Ocracoker to serve on the board.

Elsie and Irvin's house has recently been jacked up, as an added
precaution against storm tides. Like other old houses, it was once
situated close to the ground on thick trunk sections of red cedar and
live oak. The house was framed with lumber salvaged from a shipwreck. "Mr. Tommy Howard, who used to be postmaster here," recalled Elsie, "told me that the lumber came from the shipwreck of the
old *Bateman*. I can't find any record of it having wrecked. I'm sure
there were many ships that were not recorded. He always said the
lumber was from the *Bateman* and that he and Mr. Sime Garrish,
Irvin's grandfather, hauled it from the beach on a horse and cart. Some
of the timbers underneath the house still have the old spikes still in
them."

Directly across the street from their house stands a large live oak
tree known as the "Jim Dandy Oak." It was named after a shipwrecked
sailor from the brig *Black Squall*, which came ashore on Ocracoke
Beach in April 1861. Blanche Howard Jolliff, daughter of Stacy Howard, recalled the story. "When I was growing up, I always heard

different old people tell about Jim Devine. While he was shipwrecked here on Ocracoke, he began courting some of the local girls. Some of the men here didn't like it, and a squabble broke out.

"There was not a sheriff here then, but I've heard tell that Uncle William Ballance and Bob Salter and some other men got together and made Jim Devine ride astraddle a rail. Uncle William lived next door to where Elsie lives now, and one night he and Bob Salter left his house and started walking down East Howard Street. This Jim Devine was waiting behind that big oak and shot and killed Bob Salter but missed Uncle William. The next day he escaped on a schooner going to the West Indies. This was supposed to have been the last murder to take place on the island."

Also on Elsie and Irvin's property are the Live Oak Cottages, three small houses which they rent. The largest cottage, which is located next to their residence, was framed with lumber from another shipwreck, the *George W. Truitt*, which came ashore near the Ocracoke Campground in February 1928. "I was a small boy when the *George W. Truitt* wrecked," recalled Irvin. "I remember being down on the beach that day and seeing the Coast Guard take the crew off on the breeches buoy. The cargo of rough pine lumber washed ashore. They held a vendue to sell the cargo. Elsie's father and my father managed to get some of the wood and this is how the cottage next door was framed."

In the living room of Elsie and Irvin's house are five clocks. One of these is an English grandfather clock, which stands in a corner. Four other clocks sit on stands or hang on walls. "I went to watchmaking school with your father," Irvin told me. "We had just gotten out of the service and went on the G.I. Bill. The school was held in Durham then transferred to Greensboro. We both finished in about one year. At the time Elsie was working at Duke Hospital on 'Cushing,' a surgical ward. She then worked in a Greensboro hospital for several months."

By the time my father and Irvin were in watchmaking school, Elsie was well on her way as a nurse, a profession she "always wanted to go into from a very early age." As she recalls, "I had different books and magazines about nursing and those always interested me. With eight children following me, I always had to help care for them as I grew up. Two of the children died at an early age. One was only eleven days old when she died of breathing problems. The other lived until he was two and a half years old. For him, it started with an upset stomach, then he gradually got sicker and sicker. We seemed to think that he might have drunk some water that had been contaminated after a storm. We did all we could for him. There was a Dr. Swindell here at the time. He ordered glucose, but it came by the mailboat and arrived too late."

For many periods in its history, Ocracoke had no doctor. Over the years a number of doctors have come here, perhaps staying for a few years or less, but until recently none actually settled here to practice. So Ocracokers learned to take care of their sick or injured themselves, using home remedies and relying on the wisdom and experience of the old people. "Back when I was growing up," said Elsie, "and even long before, people here on the island had to treat their own ailments. They used home remedies handed down from generation to generation and trusted certain old people for advice. I remember that my family used to depend on this older lady named Miss Joannie who lived near us. A lot of the older ones, including her, used to make blackberry wine. They'd put a batch in during the spring when the berries started to ripen. They used it for diarrhea and upset stomach. I still use it sometimes.

"When my first child was born, I set her out on the front porch one warm spring day so she could get some fresh air and sunshine. Miss Joannie came by and liked to had a fit. She warned me that I shouldn't do such a thing because it would surely make her sick. They always believed that a baby should be kept inside and bundled up."

Perhaps more important than the trusted old people to the actual survival of the island's population were the midwives. As one Ocracoker put it, "Think about it for a minute. If there had not been

*One of Ocracoke's early midwives was Ester Gaskins O'Neal, known locally as Aunt Hettie Tom, who delivered approximately 550 babies between 1861 and 1898.*

someone to deliver babies over the years there might not be half the population of island people that we have today. We might even wound up like Portsmouth Island."

The earliest midwife that anybody now living on the island can recall was Ester Gaskins O'Neal, or "Aunt Hettie Tom." The tradition then was for a woman to be called by her first name and the first name of her husband. This was especially true when several women had the same first name. Since Hettie was Ester's nickname and her husband's first name was Tom, she was called Hettie Tom. Sometimes the possessive form of the man's name was used with the first name of the woman, for example, "Tom's Hettie." The "Aunt" part of the name was tacked on for respect or familiarity, even if the woman was not related to those who used that name.

Larry Williams is the great-grandson of Aunt Hettie Tom. He has a book that was given to her by a doctor who practiced at a hospital that was once on Portsmouth Island during the Civil War. A large chapter in the book is entitled "The Experienced Midwife."

Aunt Hettie Tom kept a record of all the deliveries she made. Larry's mother, "Miss" Lola Williams, kept the record book for a number of years before it was lost. Aunt Hettie Tom was supposed to have delivered 550 babies and lost only 2. Her first delivery was Polly Anna O'Neal on November 4, 1861, and her last delivery was "Miss" Iva O'Neal on November 6, 1898. "She was a good midwife," recalled Miss Iva, "but she had it hard. Her husband, Thomas O'Neal, was lost at sea. He left her with two children. She and her sister raised 'em. Aunt Hettie Tom also was a weaver, made carpets and such as that."

Aunt Hettie Tom also delivered babies on Portsmouth and Hatteras islands. She died on February 23, 1899, and is buried in an unmarked grave in one of the small graveyards along East Howard Street.

During Aunt Hettie Tom's later years, she was often assisted by her late husband's niece, Mary Jane O'Neal Garrish, who lived near her. At the time of Aunt Hettie Tom's death, Mary Jane was prepared to become the island's midwife. Elizabeth Howard is one of Mary Jane's deliveries. "I'm sure that Jane delivered after Aunt Hettie Tom died," recalled Elizabeth, "and she probably continued until she died in 1920. By that time her sister, Charlotte Ann O'Neal, had been training with her and became the island's midwife. Everybody called her 'Aunt Lot.'"

Although Aunt Lot may have assisted her sister and possibly Aunt

*Elsie Garrish, who has served the island for many years as a nurse, holds a small bag used by midwife Aunt Hettie Tom when she used to make deliveries.*

Hettie Tom during deliveries, she did not become the island's midwife until her youngest child was born. She had one son, Richard, and three daughters, Sara Ellen, Emelis, and Metta.

"Miss" Sara Ellen, Aunt Lot's oldest daughter, lived to be 104 years old. Some Ocracokers say that she resembled her mother, a "big heavy-set woman," who lived to be 96 years old.

When I visited Miss Sara Ellen not long after her 100th birthday, I found her in good spirits. She couldn't hear well, but when she did, she understood and was able to communicate quite clearly. She was dressed in a print dress with a bright pink sweater draped over her shoulders. "My mother tried to keep count of all the babies she had delivered," said Miss Sara Ellen. "She lost count around 100. She never lost a case. She had a sister that was also a midwife. Her name was Jane. I think my mother might have learned some of her stuff from her. It was Aunt Jane that helped deliver me. You see, my mother didn't start delivering until after she was married. About the only trouble she had that I know of was one time a baby started to come out foot first. She had to rearrange it before it could come out. I never did help my mother deliver. People wondered why I didn't take it up. Weren't for me!"

Several Ocracoke children once asked Aunt Lot where they could get a baby. They wanted a little sister, and they figured that since Aunt Lot was the person responsible for bringing babies to Ocracoke they would ask her. She told them to go dig up stumps, which they did, working long and hard before they finally realized that only Aunt Lot knew where the babies were.

In addition to delivering babies, the midwives sometimes helped care for the sick and injured. There were other Ocracokers who were also "good hands with the sick."

"I don't know how people got along back in them days without a doctor," continued Miss Sara Ellen. "Sometimes I reckon they fared better. You see, people's own families had to doctor their own sick. There were always different ones around that were good hands when it came to handling the sick. A woman called Miss Dory used to be a good hand. She even made this kind of salve around here that people of the island put on their sores.

"Most of the time they had to rely on home remedies. I remember one time I had the croup—tissick, we called it. My father cured me with one of his remedies. He bored a hole in a tree. The hole had to be the height of me. Then he took a lock of my hair and pieces of my toenails and fingernails and put them in the hole and plugged it up. After this I wasn't troubled with it anymore. I did have it so bad before that sometimes my mother thought that I wouldn't pull through."

She paused for a moment, but you could tell that her mind was working, trying to dredge up other bits and pieces of information from the past. Finally, she said, "When I still had the croup and the asthma, they used to give me molasses that different ones would bring up from the West Indies on sailing vessels. They give me this with soda. This helped some.

"For colds they used to give us turpentine with a little bit of sugar and you had to swallow this. They even used it on my grandmother one time when she was in the hospital.

"Then there was something with black cats." The recollection of this remedy stopped her for a moment, and she stared ahead at the wall, tapping her fingers on the arm of the chair. Finally she added, "I can't think of it to save my life. It makes me the maddest when I can't think of something like that."

Della Gaskill, Miss Sara Ellen's daughter-in-law, who was sitting with us, said, "Now she'll sit there all day until she thinks of it."

While Miss Sara Ellen was trying to remember about the black cats, Della's father, James Williams, came in the room and joined our conversation. "One thing that was supposed to keep diseases away," said James, "was to take asafetida and put it on cotton, then hang the cotton on a string in different places around the house. It was strong stuff, that asafetida.

"Then, if anybody had a pain in their head, all they had to do was get some of this real fine dust and put it in a little bag and put it on the spot and it was supposed to make it go away.

"This fellar around here used to claim that he could get warts off people with these marsh rushes. He'd take and pull 'em up and rub 'em all over the wart then put the rush right back in the ground. It had to go in the same hole.

"For a stingray sting, they'd take and cut open a live chicken—it had to be a black one, though—and they'd lay it wide open right on the sting."

"Shingles!" yelled Miss Sara Ellen. "There was something with black cat's blood and shingles. Mama used it one time on Miss Annie Gaskill."

After talking a few more minutes about other home remedies, we got on the subject of doctors. "We had a few doctors here when I was growing up," said Miss Sara Ellen. "One was this here Dr. Morgan. He was a good doctor and a smart man. He helped different ones. I used to go with a friend of mine to him while he cured her of a bone felon, a rising she had on her finger. They said he was doped up all the time. We'd have to wait for him to come out of his room before he would treat her. He had a dog. I think somebody killed it after he died."

Billy Scarborough, who died in 1982, once owed his life to Dr. Morgan. When Billy was a small boy he stuck a stick in his foot and developed lockjaw. It was Dr. Morgan who cured him. The case is supposed to have been one of the first ever to be cured in North Carolina. Billy told the story many times before he died. "One morn-ing when I was a small boy, we sat down to the breakfast table. I remember we had boiled spots, and that I couldn't eat 'em. My mother noticed that my jaw was locked. She told my father to carry me down to see this Dr. Morgan that lived on the shoreside where the ole Pamlico Inn used to be.

"It was in August and I had been running around outside without any shoes on. I stuck a stick in the ball of my foot. My mother thought that she had got most of it out, but she hadn't. So this Dr. Morgan examined me and told my father that I needed to go to the hospital. My father told him that that would be near about impossible because it would take three or four days, maybe longer, on a sailboat to get me there. The nearest hospital was in Washington, North Carolina. Dr. Morgan then said that he would take the case and do the best he could.

"The first thing that he did was to take a little instrument and pick out the rest of the stick. There was a piece still in there about as big as a match. Then he threaded a needle with a thin piece of gauze like stuff and pulled it back and forth through the hole. I passed out.

"They took me back home after this. Dr. Morgan asked my father if he had any influence with the Doxsees that owned the clam factory that was here at the time. He had heard that they might have some whiskey, and he wanted my father to get a gallon jug. He was a man, I guess you could say, that liked a little toddy. Anyway, he gave me several spoonfuls and he took the rest. Then he told my father that he would have to move me closer to where he lived over on the Point. You see, he had something wrong with his legs. They were all purple and blue and he could hardly walk, a circulatory problem I reckon you'd call it. He stayed put in his house most of the time. If anybody needed him he would help them, but they would have to get a horse and cart to tote him around in.

"So they carried me Down Point to Aunt Liza O'Neal's house, just about where Clyde Austin lives now. The first day I was there Dr. Morgan gave me some strychnine poison. He said that he was trying to kill poison with poison. I was nearly unconscious at the time, but when he gave me this I came up hollering that I had been poisoned. He tried to take my temperature with a fever glass, a thermometer you call 'em, and my jaw locked down on it and it broke in my mouth. He told me not to swallow 'cause the stuff inside was poison. I managed not to swallow and he got all of it out.

"I also had spasms. My breastbone came up like a chicken's. He would have to take the palm of his hand and beat my chest. Some of the people thought he was doing it for meanness. They didn't understand that he was trying to relax me. I knew he knew what he was doing. He was a smart man, a good doctor.

"Altogether, I was in the house Down Point for about twenty-five

days. Dr. Morgan visited me every day and night. He gave me medicine during the whole mess, some of the tiniest pills I've ever seen. He
had pills when he first came to the island, and he used to send off for
pills, supplies, such as that. They kept me in a dark bedroom with the
shades pulled down. My mother was always there and so were several
other women who helped, Aunt Pat O'Neal and some of them. They
believed that the sick should be kept in a dark place, that no light
should get to their eyes.

"My mother was always pretty good at curing us of sickness. I
remember one time I had a high fever and she used to take sassafras
leaves and tie over my forehead. This was supposed to cool the fever.

"After twenty-five days they finally carried me back home. I was
recovering pretty well by then. I did have spasms sometimes, and
they'd have to go get Mr. Piland's horse and cart to bring Dr. Morgan
way up here to our house. In another five days I was cured.

"When the Tayloe brothers that owned the hospital in Washington
heard about the case, they came over to interview Dr. Morgan. They
said it was the first case they had heard of in the state being cured.
They wanted to know how he did it, but he wouldn't tell them. I think
he done wrong by that, but he said that his father had spent a lot of
money on his education and that he wasn't about to give it away just
like that. Dr. Morgan was a smart man, though. He was from New
York and had diplomas from colleges here in the United States and
Europe."

Billy's wife, Dell, once showed me a picture of Dr. Morgan. Though
I had expected an aging man with white hair and spectacles, the
picture, which was taken only several years before he died, revealed a
young man, perhaps in his late thirties. He had smoothly shaped
features and dark curly hair. The expression on his face was relaxed
and confident, with the makings of a smile about to come forth. It was
unlike other pictures from the same period that I had seen, in which
the people looked stiff and uncomfortable with the camera.

"Billy found this picture when he was remodeling the old chimney,"
said Dell. "The old chimney and mantelpiece were part of the old

house that stood where our house stands now. When Bill was working on it, the picture fell out. I guess it had laid on the old mantelpiece until it dropped into a crack caused by the heat. Miss Sally Ann, Bill's mother, always thought a lot of that picture. Dr. Morgan had it taken here on the island, I believe. There used to be a fellar come here back then and take pictures. He lived in a tent while he was here. Anyway, Dr. Morgan gave it to Miss Sally Ann, thinking that she'd always keep it to tell people about him curing Bill."

"Dr. Morgan was a right young man when he died," continued Billy. "Not long after he cured me of lockjaw, he said, 'Billy, I've got three more months to live.' He knew exactly when he was going. This was why he came here in the first place. When he left New York, he settled for a while in Engelhard then came to Ocracoke. He thought that this would be a good place to rest. He never had a office set up here or nothing, but he'd help those that needed him when he could get to 'em. He didn't talk much about his past. He did say that he had a girlfriend in New York but she got killed and he would never have another one. I think he thought about her a lot. I didn't even know his first name. He's buried in an unmarked grave over near the lighthouse."

Aunt Lot died in January 1947. By that time there were others living on the island who could deliver babies and generally care for the sick. One of these was Lola Wahab Williams, the granddaughter of Aunt Hettie Tom. Though she did not keep count of all the babies she delivered, her son Larry believes the number to be around one hundred.

Miss Lola had little training, but she did take a correspondence course from the Chicago School of Nursing. One of her first cases occurred on her oldest brother's wedding day. She couldn't go to the wedding because of the delivery and following complications. The woman had twins: a boy, who came feet first and died, and a girl, who survived.

My mother said of Miss Lola, "She was good around the sick. If Mama, Papa, or any of our family was sick, Miss Lola was right there.

When I was pregnant with you, she came over and sat on the porch to see how I was doing. It was Saturday night and I remember her telling me, 'You're gonna have that youngun on the thirteenth.' The doctor had given me till the fifteenth or later. My sister Nina and myself flew down to Morehead City the next day, on a Sunday, and you were born early Monday morning, on the thirteenth."

Although Nettie Mae Fulcher was the first Ocracoke woman to become a registered nurse, she did not settle on the island to practice nursing. Not until Kathleen Bragg finished her nurse's training did Ocracoke have one of its own residents to come back home to practice. Kathleen was born and raised near the lighthouse in a home where she lived most of her life and where she eventually died. Her grandfather, Samuel Dudley Bragg, was one of the early Ocracoke pilots. He had a lookout tower on the shoreside near their house where he could spot ships as they approached Ocracoke Inlet. Kathleen's father, Hallis A. Bragg, was also a pilot and continued until their services at Ocracoke became obsolete.

In 1923, Kathleen left Ocracoke to attend nursing school in Rocky Mount, North Carolina. After spending three years in training, she returned to the island to begin her practice. Her test scores during her nurse's training were unequaled for many years. In addition to caring for the sick and injured, Kathleen also delivered over one hundred babies.

Kathleen began employment in 1953 with the Hyde County Health Department as a school nurse, a position she held for fifteen years. When I was in elementary school, we came to fear Wednesdays, the day that she spent at school. Wednesdays also became known as "shot days." High school boys would circulate rumors Wednesday morning, and sometimes the evening before, that a "new batch of shots" was in. The younger ones were continuously reminded about the time she supposedly broke off a needle in a student's arm. High absenteeism was not uncommon on Wednesdays.

Kathleen was dedicated to Ocracoke School, however, and anyone who remembers her walking along the road toward the old school

*Standing in front of the old Ocracoke School building, Kathleen Bragg is surrounded by Ocracoke children she delivered. (Print courtesy of Larry Williams; photograph reprinted by permission of the American Red Cross)*

building, in all kinds of weather, a large black bag in one hand, cannot help but feel a moment of love and respect for her. Her brother once told me, "She went when she was called. People depended on her."

Kathleen died in 1975. The inscription on her tomb reads "Well done thy good and faithful servant. Enter into the joys of thy Lord."

Elsie Garrish, who was at Kathleen's side when she died, then assumed the role of the island's nurse. Fortunately for the people of Ocracoke, the careers of its midwives, nurses, and doctors have tended to overlap. With the death of one, another was there ready to take on the responsibility.

Elsie left Ocracoke in 1935, two years after she graduated from high school. "I had to wait a few years," she said. "It was during the Depression and there simply was no money. I worked in one of the general stores and sold ice cream to make money for my training."

She received her training at Rex Hospital in Raleigh, North Carolina, and eventually became the supervisor of the men's ward there.
After working in a number of mainland hospitals, she returned to the
island in 1963. "I didn't really come back here to work. I've never
been employed here. What I've done, I've done for humanity's sake.
I've always been willing to help the people here in any way I could,
and I guess I've had plenty of experiences here that you don't normally find in hospital work."

Most of Elsie's unusual island experiences involve emergencies and
the transporting of patients to a doctor or hospital. "One night I got a
call to go to this house where a man was having a heart attack,"
recalled Elsie. "He had been working read hard all day long on his
house, and I believe he had forgotten to take his medicine. The house
was set back in the woods and could only be reached by a small dirt
road. It had been raining and the road was very muddy. The deputy
sheriff was there giving him oxygen, and both of us working together
managed to restore his breathing some.

"When we got ready to transport him, we found that there was no
way that the two of us could transport him on a stretcher down that
muddy road. We finally had to get him on his feet and walk him out to
the station wagon. There was no ambulance here then, and this wagon
was both the ambulance and the deputy's patrol car.

"In the meantime, the other deputy had radioed over to Hatteras
for them to send a Coast Guard boat. When we got to the north end of
the island, the boat was there. We transferred him to the boat, and
myself and the deputy went with them.

"It was just a nasty night. The wind was blowing hard and it was
still raining and cold. After we had been under way for about fifteen
minutes, the boat hit a shoal. The man was getting worse from all the
tossing about. They radioed for another Coast Guard boat to come
and pull us off, but we managed to get off ourselves a few minutes
afterwards.

"As we crossed the inlet, it got rougher. The deputy said he just
knew the boat was going to flip over. Minutes after he said that, a big

wave hit us broadside and the boat rolled on its side. The patient slipped off the stretcher and fell on the floor of the boat, cutting his head. Equipment went everywhere.

"The boat kept going, though, and finally made it out of the inlet. Then we hit another shoal. By then the man was so bad off we thought for sure he was going to die. The other Coast Guard boat got there and started towing us off, but the line broke. We somehow slid off and made it to Hatteras ten minutes or so after that. The man had gotten worse and even Dr. Burroughs at Hatteras said it didn't look good for him. They transported him to the Elizabeth City hospital and he lived."

Since there is no hospital at Ocracoke, and only recently a health clinic and doctor, over the years hundreds of patients have been transported to mainland hospitals, by whatever means available. Before regular ferry service began, patients either remained on the island to battle their injury or illness or risked the long, sometimes rough trip across Pamlico Sound on the mailboat or freight boat. If they survived the trip, they were then admitted to one of the small hospitals in either Morehead City or Washington. Many, of course, chose to remain on the island.

Visitors to Ocracoke often ask, "If someone becomes seriously injured or sick on the island, how does the person get to a hospital?" Although we now have a health clinic and doctor, more serious cases of injury or illness must still be transported to a hospital. If the case is not life threatening, the Ocracoke Rescue Squad will take the patient to a nearby hospital, usually Albemarle Hospital in Elizabeth City. More serious cases are flown out on helicopters which are based in Greenville, Norfolk, and Elizabeth City. A Coast Guard helicopter has been serving the Outer Banks for several decades. Even today, the sound of a helicopter causes Ocracokers to wonder who could be sick or injured.

Although she has never been classified as a midwife, Elsie has delivered around fifty babies, learning from practical experience during emergencies. As she recalls, this experience began long ago. "I used to help Aunt Lot get things ready for some of the deliveries she made. These deliveries were my own brothers and sister. There were seven of us in my family. Aunt Lot delivered all of them, including your daddy. A doctor visiting the island and staying in one of the boarding houses delivered me.

"One thing that always fascinated me about Aunt Lot was part of her procedure. When I got into training later, I always wanted to ask somebody about it, but was too embarrassed. She used to cut little pieces of cloth about four inches square and put them on top of the stove to scorch. Then she'd take a large, seedless raisin and put on top of the pieces of cloth, then take both of these and put on the baby's navel. I later found out that it was supposed to have a sterile drying effect and make a cleaner navel.

"Most of the deliveries I've made have been during emergencies when the woman was caught here on the island. When I get called to a patient who's getting ready to have a baby, I always check them to make sure they're not that close to having it. If they were real close, within an hour, say, I usually wouldn't send for a helicopter to fly them off, but would go ahead and deliver it myself.

"I've had some pretty unusual experiences with delivering babies here on the island. I've encountered a few cases where women didn't even know they were pregnant until the baby was born. I even delivered a baby one night and just as I was helping it through, a big dog jumped up in the bed with us. I must say, I was more shaken by the dog than the woman was with having the baby.

"Perhaps my most unusual experience was delivering a baby during the peak of a hurricane. The lady's mother came and got me late that night and said that her daughter was having labor pains. This was during Hurricane Hazel, one of the worst we've had here lately.

"The house was only a several minutes' walk away, but the storm had already hit and I clearly remember the sea tide rushing down the road just before we got to the house. We were wading up to our knees in the water and some of it even started to enter the house. I thought for sure that we were going to have to move the mother up on the second floor. We didn't, though, and the mother and the baby made out fine. He was born at the very peak of the hurricane when the winds and rain seemed to come down on us the hardest."

Most pregnant Ocracoke women now go to hospitals in Morehead City, Washington, Greenville, Elizabeth City, or Norfolk to have their children. They often leave before the due date to avoid going into labor while on the island.

In recent years health care on Ocracoke has improved greatly. In the fall of 1982 the Ocracoke Health Center opened to serve the island's medical and pharmaceutical needs. Shortly before it began operation, the National Health Service Corps placed a doctor here. Dr. Warren Silverman served as Ocracoke's doctor for approximately four years. Other doctors and physician's assistants continue to re-place Dr. Silverman, but Ocracoke has been dropped as a site for the placement of an NHSC doctor, which means that the doctor's salary has to be provided from local rather than federal revenues.

Revenues realized by the health center barely meet expenses, and the future of the center, according to some residents, is uncertain. Although in past years Ocracoke managed to survive without a doc-tor, today's circumstances are different. More and more people are moving to the island to live, including a large number of retirees, and thousands continue to visit here, placing a steady demand on the center and medical staff by both residents and tourists.

The service provided by the center is complemented by an estab-lished rescue squad with two ambulances that make local calls as well as transport patients to nearby hospitals.

Late one winter night I walked down East Howard Street to Elsie's house for a visit. As I entered the living room, the fine clocks on the walls and stands and the big grandfather clock in the corner were ticking away more or less in unison. After we had talked at length about health care at Ocracoke (I sat through two chimings of the clock), our conversation drifted into talking about old age and death on the island. This was a subject of great interest and fascination to me, especially when I was younger, but a subject from which I was never sheltered. We always had an elderly person living with us while I was growing up: a grandmother, grandfather, and great aunt. Two of these died in our house.

"Many of the Ocracoke families," said Elsie, "tend to keep their old in their homes rather than having them put in a nursing home. I guess it's something that's always been done here and people are still taking care of their own.

"As for the old themselves, even if they are sick and something of a burden to their families, I think they would still rather stay here than leave the island. The ones that do die here, die in dignity. They die in their own homes with relatives around them, and it's all very natural, no bottles, wires, and other hospital equipment hooked up to them.

"Most of the old ones that have been bedridden for a while develop pneumonia, or 'old people's friend' as we sometimes call it."

The closest funeral home is in Hatteras. When someone dies a hearse will come to the island to get the body, and the funeral will usually follow within several days. Back before the funeral home provided this service, coffins were kept in a local store. When someone died they were often buried the next day. I can remember when they were kept there, because as children we were always curious about the tall oblong boxes that stood in a corner.

Most Ocracokers are part of the Ocracoke Burial Association. When a member of the association dies, each member has to pay thirty cents. The collected amount is then given to the family of the deceased to help with funeral expenses.

There are but a few of the "old Ocracokers" left on the island. When they do get sick, the relatives sometimes still call on Elsie. Although she isn't as active as she once was in island health care, she is still there for the older ones who know her, whose families know her, and who have come to trust her. As one person put it, "Ocracoke has been lucky to have had people like Elsie over the years who they could trust, and who if for nothing else, they knew would be there to relieve some of the tension of somebody sick. It was just a matter of having someone there, someone who could comfort and reassure them."

Five-thirty on a cold spring morning. About one hundred people have gathered for an Easter sunrise service on "Billy Goat Hill," a large sand dune near the airstrip. The sky is clear with a light wind from the northeast. Beyond the surf, the sea is flat but rippled by the northeast breeze. A flock of pelicans glides just beyond the breakers, and a young couple strolls along the waterline hand in hand. Far in the east, patches of clouds are framed in the orange-red space that will be the sunrise.

Residents and tourists, young and old, are gathered around the United Methodist minister, who stands below them in a small cavity of sand. The minister begins to speak as the sun rises big and golden. A communion of bread is passed around as something is said about the beauty of this particular sunrise. Everyone is silent for a moment as they stare into the east.

On a large sand dune about two-and-one-half miles north of Billy Goat Hill, another sunrise service is being led by the Assembly of God Church. They will also hold a baptism later that afternoon in the Creek.

The United Methodist and the Assembly of God are the two established churches on Ocracoke. Though small groups of members of other denominations worship in private homes, most people who attend church and support church activities participate in one or both of the established churches.

*Residents and visitors gather on Billy Goat Hill for the traditional Easter sunrise service. (Photograph by Ann Ehringhaus)*

The earliest church records available indicate that Methodism was the predominant religion as early as 1828. The only church on the island at that time was the Methodist Episcopal Church, located near the present firehouse. Ocracoke was part of the Ocracoke-Portsmouth circuit, and the Reverend J. Atkinson was assigned as pastor.

In 1844, the Methodist Church divided into two separate churches, the Methodist Episcopal Church and the Methodist Episcopal Church, South. The Methodist Episcopal Church served the island until the Reverend A. R. Raven left the island in 1861 during the beginning of the Civil War.

The Methodist Episcopal Church, South, was established on the island in 1869. Though destroyed twice by storms and a third time by fire, the church was rebuilt and remained on Ocracoke until 1937. According to one Ocracoker, the building's third destruction came about after an old woman's prayer. She was supposed to have said that if there was any sin and wickedness in the church she hoped that God would cause it to burn to the ground. The very next day it burned!

Elizabeth Howard recalls the story of one preacher in Ocracoke's early history who used to take a drink before preaching his sermon. "This preacher had a very good delivery. He'd get in the pulpit and be a little under the influence of intoxicating beverages. One woman said that she would much rather hear him preach drunk than hear some sober.

"The same preacher wanted to borrow someone's boat so a group could go over on Hatteras Island where a camp meeting was being held. These were meetings where preaching was done out in the open. They had a space out there on somebody's property. Anyway, the man said he would get the boat for the preacher as long as he promised him that he wouldn't drink during the camp meetings, and the preacher made the promise.

"He preached every night that week, and the last night he was intoxicated. At the end of the service he called on the man he had promised to dismiss the service. The man prayed on temperance. At the end of his prayer he said that may all intoxicating beverages be thrown into the rivers. The preacher then stood up and said, 'We will now stand and sing "Shall We Gather at the River."'"

In 1883 the Reverend W. F. Parker, a presiding elder of the original Methodist Episcopal Church, established what came to be called the "Northern Church." The Methodist Episcopal Church, South, was referred to as the "Southern Church." The Northern Church was completed in 1885 and properly named Wesley Chapel, Methodist Episcopal Church. Although this building was destroyed during the hurricane of 1899, it was later rebuilt.

Both the Methodist Episcopal Church and the Methodist Episcopal Church, South, served the island until 1937 when the three branches of American Methodism united to form one Methodist denomination. The formation of the Ocracoke United Methodist Church in 1937 was something many had hoped and prayed for. The competition

*Services were held in the Methodist Episcopal Church, South, shown here in this early 1900s picture, until it was torn down in 1937.*

between the two Methodist churches had caused a recognizable division within the community.

My father was a young boy then, and he still recalls the impressions the division made on him. "I went to the Northern Church because my people did. Sometimes the preacher would have to be away from our church just as the Southern preacher did. Some people would go to the other church and think nothing of it. But there were always some who refused to go if their preacher was away. Most of these were the older ones, set in their ways. They stood up for what they believed in and you couldn't change them. I didn't agree entirely with this. I felt that something was lacking. We should have been closer. We had to live together so we should have worshiped together.

"When the children my age were growing up, they began to get the feeling that things were split up, that there was a rivalry going on, and that people were just not together in their worship. I think the older people should have been more concerned with the impression this division made on the young children. It made an impression on me."

Calvin O'Neal's family went to the Southern Methodist Church. He recalled that while some people took the division seriously, others didn't let it bother them. "All of Mama's friends went to the Northern Church," he said. "When it came time to go to church, Mama went to her church and her friends went to theirs. There was never any feelings or conflict between them.

"When I was about ten or eleven, they had Sunday School in my church at ten o'clock in the morning and in the Northern Church at two. A friend of mine went to the Northern Church. I went to church with him and he went with me. When Christmas came, there was a bag of candy for me under the Christmas tree in the other church. To me, that was the high point of my Christmas.

"Of course, some of the older ones felt different. I remember hearing Mama talk about her Uncle Bill Joe. He fought in the Civil War. Somebody came and told him that they saw his goat up at the Northern Methodist Church eating grass, and he said the goat had eaten the last of his corn.

"Some people connected the churches with the North and South during the Civil War. I've always heard that that's not why they separated."

According to my father, a dispute involving singing classes was part of the reason for the division in the church. "Some people had more money than others and could pay for these classes. They wanted to learn how to read musical notes. The other people who couldn't afford to take these classes preferred the old hymnals." Those favoring singing classes and written music formed the nucleus of the Northern Church. One churchgoer from that era alleges that on a particular Sunday morning the congregation of one church could be heard singing "Will There Be Any Stars in My Crown" while the other church sang "No Not One."

When the two churches were torn down and the lumber from both used to construct the present one, most Ocracokers were satisfied. Many had contributed to its construction. A note in the July 4, 1943, dedication pamphlet states, "Special notice is due the members of the local congregation in view of their constant efforts and persistent support of the whole building program. With very few exceptions, almost every man in the congregation and many of the women have put in actual working hours on the building."

Not all Ocracokers were satisfied, however, by the joining of the two churches. In 1937, the same year the Methodists united, a Hatteras Island group representing the Assembly of God Church came to Ocracoke to hold services. Their island audience consisted of Ocracokers who had decided to split from the Methodist denomination when it united. Though services began in the school building, they eventually were held in the yard of Elijah Styron, Sr. During the colder months, the porch of the Styron home was closed in, and this became Ocracoke's first Assembly of God Church.

In 1940 the Styrons donated a small tract of land for the construction of a new church. Bett Styron ordered the lumber and made other contributions.

James Williams, a member of the church since its inception and who has preached during the regular minister's absence, recalls the formation of the church. "I went to the Northern Methodist Church. My people always went there. When they united, some of us felt that the way of preaching we liked and thought was right was lost. We believed in the old style of Methodist preaching, in preaching the full gospel.

"I don't think that our church is right and the Methodist Church is wrong, but when you join the Assembly of God Church, you have to be saved and accept Christ as your savior."

A recent Methodist minister, Jimmy Creech, came to Ocracoke from Raleigh in the spring of 1973, breaking a string of older, more traditional "preachers." Though the Ocracoke appointment was considered out of the system of promotion and a "punishment" in some ways because of the isolation, Jimmy requested the appointment. The Methodist district superintendent was surprised but delighted and granted the request.

"I made the decision to come to Ocracoke," said Jimmy, "because I needed a change and a new situation in which to grow. The community interested me. The involvement here seemed more complete. There was an organic-like relationship, a sense of oneness among the people. The sense of membership was strong. Life wasn't as segmented as Raleigh had been.

"I think I was well received when I came here. I didn't expect anything. The people were very gracious. The old respected me because I was their 'preacher' but the young were a bit suspicious and skeptical."

One of Jimmy's priorities was to develop programs around the church to encourage more social participation among the Ocracokers, especially the youth. "I was personally interested in groups," he added.

Many new residents have found church participation a good way to enter the community. "More and more people are moving to Ocracoke," said Jimmy, "and they bring with them their particular type of worship. Many have also transferred their memberships here. All in all I think they contribute nicely to the programs and services."

The church has always provided a place for people to socialize. Years ago, according to Calvin O'Neal, it was the center of everything. "The church was one of the few public buildings where people could meet," he said. "If the children of some families didn't go to church, they couldn't go out anywhere else.

"The church is really not the center anymore. That's part of modern world influences. Our lives have become more complicated. There are more things to do."

Because we are an island, and because most Ocracokers have always lived within the boundaries of the current village, the community is well defined. This is one of the qualities that attracted people like Philip Howard. Philip's father grew up on Ocracoke, but his mother is from Pennsylvania. Although he spent some summers here, Philip moved to Ocracoke to live permanently only in 1973.

As a former seminary student, he is particularly interested in religion. "The church has a central role because the community is so well defined," he said. "We're not like other places that have outlying areas. Jimmy Creech, who used to be the Methodist minister here, said that when he was here he saw people every day from the congregation, while in Raleigh he rarely sees his congregation except on Sunday.

"Another aspect of the community being well defined is that you know who your neighbors are. We have a structure here of taking care of people without the need of a lot of agencies. There was once someone lying drunk at the end of Howard Street. No one was disturbed because everyone knew who he was and why he was there.

"Almost everybody here has someone that takes care of them. People here have had to depend on each other for so long partly because in the past so many things were difficult to get, things like parts, and even someone who knew how to do different things."

During many conversations with older Ocracokers, I found some of their fondest memories were of the ways people helped each other during times of need. In a community such as ours, people must get along with others.

From talking with elderly relatives, I learned that years ago on Ocracoke, when it came time to plant gardens, everybody would help everybody else. The Pointers would come around Creek and help the Creekers with their gardens, and the Creekers, in turn, would go Down Point and help the Pointers with theirs. Women of the island often joined together to make quilts. Or when someone needed a house built, people would chip in with materials and labor. Meals were provided for the workers.

In short, neighbors helped neighbors. Everybody pitched in when needed and knew that they could depend on others for the same kind of help when they had problems.

According to most Ocracokers who remember these times, the reason things are different today is because we are busier and spend more time trying to get and maintain modern conveniences. We are so busy, they say, that we don't even have time to visit our next door neighbors.

One Ocracoker who especially misses this quality is Ellen Marie

Cloud, who grew up on Ocracoke during the 1940s and 1950s. "That time of closeness is gone," she said. "People years ago had that togetherness. They worked hard like we have to today, but they always found time to sit on the porch and talk. Sunday, especially, was a time to visit, to get out and walk. Everybody on the island was part of one big family. Now you have to make a major effort to visit your next door neighbor."

Philip Howard thinks that television, particularly cable television, has had the most significant effect on why people isolate themselves today. "They would rather watch television than visit their neighbors," he observes.

Captain Thurston Gaskill, who retired after seventy-two years of serving as a fishing and hunting guide at Ocracoke, adds, "The visiting is lost today because of television, the automobile, and the telephone. There seems to be always something to do.

"I don't think people enjoy life as much as they used to. They think they are. But we're living in too fast an age, too fast a pace, to really enjoy things like we did when we were growing up.

"For those that want to continue living here, I'm a great believer in the word 'moderation.' It applies to every part of your life. You can have the things that you really need. But you just as well make up your mind that you can't have everything that you think you want."

Although the role of the church is not as central as it was in years past, there are still times when it brings us together to worship as a community. One of these special times is during the Christmas Eve service.

On a cold, foggy Christmas Eve night about two hundred residents and a few tourists packed into the United Methodist Church for the traditional Christmas Eve service. People were standing along the walls and side by side in the small vestibule. Since their Christmas Eve service had been held the weekend before, members of the Assembly of God Church were also present.

Some men were standing outside talking about the weather. A cold front was supposed to move over the coast that night, and the warmer air mixing with the approaching front had produced the fog. Since the fog had also forced the last Hatteras ferry to return to port, a few children wondered if Santa Claus would visit them this year.

Each Christmas a large cedar tree is sacrificed for the church's sanctuary. Though several new residents to the island had once questioned the need for cutting such a large tree every year, preferring instead an artificial one, older residents were quick to defend the tradition by saying that the Christmas tree program had been held for over one hundred years, and the large tree was a measure of the joy it produced.

This particular tree towered from floor to ceiling and extended outward to the first pew. Underneath it lay a heap of small plastic bags filled with oranges, apples, peanuts, and candy. Each Ocracoke resident receives one of the bags. The giving of the fruit and candy bags came about after problems developed years ago with the way gifts were distributed. Once it was the responsibility of adults to buy presents to put under the tree. Since some presents were more expensive than others, a few children received better gifts. Eventually this practice was abandoned for the equal gift-giving of today.

A steady rain began to fall as the service got underway. One group of children performed a Christmas play, while members of another recited individual speeches. The service came to an end as the congregation sang "Joy to the World" and held candles to illuminate the sanctuary. Following the service, many residents continued to mingle in the sanctuary, collecting Christmas bags for family and friends and enjoying the children and Santa Claus, who came despite the fog.

# Ocracoke School: One Big Family

When I began teaching at Ocracoke School in August 1982, I didn't realize how demanding the job would be. I had spent the last two school years teaching ninth-grade English at a junior high school in Hillsborough, North Carolina. Even though I had taught over one hundred students each day, I had still taught basically the same material to each of my six classes.

During my first year at Ocracoke School, though, I taught the following subjects: tenth-grade English, eleventh-grade English, journalism—which consisted of not only the study of journalism but also the publishing of a newspaper and yearbook—biology, health, physical education, and an environmental sciences program for grades kindergarten through fifth. I was also the basketball coach. Other teachers were carrying the same load—some with even more preparations.

Ocracoke School is what is known as a K-12 school—which means that all grades, from kindergarten to twelfth grade, are accommodated in the same school. The smallest K-12 public school in North Carolina, the school had an average enrollment of ninety-four students during the 1985–86 school year. Due to our size and island location, we have been the subject of many newspaper articles and much visitor interest.

Any attempt to explain the school's operation must, in fact, begin with its size. To take care of those ninety-four students there were six full-time teachers, two part-time teachers, three aides, an exceptional education teacher, a volunteer chemistry teacher, the principal, who also taught several classes, a secretary, and a janitor.

Kindergarten and the first and second grades were housed together in a room connected to the gymnasium, while the third, fourth, and fifth grades were taught together in a double-wide trailer that the Hyde County Board of Education had obtained as a forfeiture after the former inhabitants were convicted of drug dealing. The sixth, seventh, and eighth grades and the high schoolers attended classes in the main school building and an old trailer adjacent to the main building.

The main school building was completed in the summer of 1971, while the gymnasium and adjoining classroom and shop were constructed in 1977. Although many residents were pleased that Ocracoke finally got a new school, others were sorry to see the old one, which had been built in 1917, torn down. The old school, with its sturdy wood frame and white-painted clapboard exterior, had withstood constant use and abuse by both humans and nature. According to many of the decision makers, however, it had served its purpose. During the last few years of its existence, there were continuous problems with the electrical and plumbing systems, as well as the overall upkeep of the building.

Since the construction of the main school building, however, some have regretted not remodeling the old school. Those involved in the tearing down of the school remark quite often that "you just can't get lumber like that nowadays." Many at Ocracoke will always think that its destruction was one of the biggest mistakes ever made here.

The first record of a school at Ocracoke was in a deed dated February 4, 1808, in which William Howard, Sr., sold to the subscribers of the schoolhouse a piece of land for the purpose of getting firewood for the school. The subscribers were allowed to cut all trees except live oaks and cedars, important timbers for house and boat building. The subscribers themselves were residents of Ocracoke who had contributed money for the construction of the building. At a later date when a new building was to be constructed, the subscribers each gave from five to twenty-five dollars, totalling $517.50.

Between the early 1800s and 1917, a number of schools in different locations, both public and private, existed on Ocracoke. Included in these was a school for the children of men who served in the United States Lifesaving Service. Many of these schools had only one teacher.

In the early 1900s the downstairs section of the Oddfellow's Lodge (now the Island Inn) was used as a school for grades one through eight. Even though a permanent school was finally built in 1917, students who wanted to finish high school still had to leave the island. Ocracoker Elsie Garrish recalls the transitions she went through to complete her education. "From grade one through grade six I went to school here at Ocracoke. They had school through the eighth grade here then. During my seventh-grade year, I went to Hatteras to spend a year with my uncle and went to school there. I then returned to Ocracoke for my eighth-grade year.

"Because Ocracoke School didn't teach the ninth grade, I had to leave the island to continue my education. Like a few others around here, I went to Washington, North Carolina, and attended Washington Collegiate Institute, which was a Methodist boarding school. Some others went to the Farm Life School in Vanceboro, North Carolina.

"We stayed in dorms and only got home at Christmas. I worked for part of my tuition and board. There was a lady who lived in the mountains that also paid part of my tuition. I never did know who she was. It was someone that wanted to see me get my education. The dean of the school knew, but he wouldn't tell me.

"I returned to Ocracoke School for my tenth-grade year because that's the year they had the first high school here. That year's eleventh grade, the Class of 1931, was the school's first graduating class. They were Lucy Garrish, Mabel Fulcher, and Russell Williams. You only went through the eleventh grade back then. I graduated the following year with ten other students. We were one of the big classes.

"I was in high school during the Depression. Like everywhere else, we had it tough. A lot of times we had to go gather wood to burn

The first graduating class from Ocracoke School was the Class of 1931. Standing on the front steps of the old school, they are (top to bottom) Russell Williams, Mable Fulcher (left), and Lucy Garrish, who was also the class valedictorian. On the bottom step is principal David Taylor. (Courtesy of Lucy Garrish)

because the school had run out of coal. On the real cold days they held classes around the potbelly stove.

"I think the students were closer back then. You see, they were all mostly local people who were born here. We had two high school teachers, Selma Wise and Graydon Ring, and the principal, David Taylor, who also taught. You had more personal attention."

Lucy Garrish, who was a member of the first graduating class at Ocracoke School, also gave the valedictorian speech. The speech, entitled "History of the Senior Class," is worth reprinting here for the insight it gives into that first year of high school for its forty-six pupils.

On September 3, 1930 school opened at Ocracoke. For the first time in its history high school work was to be done at Ocracoke.

When school first opened there was no library or laboratory in our school. There wasn't enough desks for the students, and teachers. We had only two high school teachers at first. They had to teach all the high school subjects. But soon another teacher was added to our school, and we had three high school teachers. Mr. David B. Taylor, principal, Mr. Graydon Ring assistant, and Miss Selma Wise.

The opening of school brought together to finish their high school work at home, all the boys and girls who had been going away to boarding schools. There were about forty-six pupils in high school. There were only three pupils in senior class. Although our school wasn't equipped as high school should be, we went to work with high hopes and determination to make our high school life count for something.

A few weeks after Christmas an addition of two new rooms was begun on our building, which was to make it more convenient for the teachers, and pupils, because the rooms were so crowded.

New laboratory equipment was also added to our high school.

We had not been able to do science work before, because of a lack of equipment.

Our library was first supplied with books that the teachers and students brought, then a lot of new books were given by patrons of the school. Through state aid over a hundred new books were added, and we soon had a good library for such a small school.

About the beginning of the spring term we organized for the first time. This being the first time in the history of O.H.S. that any class had organized. We elected Russell Williams, President, Lucy Garrish, Vice President, and Mable Fulcher treasurer. We selected purple and gold for our class colors, violet for our flower, and chose for our motto, "Let us be known by our deeds."

On March 30, 1931 the juniors entertained the seniors, by giving us a banquet. It is an event that will always be remembered by us seniors, first, because it was the first time this had happened on Ocracoke, second, because the juniors took so much interest in it, and it was arranged so well by them.

The school work has runned very smoothly this year, excepting only a few incidents that occurred, that teachers had some trouble with. There has been a few storms this year when the students couldn't get to school; also the influenzy spreaded over the school so that it had to close down for a week.

The high school students have responded gladly in their H.S. work this year, and have tried their best to help make the school a success.

In our first year at O.H.S. we have perhaps not done the best work that we could have done; we have perhaps not set the best examples for those who follow us, and our mistakes have been many to be sure, but remember we are the first to graduate from Ocracoke. We have had no other whom we could follow. We have had to blaze the way as the first senior class. A great responsibility rested upon us, that of setting worthy examples for those who will follow us. We have constantly striven to keep ourselves upright and to make ourselves worthy of the great and noble school which we hope Ocracoke will one day be. Let us hope that as the years go by, those who follow in our footprints, will profit by our mistakes, build where we left off and make greater and nobler standards for O.H.S than it has been possible for us, who blazed the way to make them.

The students and faculty of our school today sometimes refer to themselves as "one big family." In an environment where everyone knows everyone else, there is daily interaction among younger kids, older kids, teachers, family members, and other people in the community. An inherent flexibility also allows everyone to use the facilities, equipment, and other materials with minimal supervision. "We're not just a school," said Becky Cornette, a high school aide. "We're a family with the squabbles, sibling rivalry, and pats on the back. We cry and celebrate together."

A former exceptional education teacher, Lynn VanOrsdale, added, "The real Ocracoke is so much more than what people see on a fast summer trip. Attachments here run deep. In our school, before you even realize it, these kids have crawled into your soul."

While a fourth-grade student, Shane Bryan once observed, "Our principal also teaches. Most principals do not teach classes. Our principal knows the kids. Some principals don't know the kids."

Another student, fifth grader Serina Paul, added, "Most other schools call their teachers by their last name, but all of our grades call our teachers by their first names."

Ocracoke School is not perfect, of course. Like other schools, we have our problems. And every year we face tougher challenges as we try to adapt to the growing demands placed upon us by state and federal programs.

A recent principal, Ernest H. Cutler, who came to Ocracoke from the Hyde County mainland in 1976, faced many of the same "small school" problems each year. "Working in a small school is much different from working in a large school," he observed. "In a small school you need to be prepared to handle a variety of problems. A small school does not provide the luxury of specialization.

"Working in a small school such as Ocracoke can be very rewarding as well as frustrating. If you really care about children, you get so close to them and their problems that you can burn out pretty quickly. You laugh when they laugh and you hurt when they hurt. You have a greater responsibility than you would have in a large school. You reach a point that you begin to question your effectiveness.

"Small schools are generally not cost effective when compared to large schools. Most resources are allocated to schools on the basis of students numbers. This creates problems for small schools. It costs more money to get the job done.

"Most small high schools also have limited course offerings. Today we see a national concern for return to the basics. Most small schools never left the so-called basics. This was a necessity, not an option."

One of the most frequently asked questions by people outside the Ocracoke community is "What do the students who graduate from Ocracoke School do after graduation?" Relatively speaking, we are not unlike most high schools, in which a certain percentage of students go to college, others join the military, and still others enter the work force. In recent years more and more Ocracoke School students are choosing college.

One year after the eight students in the Class of 1985 graduated, one was a student at Guilford College in Greensboro, North Carolina; one had joined the Army; four were living and working at Ocracoke; and two were sailing on an extended adventure in the Caribbean.

Shortly before she graduated from Ocracoke School along with seven other seniors, I asked Suzanne Lewis of the Class of 1986 what she would miss about our school. "One of the best things is how close everybody is. I also like the individual help we could get. During my senior year I was the only student in French II and Algebra II. I hope the set up of the school stays the same. If I could wish for anything, I guess I'd wish for more sports."

As they move up through grade levels, students become increasingly aware of the advantages and disadvantages of small schools. Many, like Suzanne, wish for the sports opportunities and other extracurricular activities found at larger schools. Though our main sport is basketball, attempts to provide other activities such as softball and track continue.

When I was a student at Ocracoke School, our only organized sport was basketball. At the time we had no gym and had to play on a small outdoor court, usually in all kinds of weather. Sometimes we had to crack ice on the court before we could play; other times we played at night under a single streetlight located at half court.

Our basketball opponents were teams like Hatteras, Manteo, and a few mainland teams. We were always excited to play indoors in their nice gyms. We didn't have an activity bus then and had to travel in private cars, often spending the night because we couldn't reach the late Hatteras ferry in time. After one game, we got stranded at Hatteras for two days because a fierce winter storm prevented the ferries from running.

From grade one through grade eight I went to school in the old building, before it was torn down to make way for the present one. The old school was divided into six sections: two large high-ceilinged rooms on the southeast side for the elementary grades, a central library, and three large rooms on the northwest side for the high school. The bathrooms were located in a structure outside and to the rear of the library. In addition to the main building, a small "recreation hall" stood to the east of the school.

While the old structure was being torn down during the 1970–1971 school year, we had classes in the Methodist Church Sunday School rooms. This change of setting went better than most of us expected. The elementary grades were taught in the classrooms downstairs, while the high school grades attended classes upstairs. Occasionally we'd have to leave school early because a funeral was scheduled to take place. Although I don't remember it happening, one story that came out of that year at the church was about the several elemen-

*The old Ocracoke School building was built in 1917 and torn down in 1970. To the school's right is the recreation hall. (Courtesy of North Carolina Division of Archives and History)*

tary students who were discovered in the sanctuary, eating their lunch and gazing intently at a dead body as it lay in a coffin.

For as long as I can remember, school has been released early for funerals. As a matter of fact, one student, when asked to write an essay comparing the advantages and disadvantages of going to a small school like Ocracoke School, wrote, "One of the best things about going to school at Ocracoke is that you get out every time there is a funeral." In addition to paying respect to the dead, this tradition came about because of the close proximity of the church to the school, the need for parking spaces and easy movement of the funeral procession, and a desire to maintain a peaceful setting without noisy children nearby. When a funeral is scheduled at two o'clock, as are most funerals, the students are released for the day at one-thirty.

I began the tenth grade in the new building, which, unlike today, housed the entire school. At the time we presented no space problem because the entire school enrollment was approximately seventy students.

*Alice Ronthaler displays a seashell collection for her students, who are seated in a classroom in the old school when this picture was taken in the mid-1950s. Along with her husband, Theodore, who was the principal, Mrs. Ronthaler taught at the school from 1948 to 1962. (Print courtesy of Larry Williams; photograph reprinted by permission of the American Red Cross)*

The first few years in the new school posed many challenges, especially for the upper grades. The building was designed with three large classrooms which opened into a central library, and most of the time you could see and hear what everyone else was doing. If someone entered the school and walked into the library, students and teachers alike would often look up to see who it was.

High school students were also allowed to put aside the old traditional desks and make their own seats, which could be as comfortable as they wished. Some of us designed and made some pretty interesting seating arrangements.

In the spirit of the new "open space" setting, the curriculum was opened up to allow students more freedom to choose their own

*The present main building of Ocracoke School, built in 1971.*

program and to work at their own pace. Although the system worked well for some, many students took advantage of the inherent freedoms and moved through high school with little effort.

Before the gym was built, graduations were held in the Methodist Church. As I look back now on that spring night when the seven of us marched up to the altar where we sat facing the audience, I realize how much I had to learn. I had spent very little time off the island. I had made regular trips to Manteo, Elizabeth City, a few visits to Norfolk and Raleigh, and gone with school groups to Williamsburg and Washington, D.C. The Washington trip took place during my ninth-grade year and was the first time that many of us had been to a big city.

Trips off the island are still something special for many Ocracoke kids. With the increase in tourism, our students are not only being exposed to other life-styles but they are also traveling more. "The isolation factor has changed," observed Karen Lovejoy, who came to the school in 1978 as its first exceptional education teacher. "It's not so strange to leave and go places anymore.

"More students are traveling on their own. We even have high school students who have spent time studying in France, Germany, and the Netherlands."

Karen's husband, Dave Frum, added, "One of the unique things about the young people here is that they are more responsible for themselves than most young people their ages elsewhere. These kids have jobs throughout high school, and even earlier ages. They are working to pay off cars, boats, crab pots, and other things."

Although the busy summer season brings young vacationers of all ages, it is the lengthy school year that can sometimes be socially confining. "The social group is so small," said one parent, "that if you don't belong you're left out of the whole school."

A frequent complaint, especially during the winter, is that there is little to do on the island for young people. According to Miss Nora Gaskill, wife of Captain Thurston Gaskill, the young people today have to do what she did when she was growing up during the first decade of the 1900s: "They have to make their own amusement like we did."

Ocracokers young and old have always entertained themselves. Before the 1950s most social activities centered around the church. Young people also gathered at various houses, cooked fudge, sang, and danced. "Ocracokers have always danced," said Ellen Marie Cloud, who grew up at Ocracoke during the 1950s. "There was always somebody in every crowd who could play an instrument. They had square dances at the Pamlico Inn, the Island Inn, and there was a place that Stanley Wahab built called the Spanish Casino. Everybody went to the dances. You might be swinging a seventy-year-old man or twelve-year-old boy."

Most of Ocracoke's musicians were influenced by family members who passed along their talent to the next generation, who continued providing music until another generation came along. One early fiddle player was William "Wid" Williams, whose son, Sam Keech Williams, also played the fiddle and tap-danced. After Wid Williams, another fiddle player, Tom Neal (O'Neal), took his place.

During Tom Neal's fiddling days, a larger group of Ocracokers, influenced by Jimmie Rodgers, formed a band known as "The Graveyard Band." The name stuck because most of the group were brothers

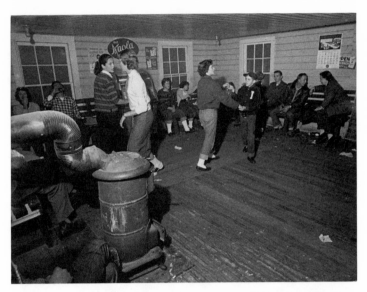

*A popular teenage hangout during the 1950s was Old Jake's, where Ocracoke's young people often danced to juke box music. (Print courtesy of Larry Williams; photograph reprinted by permission of the American Red Cross)*

and cousins from the Garrish family, who lived close to the Howard graveyard (next to the British Cemetery). The band also practiced evenings in an area near the graveyard.

The Graveyard Band existed from the 1920s to the 1950s. As the original members dropped out, others were added. The Garrishes included Robert Lee, Jakie, Junior, Jule, Charlie, and Powers. Others were Ansley O'Neal, Willie Hunnings, Lawrence and Maurice Ballance, Roy Parsons, and George Jackson. Although my father played but a short period with the group, his younger brother, Maurice, continued playing. Maurice still plays occasionally with Edgar Howard, who grew up at Ocracoke, but who, along with his brother Walter, left to pursue a career as an entertainer. Edgar eventually played banjo for such entertainers as Milton Berle.

"The 1950s brought the teenagers alive," continued Ellen Marie.

*"Old Jake" Alligood. (Courtesy of Margueritte Boos)*

"Except for square dancing, most dancing was for adults with orchestras."

A popular teenage hangout during the 1950s was "Old Jake's," half of a Quonset hut which was used as one of the barracks at the Navy base during World War II. The proprietor, Jake Alligood, had a juke box there and sold soft drinks and other snacks. "Going to Old Jake's was a every night thing, except Sunday," recalled Ellen Marie. "We danced by the juke box. Most of the guys would not dance except for square dancing. We girls would dance with each other.

"Old Jake was almost blind, but he knew who you were before you shut the door. They had movies in the old Wahab Village Hotel. A theater was in one part and a skating rink in another. We'd go in Jake's before the movie, buy a drink, a pickle, and parched peanuts. The film would break many times during the movie, and when it did people would start rolling their drink bottles on the floor.

"Jake was a very good and patient man. He had to be to sit in that place, night after night, and listen to a crowd of teenagers."

During the winter Ellen Marie and others her age would sometimes steal a chicken. "We waited until people went to bed. Of course, when you jumped in there and grabbed the chicken by the legs the lights would start coming on in the houses. We wrung his neck, then we had to pick him and clean him. We then took him to somebody's house and had a chicken stew. Sometimes it would take forever to cook him he'd be so tough. People just knew in the wintertime that we were going to steal a chicken. It was fun."

During the 1960s, some descendants of the Graveyard Band formed a group and began playing rock and roll music. Three of the members, Martin, Kenny, and Lee, are sons of original Graveyard Band players Powers and Junior Garrish. Other members included Jackie Willis, Ronnie O'Neal, and later Frankie Garrish, David Styron, and Michael O'Neal. During its early years the group was called the Cousins and the Gallon Jugs. Later the name was changed to the Graveyard Band Revived in honor of the original band.

Part Three      Building Bridges

On a hot late summer morning, Dave Frum of the National Park Service and I drove down a dirt road near the Ocracoke Campground to the soundside. An orange-red sun, clearly defined in the humid air, was rising behind us, and light breezes from the northeast occasionally rippled the calm water. We stopped within fifteen feet of the sound where the road ended, unloaded a sixteen-foot canoe, placed it in about eight inches of water, and began paddling-poling along the edge of the salt marsh. A mixed flock of seagulls, willets, and plovers had gathered on a dry shoal about seventy-five yards from the bank. Several took to the air and flew off into Pamlico Sound. These are only a few of the approximately 350 species of birds that have been seen on the Outer Banks.

Though one of the most productive and beautiful areas on earth, the salt marsh is not normally a part of the average coastal visitor's vacation. Hiding within this muddy and sometimes malodorous environment are vast quantities of life that reveal themselves only to the observer who decides to get his feet dirty.

We adjusted ourselves in the canoe and followed along a narrow gully that cut close to the bank. The tide was high. A thin slime of brown algae covered the bottom. This same slime appears a greenish color when the tide is out. Marsh periwinkles were plentiful on the stalks of the *Spartina alterniflora* which stood in continuous stands all along the bank. Tiny spider webs, sagging with dew, were strung among the stalks. Dave pointed to a small stand of coastal broom sedge on a slightly higher section of the bank. It stood directly in front of a growth of red myrtles and salt marsh elders.

The shoreline here is relatively straight but tends to curve from our entrance point east-northeast until it reaches a small bay that cuts east-southeast into the bank. We followed along the edge of this small bay, paddled the canoe up to the muddy bank, and stopped. The usual stand of *Spartina alterniflora* was replaced here by a clump of chickenclaw saltwart, or glasswort, which covered the thick mud, its fibrous roots exposed where the tide had eroded the bank.

We got out of the canoe, pulled it up on the bank, and began walking inland over a flat fieldlike plain toward a growth of shrubs and trees that started just out of reach of the tide. As we walked, we noticed that the gnats, mosquitoes, and greenhead flies that were part of the usual summer marsh experience were missing. We had had a pretty dry summer.

We bent down to examine a plant with tiny purple flowers that we had noticed from the canoe. There were other, similar plants nearby. "Sea lavender," said Dave. "From a distance they appear like a purple mist on the marsh."

Dave and I continued walking, stepping on more chickenclaw saltwart. We stopped for a moment to examine a salt marsh aster, a small daisylike flower that looked much too fragile for the often tide-swept salt marsh. We wondered how it could have possibly survived the latest northwester that drowned the marsh with a higher than usual tide.

As we approached the line of shrubs marking the end of the field, we were confronted by a stand of black rushes, or needle rushes, that stood like guardians before the ascending thicket and the taller trees beyond. These plants, though green, brown, and gray at different times of the year, appear as dark, almost black areas on the marsh when viewed from a distance. They have thin stalks that end in sharp points and branched, brownish flowers. I've been stuck by them many times while tramping through the marsh. They are also one of the greatest dangers in the life of a pair of waist boots.

We chose the clearest opening and proceeded inland, pushing aside the rushes and stepping on downed stands of them and *Spartina alterniflora* to avoid small puddles of brackish water. The bank of higher land where sea-myrtle, yaupon, red cedar, loblolly pine, and live oak stood, was only ten yards away. We stopped once again to examine a small colony of cattails which we had eyed from the water. "Where you see these," explained Dave, "you know the freshwater line begins." The tall flat leaves of the cattail can reach a height of eight feet, and the spikes, the brownish flowers referred to as tails, are three to twelve inches long. The lower part bears the female flowers while the higher part bears the male flowers.

The latest big tide had spread a layer of seaweed, driftwood, and other flotsam over the marsh, ending with a cluttered line near the cattails. There were bits of trash, a large cork from a fisherman's net, and a tall piece of bamboo with a red rag tied at the top to mark the location of a net set somewhere in Pamlico Sound. In the middle of this collection was a bright red and white kite with a trailing string that led up over the edge of the marsh and into the trees.

We searched among the cattails, rushes, and flotsam for the swamp rose mallow, one of the most beautiful plants on the marsh. We finally found it, a large green plant with pink flowers, almost hidden from view by the tall leaves of the cattails. After examining the flower itself closely, we continued to the bank and stepped up into the forest of red cedars, loblolly pines, and live oaks. This is Six Mile Hammock, a name it has retained since the eighteenth century when early settlers named the location because of its distance from Ocracoke Inlet. This chunk of maritime forest is one of the most beautiful areas on the island. It is also the site of some of the largest live oaks on the island, one in particular several feet thick. None of the trees is exceptionally tall since they are continuously cropped by the prevailing winds. They fit together like an abundant stalk of broccoli.

We returned to the canoe and began to paddle back toward the truck. A small flock of common egrets flew over, amazingly white and graceful in their flight. We drifted for a moment in a small bay where I had been only a week before with Uriah and Sullivan Garrish fishing for mullets. Other fishermen teased us when they heard that we had been so close inshore. "Don't tell me you crowd have been in there again after them ole mashy mullets," one said. But Uriah and Sullivan had made some good sets far inshore, and occasionally they would want to "check it out." Most of the time all we found were a few very large mullets, more brown than silver due to their continuous presence in the dark, nutrient-rich water, and therefore referred to as "mashy." Dave and I saw several mullets jump. "I'll have to tell Uriah and Sullivan about them," I said.

Life was rich and abundant on the bottom as we stared down into the murky water. We saw countless minnows; an occasional horseshoe crab; a banded water snake; blue crabs scavenging anything that looked edible; snails; a diamond-backed terrapin; a small stingray; and mullets that shot through the water, disturbing the quiet and slower pace of existence. "Do you think the old-timers know the great value of this marshland?" asked Dave.

"Yes," I said. "They've always known it. But they didn't realize it from reading about it. They discovered the value by doing what we're doing now, looking and seeing the coming and going of life here. It doesn't take long to see the connection between the small minnow that swims in the quiet, safer water and the fish that is caught later when it has matured."

From a distance we saw a yellow-crowned night heron fly along the edge of the trees we had just visited, continue southward, then settle in front of us on one of several old stakes stuck down in a small bay not far from the truck. As we paddled toward the stakes, other herons flew up and took roost in the nearby trees. These night herons don't show themselves much during the daylight hours. They hunt mostly at night and can be identified by their call, a single "kwawk." As we approached the one remaining heron, it too flew off to join an increasing flock that appeared to be settling in for the rest of the day.

Our last stop would be to examine the stakes. They had been stuck at the head of small bays such as this one by Ocracoke fishermen who tied their boats close to nearby camps. These camps were once used so the fishermen could live and work near the areas they fished. When the National Park Service acquired most of the island, the camps were eventually torn down. Usage of the small bays to harbor boats also soon ended.

With the exception of the 775 private acres comprising Ocracoke Village, the whole island of Ocracoke is part of the Cape Hatteras National Seashore, the first national seashore park established in the United States. The acquisition of the seashore began on August 17, 1937, with an act of Congress. A minimum of 10,000 acres was to be acquired with public and private funds. By 1952 the minimum was met, the state of North Carolina conveyed to the federal government lands they controlled, and, on January 12, 1953, the Cape Hatteras National Seashore was formally established. The original area totalled 12,414 acres within an 80-mile stretch of the Outer Banks. Today that amount has grown to about 30,000 acres.

Included in these 30,000 acres are two tracts of land on Ocracoke Island. The first tract runs from Hatteras Inlet southwest, covering the entire stretch of beach, to Ocracoke Village. The second tract is located along the northern part of the Creek where the National Park Service facilities are located.

The Ocracoke land was purchased from various residents, many of whom were furious because they had to sell their land. I remember hearing my grandmother talk about her family losing to the "government" much of the land near the Ocracoke Campground. Some of this was the Six Mile Hammock area, one of the highest areas on the island. Uriah Garrish once said, "I'd like to own that Hammock, have a house on it, and be a young fellar."

People needed to blame someone for the sudden change of ownership. They didn't know the poor fellow sent out by the government to offer them a standard price for their land; and it certainly didn't matter whether they liked the transaction or not.

The Ocracokers soon learned that an agency of the federal government, the National Park Service, would be the agency administering their former lands. The land would become part of a national park for the "benefit and enjoyment of all the people." The United States Government. The Government. The National Park Service. Someone to blame.

Some of the bitterness was eased when local men were hired to plant grass and erect sand fences along twelve miles of dunes on Ocracoke Beach. A portion of this beach work had already been done in the 1930s by the Civilian Conservation Corps under the Civil Works Administration.

Eventually more of the local men were hired, the grass got planted, the state of North Carolina completed the beach highway, a small campground was set up in the village, and tourists began thronging unremittingly to the island.

As it is in other parks the National Park Service presence on Ocracoke today is divided into three areas: protection, interpretation, and maintenance. Each division has a responsibility for the resources and the visitors who use them. A few Ocracokers have permanent jobs and others have seasonal work during the busy summer months. Few Ocracokers try to make a career with the park, however. Many say it's too difficult to get job security and that you never know when you'll be laid off or sent away from home to work at another park.

Though feelings toward the National Park Service are sometimes mixed, most residents are aware of the important role it has had in preserving Ocracoke Beach. I have often heard comments like, "No telling what that beach would be like now if they hadn't come in and took over," and "It would be another Nags Head. You can be sure of that."

But sometimes National Park Service policies toward management of the island's resources conflict with Ocracokers' view of them. Much of the conflict stems from the historical, unrestricted use of the land before the Park Service came to town. At times, Ocracokers resent the new restrictions, which are necessary for the protection of the resources and the visitors themselves, and they sometimes feel that they must compete with "outsiders" for usage of the land.

Park ranger Judy Ballance Lawson has been working with the park since 1973. For her, these occasional conflicts with Ocracokers, her own people, are particularly hard.

On a warm August evening in 1980 I went with Judy on her night beach patrol. We left the village and entered the Cape Hatteras National Seashore by the road that leads from Highway 12 to the south point of the island and Ocracoke Inlet. The sand road is soft in places, depressed in others. Travel over the road often requires a 4-wheel drive vehicle. Some Ocracokers, however, experienced in driving in soft sand, take ordinary cars and trucks just about anywhere they want to go on the beach. The off-road vehicle traffic has steadily increased in the park over the years. This increase has brought about greater strains on the resources. To prevent aimless driving in the south point area, the Park Service has established a marked route that leads to the inlet. Occasional signs warn drivers to keep out of certain areas. "One thing we're trying to do," explained Judy, "is to get the grass to catch and grow on either side of the road. A lot of this road floods when we have a storm or big tide.

"It takes a while for people to get used to following a road on the beach just like they'd follow any other road. When they get out on the beach they sometimes have a tendency to go wild."

When we had traveled about a mile, Judy quickly switched on the siren and blue light, veered off the route, and headed toward a large dune along the soundside. "Dune busters," she said. Two jeeps suddenly appeared on the top of a dune, lodged for a moment in the soft sand, then made an awkward descent to the bottom. Judy was waiting for them. It is against Park Service regulations to travel off marked routes, and especially to drive over sand dunes, so crucial to barrier island protection. The violators pleaded with the ranger, insisted that they didn't seen the signs, weren't aware that they weren't supposed to drive on the dunes, but finally accepted the citation.

We proceeded on toward the inlet, passing numerous signs that said "Tern Nests, Keep Out." These signs are placed in this area in the late spring to protect such nesting birds as the least tern, black skimmer, common tern, gull billed tern, and others. Most people who come in contact with these protected areas respect the reserved space, especially when they see the birds with their eggs and young chicks. The birds are also protective of their nests and have been known to dive at observers who get too close.

We arrived at Ocracoke Inlet as the sun set over Portsmouth Island. Several trucks were parked near the waterline. Men and women were fishing in the surf, and children were building sand castles and playing games in the sand. Judy made a wide swing past the vehicles, greeted them casually, then headed north. She drove up to the base of a large dune that had been lapped by the ocean during the previous winter. During the summer months, with the prevailing winds from the south and the sand supply consequently driven onto the island, a large acre or so of land had spread out approximately 200 yards southwest toward the point of Portsmouth Island. Where the fishermen and their children were now, a channel of water had once run, deep and powerful.

Between Ocracoke Inlet and the Ocracoke Airstrip (a distance of about four and one-half miles) we saw few people. At the airport an unusually large number of people were still swimming in the protected area even though the Park Service lifeguards were off duty. This is always the busiest beach location during the summer season because of its closeness to Ocracoke Village and the available lifeguard protection. This protected beach was established in 1978. Another protected beach at the Ocracoke Campground remained in operation until it was closed in 1980.

A distance of three miles separates the Ocracoke Airstrip (sometimes referred to as Ramp 70) from the Ocracoke Campground (Ramp 68). This area is closed to vehicles between Memorial Day and Labor Day. In near darkness we left the beach and pulled into the campground so that Judy could check with the night teller for any problems. The 136-site Ocracoke Campground has undergone major changes in the last few years. New comfort stations and showers were installed, replacing pit toilets and the few showers which depended on chlorinated groundwater from a shallow well. Several miles of water lines now connect the campground to the village water system.

While many campers welcome the improvements, others lament the loss of the primitiveness that had distinguished the Ocracoke Campground from others in the seashore. They also complain that the campground, like Ocracoke Village, is becoming too much like the rest of the Outer Banks.

After checking with the night teller, we made a slow circle through the campground, stopping once so Judy could tell a camper to move his car back onto the pavement. "Some people are afraid to walk a few extra steps," she said. We continued on the patrol, entering the beach again by the same ramp. A dull yellow moon was rising over the ocean. She drove carefully. "Probably be a few couples walking around tonight," she observed.

After clearing the campground area, we began to notice an unusually large number of ghost crabs scurrying back and forth between the dunes and the sea. "We've had a few turtle crawls around here somewhere," added Judy. "Kenny found one a few weeks ago." For centuries the loggerhead sea turtle has found its way to these shores to lay eggs. On moonlit nights during the warmer months female turtles crawl out of the ocean and up to the dune line to make their nests. The rangers can tell where a turtle has come ashore by the tracks she makes with her flappers as she struggles to reach the dunes. Once there, the turtle digs a hole approximately ten to twenty inches deep with her flappers and deposits anywhere from fifty to one hundred and fifty golf ball–size eggs. She then covers the nest and returns to the sea.

Sometimes the rangers dig up the nest, count the eggs, then rebury them. They check the nests regularly for any damage from ghost crabs, one of the main predators of turtle eggs. One year, as an experiment, the rangers moved several nests to a sandy site in the village near their maintenance yard. When Sherry O'Neal, a Park Service maintenance worker, came to work one morning she met some of the hatchlings as she opened the yard gate. Their tiny flappers were busily scratching the marl yard, heading southeast toward the sea.

The hatching period is approximately seventy-five days. When it was time for my brother Kenny, who was also a park ranger at the time, to check the nest that Judy had mentioned several months before, I went with him. We approached the nest from the highway, walking over the dunes to the marker that had been put there several months before. The nest was higher on the dune than I had ever seen one before. As an October moon shone down on the ocean, I held the flashlight as he dug the nest. "They should be ready to hatch," he said, digging carefully with his hands to prevent any damage to the eggs. When he finally reached egg level, he pulled up several of the spongy-feeling eggs to examine them. Most were not formed. Others had been cracked open, revealing bits of yoke and half-formed turtles. "I don't think this nest is quite ready," said Kenny. "Some of them have hatched, but the nest doesn't look too healthy."

After covering the nest, we searched nearby for the presence of ghost crabs. Several holes close to the nest confirmed our suspicions about the little vandals. "Those things are everywhere this year," said Kenny.

Although some of the eggs hatched, it's hard to say how many of the hatchlings made it to the open ocean. Most don't survive. Those that hatch are threatened by ghost crabs and shore birds before they get to the water. Once in the water, the tiny turtles have other predators to deal with. Some must survive, of course, and of these perhaps a few find their way back to our shores to lay their own eggs.

Between the campground and Hatteras Inlet (a distance of about ten miles) the beach gradually narrows, especially at a point about halfway between the pony pen and the inlet. This area is causing great concern among Ocracokers, Park Service officials, and the North Carolina Department of Transportation.

In the winter of 1980 the ocean finally reached and began pounding away at a two-mile section of dunes not far from the Hatteras ferry docks. A major break in the dune line occurred on a stormy December afternoon as Judy, Dave Frum, and I were there to investigate the damage. An east-northeast wind had been strong for several days, pushing high seas on top of an already big tide. Although northeasters are a normal part of winter weather, this particular one seemed more severe since the sea had broken through the dunes and covered the road six inches deep in many places.

Although it seemed a real possibility, the road itself was not washing out. Huge breakers continued to slam into the dunes, meeting some resistance before surging upward and eventually over the sand barrier. Clumps of American beachgrass and sea oats, along with small red cedars and red myrtles, once part of a peaceful back dunefield, were uprooted and carried across the road by the surge. A small side road that leads to the Pamlico Sound was filled with water, providing a shallow, watery connection between sea and sound, and suggesting a potential inlet. Tons of sand were being displaced by the surge, much of it already covering the road.

When the storm finally abated several days later, large deposits of sand and grasses with exposed roots covered the road and shoulders. The bases of many shrubs that were higher up on the beach were also covered by the deposits.

Many people assumed that the road was doomed and that even the entire north end of the island was going to wash away, but what we were seeing was part of a process that has been repeated periodically for thousands of years. "On a healthy barrier island you have overwash passes," explains Duke University marine geologist Orrin Pilkey. "During a storm this overwash goes right on through them. The old creeks along Highway 12 at Ocracoke are probably old inlets, old overwash passes." Ironically, according to Pilkey, the building of artificial dunes has probably increased the rate of erosion on the front side of the island. "All of the storm energy comes up against this dune line, and the reflection causes sand to be brought back out to sea," he says.

East Carolina University geologist Stan Riggs has also recognized the problems associated with the artificial dunes at Ocracoke. Accord-

*Erosion along the Cape Hatteras National Seashore eventually claimed the old Hatteras Inlet Coast Guard Station, pictured here in this 1955 photo. (Courtesy of National Park Service, Cape Hatteras National Seashore)*

ing to Riggs, the beach face off Ocracoke descends to about twenty-five feet before it flattens off to a shelf which gradually slopes to the edge of the continental shelf. "This beach ramp absorbs the energy," explains Riggs. "You also have offshore bars, which are part of the ramp, that help break this energy. The beach face, or ramp, gets steeper and steeper because of the artificial dunes. Without the dune ridge you would have smooth overwash and therefore maintain a more normal, gentler profile."

Pilkey also explains that the "artificial dunes have had a profound effect on the vegetation, allowing it to move closer to the beach, temporarily causing the vegetation to be in a place that it doesn't want to be."

Despite the winter storms and hurricanes that have raked Highway 12 all along the Outer Banks, we have had few problems with the road actually washing out. When the highway was completed in the 1950s, a line of protecting sand dunes was already in place. With the exception of a few areas on Hatteras Island and the north end of Ocracoke, the highway and much of the dunes have remained intact.

Incidents of ocean overwash at Ocracoke's north end often raise questions about the Park Service's policy toward beach erosion. The current policy is not to renourish the eroding beaches, not to interfere with the complex processes involved in seashore dynamics. This, of course, doesn't mean that the Park Service wouldn't work with the North Carolina Department of Transportation if access problems, such as ocean washovers and highway washouts, impeded travel along the Outer Banks, much of which is part of the Cape Hatteras National Seashore.

Threats to Highway 12, as well as other travel problems in the park, ultimately fall on the desk of the superintendent. Thomas Hartman has inherited some large problems since coming to the area in the fall of 1981 from Cumberland Gap National Historic Site. Problems such as saving the Cape Hatteras Lighthouse, proposed jetties at Oregon Inlet, the deterioration of existing park facilities due to the harsh marine environment and extensive visitor usage, and ocean overwash and erosion of the sand dunes all require potentially huge budgets to manage.

As an administrator, Hartman often sees it all from a financial perspective. "Concerning the dune problem at Ocracoke," he said, "as in other areas of the park, I think it is a question of awareness. We are more aware of the seashore dynamics now than before. We have a problem created during the time in the 1960s and before when we had a large budget to work with and when we also thought that we could handle the ocean. We're now able to see that it's a much more difficult issue."

Every national park tends to have some natural or historical landmark that attracts the eye of the tourist. One of Ocracoke's biggest attractions, and one almost synonymous with the name of the island itself, is the Ocracoke wild ponies. Although their origin is uncertain, the most common explanation is that they are descendants of shipwrecked horses, perhaps from Spanish ships, during the early explorations along the Outer Banks. It is almost certain that the horses are of Spanish origin.

In recent years many facts have been gathered about the history of the horses. Ocracoke district ranger Jim Henning and his wife Jennetta have spent a great deal of time researching and caring for the horses. Henning came to Ocracoke in 1974 from Bodie Island, the northern end of the Cape Hatteras National Seashore. Being district ranger on Ocracoke has often been regarded as a difficult assignment. Henning has enjoyed the move, especially, as he found out later, the chance to work with the horses. Before his arrival no records were kept on the horses, they received little medical attention, and their penning and pasturing were much less structured.

One of Henning's first tasks was to prove the Spanish ancestry of the horses. After researching and working with veterinarians, he was able to identify a number of physiological features typical of Spanish mustangs, including one fewer lumbar vertebra; greater density of bone (five to ten times greater); ability to carry more weight relative to size; little leg trouble; walls of hoofs more concave and less flat-footed; wide forehead and short, strong neck; long, flowing mane and tail; hot blooded; and good tempered.

Because the Ocracoke ponies are inherently good natured, their "wild" name tag is often deceiving. Recently several of them have been used for horse patrols on the beach, particularly during the busy summer season. While most parks have mounted horse patrols, this is the first time horses, especially native horses, have been used for patrol by the Park Service at Ocracoke. They not only provide the ranger division with better accessibility to beach areas but also promote good public relations.

Approximately twenty horses now make up the Ocracoke herd. When settlers first came to the Outer Banks, one of the main reasons was to take advantage of an area where livestock could graze and roam freely. In 1733, for example, Richard Sanderson acquired all of Ocracoke Island from his father, including the "stock of Horses, sheep, cattle, and hoggs." In later years, as more people began to settle

*During the 1950s, Captain Marvin Howard (on horse at far left) organized Ocracoke's mounted Boy Scout troop. Each scout tamed and cared for his own pony, which came from the Ocracoke wild pony herd. (Print courtesy of Larry Williams; photograph reprinted by permission of the American Red Cross)*

on the island, they acquired their own livestock, and early wills included the transfer of livestock to beneficiaries.

At one time several hundred wild ponies ran free all over the island. Some of these ponies were caught, penned, and tamed by Ocracokers, who used them for transportation. Several were also used by the Life Saving Service to haul beach equipment and conduct patrols.

Up until the late 1950s, an annual Ocracoke event, usually on the Fourth of July, was the penning of the wild ponies. The ponies were caught, penned, branded, and then released. The brands were registered with the register of deeds office in Swan Quarter, and for many years the registration fee was only ten cents. Some of the ponies were sold at an auction, usually for a price of fifty to one hundred dollars.

In the middle 1950s, Captain Marvin Howard, a native Ocracoker who had spent many years away from home sailing throughout the world, retired and returned to Ocracoke. Soon after his arrival, he came up with the idea of forming the only mounted Boy Scout troop in the United States. Beginning with about fifteen scouts, his plan was for each boy to have his own pony. The scouts first bought ten ponies. Each scout was responsible for catching, penning, and taming his pony. The boys were required to work at odd jobs to get money for the care of their animals.

According to several of the former scouts, the ponies were often difficult to catch because they were about as comfortable in the water as they were on land. Also, after they were caught, it took a while for the ponies to learn to eat oats and other normal horse food. In their wild state they had been used to roaming the beach, eating salt and beach grasses, and digging holes in the sand with their hoofs to get fresh groundwater.

Eventually the mounted troop was formed, consisting of just about every scout-age boy on the island. In addition to participating in the annual pony pennings, they also marched in parades and did other scouting activities, all with their trusty ponies.

By 1957 the future of the other wild ponies had gained the attention of the North Carolina General Assembly. A bill was passed that year to require all Outer Banks livestock, including ponies, to be penned. The major point of contention was erosion and loss of vegetation due to the roaming livestock. Luckily for the Ocracoke Island scouts, an amendment to that bill exempted their horses from this requirement.

The Park Service, too, was beginning to have doubts about the wisdom of allowing the ponies to remain free. A new highway was to be constructed, and the ponies might wander onto the roadway. Upon hearing this, Captain Howard came to the rescue of the Ocracoke ponies, pointing out their long years of service to Ocracokers and the life-saving service and their current use by the scouts. After all, he reasoned, what better way to prevent juvenile delinquency and teach morality to the scouts?

The mounted Boy Scout troop lasted only a few years, though. As the original members got older, the group started to break up. In

*Park ranger Howard Bennink stops during his horse patrol long enough for Todd Mugford to pet one of the Ocracoke Wild Ponies which are being used on patrols by the National Park Service.*

1959 the remaining wild ponies were confined to a corral near the present location, ending the many years of pony pennings. The construction of Highway 12 down Ocracoke Beach was underway, and the wild ponies would never again roam freely.

The remaining herd of approximately twenty horses is today cared for by the National Park Service rangers. They are fed and watered daily, and a veterinarian is sometimes called in when medical attention is needed. Though confined within three miles of fence, the ponies are still wild and can be seen in their 160-acre pasture, located about five miles south of the Hatteras ferry docks.

On a cold December afternoon near sunset, Dave Frum and I again went for a walk on the marsh in the same area that we had visited earlier in the summer. A strong wind blew with increasing gusts from the northeast. We parked near the campground and took a small path that led to the marsh. After passing through stands of live oaks, pines, red cedars, yaupons, and myrtles, we eventually reached the cattails and salt-water grasses at the edge of the marsh.

Our first impression was the consistent brown color of the marsh grasses. The sea lavender flowers had died and turned a dull brown, blending with the coastal broom sedge, cattails, black needle rushes, and saltmeadow cordgrass.

As we crunched over the dead marsh grasses, lying flat after being combed by the recent high tides, we noticed a collection of flotsam that included a bright green channel marker, some bottles, net corks, and several pieces of bamboo. We passed a small pond about as big as a bath tub. Several other similar-sized ponds were nearby. "Good place for teal," observed Dave.

When we reached the water's edge, we followed the shoreline as it cut into a small cove. A duck blind constructed of red myrtle limbs was situated at the head of the cove. Empty bright red gun shells were scattered on the ground nearby. Although no one was in the blind, about one dozen decoys were bobbing in the water. A dead loon floated next to the bank.

After passing the blind, we stumbled on a loggerhead sea turtle that had crawled onto the bank; it was about three feet long and its shell was covered with barnacles. Thinking first that it was just having difficulty, we gently placed it back in the water. Within a few minutes, however, it swam back toward the bank. "Something must be wrong with it," I said. The turtle seemed determined to get back to the muddy bank and continue with its original purpose.

In the growing darkness we headed back across the marsh to the path. A steady rain had started to fall. We were silent for a while, thinking about the turtle, wondering why it was determined to make a landing. Our answer came two days later when several hunters reported a dead sea turtle lying in the marsh. We then realized that the turtle had been in the process of beaching itself to die slowly in the marsh, a marsh that would, for the most part, come back to life in the spring.

Most people who live on a barrier island watch the weather and seasons more closely than those who live inland. Ocracokers realize that changes in the weather can mean delayed ferry schedules, a difference in the number of tourists who visit, and whether or not they'll be able to check their crab pots or fish their nets.

Long before an identified cold front approaches the North Carolina coast, fishermen begin speculating on when the front will move across the island, how strong it will be, and the number and kinds of nets to use to catch the most fish. Cold fronts get fish on the move, and the accompanying strong winds often stir the bottom sediments, making it more difficult for fish to see the net.

The one time of the year when Ocracokers are especially attentive to the weather is during hurricane season. After a number of hot August days with little or no rain and wind, conversations like the following are common:

"All this hot weather's going to lead to something."

"It can't keep on like this. Something's got to give."

"There's a lot of turbulence around. You can look at the clouds and tell there's something brewing down there."

"Down there," of course, refers to the Caribbean and other areas of the Atlantic Ocean, and "what's brewing" is likely to be a hurricane. As areas of tropical disturbance are identified, weather watchers keep their eyes and ears open for any developments that could mean strengthening and movement toward the continental United States.

Before radio, television, and advanced weather-tracking technology, Ocracokers, like others concerned with and greatly affected by the weather, relied on various signs learned from years of nature watching. In addition to continuous hot August days and the presence of turbulent-looking clouds, other indicators, such as mud fiddlers leaving low marshland where they usually live to crawl toward higher ground, were thought to be signs of an approaching hurricane.

Generations of Ocracokers lived with the annual threat of hurricanes. Since they could expect little advance warning of an approaching storm and transportation was slow, very few, if any, early residents evacuated the island. Most accepted the potential dangers, secured their homes, boats, and other possessions as best they could, and then rode out the storm. According to those who have knowledge of past hurricanes, no resident has ever died at Ocracoke as a result of a hurricane.

Most people who now live at Ocracoke have never experienced a "bad" hurricane—at least not the hurricanes that stand out in the minds of those life-long residents who remember the hurricanes of the 1930s and 1940s, and even the powerful one in 1899.

According to reports from the observer at the Hatteras Weather Bureau, the 1899 storm was one of the worst in the memory of anyone living at Hatteras at that time. The observer, S. L. Doshoz, also wrote that Ocracoke was hit as badly as Hatteras.

Effects of the hurricane began on August 16 with easterly gale force winds, which eventually reached hurricane strength during the early morning hours of August 17. By one o'clock that afternoon, the winds had gradually changed to the northeast and reached 93 miles per hour, with occasional gusts up to 120 and 140 miles per hour. After a brief lull in the hurricane that night, the wind shifted to the east-southeast and increased once again to 60 and 70 miles per hour. Gale force winds from the south and eventually the southwest blew throughout the day on August 18, and squally weather continued even on the following day.

The observer also included in his report that the tide had reached one to four feet in most houses (over land the tide was supposed to have been from three to ten feet), and that not only homes but also boats and fishing equipment suffered extensive damage. Though no lives were lost at Hatteras, the observer wrote that a pleasure boat at Ocracoke was destroyed, and several people from the boat, who were from Washington, North Carolina, were drowned. Countless chickens, hogs, sheep, and cattle were also lost.

Before their deaths, I talked with "Miss" Sara Ellen Gaskill, then about 100 years old, and "Miss" Lillian Jackson, almost 90 years old, about the 1899 hurricane. To them the "old August storm" was one of the worst to hit Ocracoke. "It seems like to me," recalled Miss Sara Ellen, "that the ole August storm was the worst one we ever had. The day before it hit that night was a pretty time. The sky was clear and the sun was out pretty. We didn't have too much of a way to be informed that a storm was about to hit in those days. There was a Coast Guard station down toward Hatteras Inlet called the Cedar Hammock Station. This was before they built the one here in the village, and sometimes some of the men from that station would keep us informed.

"When it hit that night, we had to leave home because the tide started to come in our house. I lived with my mother and father at that time in a house not far from the water tower. Anyway, when it hit, we left and went over to this old woman's house called Miss Arcade. Her house set on high ground, and I reckon a lot of people knew this because the house was packed. I believe Lillian was there."

"Oh yes," said Miss Lillian, "I was there. I'll never forget it. That's where we spent the night, too, me and Mommie. Poppie and Buddy were down below fishing at the fishing camps when it hit, and we were there by ourselves. About the time the tide started to come in our house, Uncle Howard, Sara Ellen's daddy, came and got us and took us over there with him and Aunt Lot. I believe Sara Ellen was there with 'em too.

"Well, weren't long 'fore the tide started to come in their house too, and we finally had to clear out and go to Uncle Kit's and Aunt Nancy's.

Uncle Kit weren't there but Aunt Nancy was. Not long after night, the tide even come in their house and we had to get out of there and go to Miss Arcade's.

"Ole Jones had just started to build his house near there, and the lumber was strewed everywhere. When we started to wade over there, Uncle Kit put me down and I got straddled on a piece of that board. The tide was a-swirling around and they had to grab me, for I reckon if they hadn't, the tide would of swept me out.

"Miss Arcade's house was on high land, you see, and when we got there, youngerns, the house was packed. Let's see, there was Miss Mid and all them, Miss Missouri and all them, and I don't know how many more. There was so many there that the boys and men had to get down on the floor and under the beds to give the womenfolk a place to sit down.

"And during the hardest of it—youngerns I'll never forget it—Miss Annie Gaskins started praying. Weren't no time after she had prayed that somebody went out and said that there weren't a drop of water to the step. It had gone out that quick.

"It was a mess when we got back to the house. The tide had gone clear past the weatherboarding on the house and the inside was the biggest mess anybody'd ever seen. Youngerns, that was a bad storm.

"Next day, Poppie and them had to tie their boats to the trees and travel up. They had to wade up to their waists in most places along the ole tracks they used to go back and forth on. In some places Poppie would have to carry Buddy on his back it was so deep."

My grandfather, Elisha Ballance, was with Miss Lillian's father and brother when they were trapped at the fishing camps located ten miles north of the village. When the full strength of the hurricane hit, my grandfather and seven other fishermen had to take shelter in small valleys of a nearby sand dune. After being stranded without food or drink for several days, they were finally able to walk back to the village on Friday, August 18. As they waded through water sometimes four feet deep, they counted approximately one hundred cattle and horses that had drowned.

An article that appeared in the August 21 edition of the *Washington Gazette* reported that the "whole island of Ocracoke is a complete wreck as a result of the fierce storm which swept the entire coast of North Carolina." The article also stated that waves twenty and thirty feet high pounded the beach, and the tide was four to five feet all over the island. Thirty-three homes were also damaged, many boats were sunk or destroyed, and there was "much suffering" due to a lack of food and drinking water.

There are many stories associated with the 1899 hurricane. My grandfather told me that two porpoises swam out of the ocean and onto the flooded island. After getting lodged in the fork of an oak tree, they finally broke loose and swam on into Pamlico Sound. Another man, Isaac "Big Ike" O'Neal, reported that when it appeared their house was going to wash off the foundation, his father told him to chop a hole in the floor to relieve the pressure of the rising water. After the hole was chopped through, the water rushed up toward the ceiling, carrying with it a duck that had been trapped under the house by the rising tide.

Some Ocracoke houses were built with trapdoors, or at least holes bored in the floor, to allow water to come in, thus preventing the house from drifting off its foundation. My grandfather had a trapdoor in his house. During one hurricane when he opened the door to allow water to enter, he found one of his cats clinging for dear life to the hatch's underside. One house during the 1899 storm did break from its foundation and drift across the Creek.

Although no one is now living at Ocracoke who experienced the 1899 hurricane, there are still many who remember the almost equally destructive hurricanes of the 1930s and 1940s. The following accounts, written on the wall of a previously abandoned house here, give some idea of the size and destructiveness of these storms.

*Hurricane—August 22, 23, 1933*

6 p.m. August 21. Storm warnings. Northeast winds all night. Barometer falling.

August 22—Mailboat started to Atlantic, but returned. Inlet too rough. Strong Northeast winds until 11 a.m. Walked to beach during lull in storm to view washed up "Victoria," wrecked 1925. Water knee-deep between village and beach. Storm warning in afternoon. Barometer falling. Tide very high.

5 p.m. Water coming into yard.

10 p.m. Water to second step.

12 p.m. Water to sills. Barometer 29.51.

August 23

3 a.m. Winds shifted to Northwest.

4 a.m. Winds shifted to West. Barometer 29.06.

8 a.m. Winds shifted to Southwest. Water dropping.

Barometer rising. Major damage: Front of Anderson cottage blown out. Lum Gaskill's fish house washed out to sea. Gary Bragg's dock gone. Pamlico Inn dock badly damaged. Dance Hall at end of dock swept away. In lake "Marie" badly damaged and sunk. "Eleanor M." slightly damaged. Bad mess at government dock. Most small boats in lake sunk or smashed up. Debris all over island.

*Hurricane—September 15–17, 1933*

Worst storm in memory of oldest living inhabitant. Winds estimated at Hatteras at 122 m.p.h. Barometer fell to 28.28. Lowest known locally.

Saturday a.m.—September 16—Tide flooded island. Many people took refuge in light house. Water stood 7 inches above floor in this cottage. Porch torn off by wind and tide and demolished. Roof over cistern blown off. Fence swept away. Surf against house reached the eaves. Worst damage ever to trees. No lives lost on Ocracoke.

*Hurricane—September 14, 1944*

Storm warning—September 13, 1944

Day calm and hot. In evening, 14 fishboats came into lake for shelter.

September 14

5 a.m. Winds rising: Northeast

7 a.m. Winds reached 75 knots. Anemometer on water tower at Naval Base carried away. Later wind estimated at 100 knots. Barometer 28.40

7:30 a.m. Winds shift to Northwest. 14 foot tides. Island completely under water. Most fishing boats blown far ashore, causing considerable damage to boats and docks. Mailboat tossed ashore close to coffee shop.

Six houses completely demolished.

Pamlico Inn damaged beyond repair.

Extensive damage done to Gary Bragg's home.

3 feet of water pounding through this cottage. Porch blown off and front windows shattered, and front door blown in. Practically all furniture upturned and much of it washed into kitchen. Kitchen window smashed. Front room floor torn up.

9:25 a.m. Wind velocity dropped.

Completely calm by 12:30 p.m.

Far worst storm ever to strike island.

No lives lost.

Ocracoke was hit hard by hurricanes during the 1930s. According to one old resident, such storms swept over the island in 1931, 1932, and two in 1933. The two 1933 hurricanes lashed the North Carolina coast within a few weeks of each other, causing considerable damage to structures and vegetation. Because little rain had accompanied these two storms, the standing salt water was gradually absorbed by all forms of plant life, eventually killing much of it. Drinking water also became contaminated, causing the death, according to my father, of his brother, who had drunk some of it following the storm.

*The mailboat* Aleta *and another vessel* Miss Willis *are high and dry in front of the Island Inn after the 1944 hurricane. Other boats are cast up near houses in the background. (Courtesy of North Carolina Division of Archives and History)*

The September hurricane of 1933 was, at the time, the worst one to hit the island in the memory of anyone living here then. Sullivan Garrish was trapped at the fishing camps ten miles north of the village during this hurricane. "During the worst of the storm," he recalled, "I had to get out of the camp and get on the roof. I climbed to the leeward side of the roof and hung on. Even the chimney blew down. A boat broke loose from where it was tied near the camps and drifted out into Pamlico Sound. When the wind shifted and went to the northeast, the boat returned to the same spot."

Perhaps the most talked about hurricane in Ocracoke's history is the 1944 storm. "You couldn't ask for a prettier day," said one man, referring to the hot, calm day before the hurricane hit. "It didn't seem like we'd be getting anything like we did." Ocracokers got the word of the approaching storm from Navy personnel who were stationed at the naval section base here during World War II.

After the wind shifted to the northwest on the morning of the hurricane, the tide spread all over the island. Water rose two to four feet in many houses, and some residents opened both the front and back doors to let the tide roll on through. "When the tide started to come in our house," recalled my mother, "we thought it was raining in the windows. It was actually coming through the floor. It even washed through the windows when the tide got that high. We waded around in it for a while then went upstairs. When the tide finally went down, there was a muddy mess on the floors."

Uriah and Maude Garrish, who live near the western entrance to East Howard Street, watched a big fishing trawler carried within a few yards of their front door. Other large boats were cast ashore near the Island Inn. After the tide rose and fell within their house, they heard a flapping noise in the bedroom. Looking under the bed, they found a stranded hogfish which had been brought in by the tide.

When the storm was finally over, the amount of standing water all over the island was so great that some residents, including Uriah Garrish, tied boats to their houses so they could get around.

Reports issued after the storm indicated that the wind reached 105 miles per hour and the water level in most houses was two to four feet. Three boats were damaged beyond repair, all docks were badly damaged except the Navy dock, and the island's power plant went out after the generators were flooded.

Within my own lifetime, I can faintly remember experiencing the minor hurricanes of the 1960s, as well as hearing stories about Hurricane Hazel, which hit the North Carolina coast during 1954. My mother had gone to Morehead City before Hazel struck because she was expecting the birth of my brother Kenny. My mother's parents were also with her, leaving my father to board up our house.

Although the hurricane's strength lashed Morehead more than Ocracoke, the island still felt the effects of the storm. "After we boarded up the house," he recalled, "I caught the chickens, put 'em in crates, and moved 'em in the house. I stayed with Mama during the storm. When I came back home, the chickens had gotten out of the crates and were all over the house. When I walked into the dining room, they were standing on top of the china closet staring at me."

None of these, however, are as clear to me as Hurricane Gloria, which ripped across the Outer Banks in late September of 1985.

*Boats cast up on the north side of the Creek during the 1944 hurricane.*
*(Courtesy of Maude Garrish)*

Although we had been watching Gloria's developments for several days, not until Wednesday morning did we realize for sure the likelihood of being in the path of the hurricane. A group of us—students, teachers, and a few parents who had come to the school to pick up their children—stood around the school library television, watching the radar picture of the white blob that had increased in size overnight. Gloria was being described by some as the storm of the century. Many of our students and a few teachers were already on their way to higher ground.

As evacuation notices went out later that day, streams of traffic began to increase all along the Outer Banks. All ferries from Ocracoke to Hatteras and the mainland were running full.

After a long twenty-four-hour evacuation period, in which approximately one thousand residents and tourists left Ocracoke, the ferries finally stopped. The last ferry left for Hatteras around noon on Thursday. For the one hundred or so of us who chose to remain on the island, we would have a long night of waiting and "battening down the hatches."

The threat of Gloria was so great that even Ocracokers who had witnessed the hurricanes of the 1930s and 1940s decided to evacuate. Those of us who were left had our own reasons for staying; I'm still not sure why I stayed, but my decision had a lot to do with my role as a county commissioner. Our risk was also increased because our deputy sheriffs, doctor, Coast Guard personnel, and others involved in public safety had evacuated.

One of the deputies left me his patrol car and the keys to the jail so that I could maintain contact with the Hyde County mainland. On that Thursday afternoon as the skies darkened and rain began to fall, Monroe Gaskill, another Ocracoker who stayed, and I traveled throughout the village making a list of the people left on the island. Our numbers, which totaled approximately one hundred, were more accurate than local and national news reports that claimed only ten, twenty, or thirty people left on the island.

After positioning my personal car and the patrol car on a high spot of land, I returned to my house for the night. I had with me a National Park Service walkie-talkie and communicated regularly with Jim Henning, district ranger for Ocracoke, who had stayed with his family in the Park Service living quarters at the lighthouse.

My mother and father also stayed on the island and spent most of that Thursday like any other day. My father received a phone call from a reporter who wanted to know how he felt about being stranded on the island. Was he afraid? How did the sky look? How did the wind sound? My father, who had just finished supper and was settling down to watch television, replied that he was doing fine and that he was in the process of doing away with a big bowl of rice pudding.

Shortly after settling in the house for the night, I began a journal which I continued until the peak of the hurricane drew my attention from it.

September 26, 1985

7:51 p.m.

We still have lights, even though they have been going off and on for a few seconds. The wind has increased to gusts of about 50 miles per hour. All this wind happened within the last two hours. It's been calm most of the day. The phone keeps ringing.

8:35 p.m.

Just got a call from Sheriff Dale. He felt that the eye of the storm was going to land somewhere between the mainland and Ocracoke. I told him that everyone had settled in for the night. He said that the National Guard was going to send a helicopter over first thing in the morning.

8:51 p.m.

I'm sitting here in the front porch swing. It's very hot in the house with all the windows closed. The power is now out and has been for about twenty minutes. About the loudest thing I hear other than the wind is the roar of the ocean. I'm sure there must be some overwash, and I keep turning my head back over my shoulder to look down the road, thinking that any minute a surge of ocean water might be coming down the road toward the house.

9:45 p.m.

Just killed a cricket in the kitchen. He was making so much noise that Mama couldn't sleep. They have just gone to bed. The wind continues to gust in the forty to fifty miles per hour range.

Got a call from Doug Hoell of the North Carolina Division of Emergency Management. He said that the Dare County Coast was getting lashed pretty badly. He also seemed to think that Hyde County might be hit the hardest. Many people on the mainland of the county have taken shelter in the high school gym there.

10:35 p.m.

Jim just called to say that his phone was still working if I needed him. Also had several calls from other people who wanted to know how things were.

I had to go out back to nail some backporch windows. The strong gusty wind felt good. I almost got jolted to the ground several times. I made a quick survey of the yard. A few limbs were down but no major damage. Fowler O'Neal's television antenna was still there. Our house appears to be handling the wind quite well. We are lucky to be surrounded by trees.

I continue to check for any incoming tide—the big worry at this point.

10:47 p.m.

The temperature is 70 degrees and it's now started raining. It's hot here in the house. Time for the front porch swing. There are still a few cars going by.

10:51 p.m.

Got a call from my cousin who lives in Alaska. She tried to call some of her other relatives but there was no one there. She said, "I called the sheriff's department and they told me that you were one of the few left on the island. We kept seeing it on the television."

11:26 p.m.

Two reporters called. Want to know if they can keep calling back. Sheriff also called again and said that the hurricane seems to be heading out to sea more and that we might just get the weak side of it.

11:49 p.m.

I called Doug to give their office an update. He said that the helicopters were standing by. Also got a call from a woman who said that everyone there was thinking about everyone here.

12:15 a.m.

The eye approaches Ocracoke! Just got the latest advisory from the National Weather Service. Gloria is now located about 50 miles south of here. The eye is moving quickly at about 25 to 30 miles per hour. They also announce that the boats are high and dry in Buxton Harbor; that all the water has been sucked out. I give Jim a call to discuss the situation.

12:28 a.m.

Got a call from Doyle Kline, assistant superintendent of the Cape Hatteras National Seashore. I also call a few people here to give them updates.

The weather appears to be much calmer right now.

1:05 a.m.

Jim called me on the radio. We both feel that the eye is upon us right now. The wind seems to have died down to around 20 to 30 miles per hour and the sky seems somewhat lighter. Jim's wife said she even saw a star. I went down to the edge of the Creek. The water level is the same as the ground level in front of the post office. Our boats are still OK.

1:12 a.m.

Jim called on the radio from his vehicle. The eye conditions seem to prevail, but there does appear to be a shift of wind to the northwest. He said that he met some water coming up the road.

1:28 a.m.

Still no sign of the tide. I have made many trips to the back door to check for it. Winds have increased slightly to around 30 miles per hour.

1:41 a.m.

The storm appears to be taking a new hold out of the northwest. I guess the tide will soon follow.

1:47 a.m.

The tide's beginning to come up in the backyard! I just watched it roll in from the yard in back of us.

2:55 a.m.

A couple of feet of tide in the backyard. It's about ready to come in the house. Mama and Daddy have gotten up, and we're putting things up so the water won't ruin them. We'll probably lose the rugs.

Mama has just made coffee. She doesn't seem worried. She said, "Well, if it comes in we'll just have to wade around in it."

Although I wasn't able to return to the journal, I do remember the three of us scurrying throughout the house, moving furniture around and checking the water level through several holes my father had bored through the floor. After coming within a few inches of entering the house, the water leveled off and gradually receded. Our floors were spared.

Shortly after the tide started to fall, my mother and father went back to bed and slept until daylight. I remained up, talking on the phone, trying to snatch a few minutes of rest, and thinking about what I'd have to face in the morning.

As the hurricane passed offshore, the winds dropped and the clouds began to open up. Soon after daylight the sky cleared and the air was cooler.

A quick survey of the village revealed some damage, mostly a few boats tossed around, shingles blown off roofs, and some trees down. Water stood throughout the village, and debris was scattered everywhere. Approximately twenty houses, as I found out later, had been flooded with as much as eighteen inches of water. Most of these houses were in the southern part of the village near the lighthouse.

Perhaps the most destructive slap at the island was at Ocracoke's north end, where a two-mile stretch of highway was covered with anywhere from two to four feet of sand. This problem would have to be a top priority, especially since the northern route is our main transportation link through which food, fuel, and other necessary supplies flow.

By noon that day it was apparent that no one needed medical attention, nor were there other life-threatening situations. Numerous news helicopters buzzed over the village, landing occasionally to interview anyone who appeared to have weathered the storm. Other helicopters brought the governor, lieutenant governor, and other state government officials to the island for a visit.

Though we were without power for approximately twenty-four hours, it was eventually restored when our own village generator was put into operation. The main service line that runs down the Outer Banks was damaged and would take several days to repair.

Most of us spent at least a week getting things back to normal. Some establishments lost several weeks of business, and other closed down for the season.

Since the amount of damage wasn't as great as everyone had expected, many residents were sorry they had evacuated the island.

Most of us spent at least a week getting things back to normal. Some establishments lost several weeks of business, and others closed down for the season.

Although Ocracoke had been spared the brunt of Hurricane Gloria, there is always the next hurricane to worry about. Increased development along all coastal areas, as well as the popularity of "weathering" a hurricane, will continue to pose additional problems. We often ignore the experiences and lessons of past hurricanes. As one elderly man warned, "If one hits in here like I have seen 'em, you'll see a mess. Talk about a two-by-four in the water."

Most people who lived at Ocracoke during World War II didn't realize at first how serious a war was being waged just offshore of their home. Not until the ships started burning and the cups and saucers began rattling on the tables after the German U-boat torpedoes and the United States Navy depth charges went off did Ocracokers understand that something big, powerful, and frightening was taking place nearby.

The sea war off the North Carolina coast began to intensify soon after Hitler declared war on the United States in December 1941. Shortly after this declaration, he put into operation a plan to strangle the shipping lanes along the East Coast. Much of the oil, iron, coal, lumber, and cotton crucial to the war effort passed just offshore of Ocracoke.

The first few months of 1942 proved to be the most disastrous to shipping. Though only six or eight U-boats were operating off North American waters at this time, they were clearly taking advantage of American inexperience in antisubmarine warfare. The U-boats were scattered along 2,500 miles of coastline between Maine and Texas, making their detection almost impossible by the few antisubmarine vessels of the U.S. Navy.

Ships were easy prey as they continued to sail in the shipping lanes, unaware that nearby U-boats were listening to their radio traffic about positions. Coastal towns, as well as the ships themselves, failed to black out their lights at night, thus providing the U-boats with silhouetted targets.

Suddenly bodies and wreckage and other flotsam cast from ships torpedoed offshore began showing up on the once-clean beaches. By the end of January 1942, approximately twelve ships had been lost off the North Carolina Outer Banks. The number dropped to nine vessels in February, but climbed to twenty-five vessels in March and twenty in April.

One of the vessels lost during the disastrous month of March was the freighter *Caribsea*. The second mate on the freighter was James Baum Gaskill of Ocracoke.

Jim Baum was born at Ocracoke on July 2, 1916. His parents, Bill and Annie Gaskill, ran the Pamlico Inn, a small inn located on the northwest shore of the village near Springer's Point. After growing up on the island, Jim Baum left Ocracoke and eventually received his master's license. As the United States got involved in World War II, he joined the merchant marines and shipped out on the *Caribsea*.

While sailing in the shipping lanes off Cape Lookout in early March, the *Caribsea* was torpedoed by a German U-boat. Shortly before the vessel's destruction, Jim Baum had been on watch, but had retired to his quarters. He was lost with the ship. His framed license, attached to a small piece of the ship, drifted ashore on Ocracoke Beach and was recovered by his cousin, Chris Gaskill. A day later the ship's nameplate, attached to another piece of the vessel, drifted into Pamlico Sound and washed up to the dock of the Pamlico Inn. The piece of wood bearing the nameplate was later used to construct a cross that stands today on the altar of the Ocracoke United Methodist Church.

The U.S. Navy soon realized that it needed more help to deal with the U-boat menace. To increase patrols it borrowed vessels, even private yachts. The Royal Navy also sent twenty-four antisubmarine trawlers that had been involved in fighting U-boats off its own shores. One of these vessels was the *H.M.S. Bedfordshire*, commanded by Lt. R. B. Davis. Along with three other officers and thirty-three men, the

*Bedfordshire* left England for the United States in February 1942. After a number of delays, the ship finally arrived at its station around the end of March.

The former sea-going commercial fishing vessel was 170 feet long, outfitted with four-inch, quick-fire deck guns, a 303 caliber Lewis machine gun, and eighty to a hundred depth charges. By the time the ship began patrolling off the North Carolina coast, submarine activity had decreased. In addition to the added help from the British, other security measures were also being developed and employed by the U.S. Navy.

On May 11, 1942, shortly before midnight, the German submarine U-558 encountered the *Bedfordshire* off Cape Lookout. The British vessel was hit by a torpedo and went to the bottom. There were no survivors.

On the morning of May 14, only a few days after the *Bedfordshire's* destruction, two bodies were taken from the surf by Coast Guardsmen from the Ocracoke station. The bodies were then transported to the village and stored in a small building in back of the Coast Guard Station.

Not only was the fate of the *H.M.S. Bedfordshire* similar to the *Caribsea*, but there were also some eerie incidents that took place, again involving Ocracokers. In one of these Wahab Howard had chanced to meet one of the officers of the *Bedfordshire*, Sub-Lieutenant Thomas Cunningham, while in Norfolk on business. Wahab's widow, Elizabeth Howard, has told the story of her husband's impressions many times. "Wahab met Cunningham in a restaurant in Norfolk. They shared a table together because the restaurant was full when Cunningham and another British sailor came in. During the meal Wahab kept noticing Cunningham's gold watch and ring. He remembered it later when Cunningham's body was found."

At the time of Wahab's meeting, the *Bedfordshire* had been tied up at the Navy base in Norfolk. Approximately a month later the vessel had been in port again, this time in Morehead City. While it had been there, another Ocracoker, Jack Willis, had had a chance meeting with

Cunningham. "I was with my father in Morehead City when I saw Cunningham. He was in a drug store pretending to shave off his beard with an electric razor. I remember he had a thick black beard."

One of the main jobs of Aycock Brown, a special investigator for the Office of Naval Intelligence during World War II, was to identify bodies. Shortly before he died, Aycock Brown and I talked about the *Bedfordshire* incident. He too had met Cunningham while the *Bedfordshire* was tied up in Morehead City. Brown had gone aboard the ship to request some British flags and a detail of pallbearers to assist with the burial of four crewmen from the *San Defino*, a British tanker which was torpedoed off Cape Hatteras on April 9. Although men from the *Bedfordshire* could not be spared, since the ship was scheduled to leave shortly, Cunningham had given Brown six new Union Jacks. He also gave him an empty rum jug that had attracted his eye, and which Brown always kept as a souvenir of the experience.

After the two bodies had been recovered from the surf, Brown was called to the scene. Within a short period of time, Brown, Wahab Howard, and Jack Willis discovered that one of the bodies was Thomas Cunningham, a man all three had recently met. The other body was that of Stanley Craig, a telegraphist aboard the *Bedfordshire*. "I remember going down to the station to use the telephone," recalled Jack. "They brought in two men who had washed up on the beach. They had 'em on the back of a truck. When they pulled up the canvas, I recognized one of 'em. He had on a turtleneck and looked pretty normal. His beard was still coal black. It was Cunningham, the one I saw in Morehead City."

Aycock Brown was in charge of the funeral detail. "There were no coffins to be had on the island," he recalled. "Lumber was hard to get. We had to use what we could to bury them in." After making a number of inquiries, he managed to locate several coffin-shaped "sink boxes." In normal times these boxes were placed on sand bars so hunters could lie down at water level to shoot unsuspecting ducks and geese.

According to Elsie Garrish, her father (and my grandfather), Elisha Ballance, gave the burial detail one of his coffin-shaped boats. "Papa had what they called an old scow flat," she said. "They came to him and asked him if they could have it to bury those sailors in. He gave it to them, saying that he had boys in the service and only hoped that if it was needed that somebody would do the same for him someday."

The Williams family donated a small tract of land next to their own cemetery as the burial site for the British sailors. Cunningham and Craig were buried there in the old sink boxes, each draped with one of the two remaining flags that Cunningham had given Aycock Brown.

Approximately a week after the burial of Cunningham and Craig, two other bodies were found floating in the ocean. Although the bodies were in bad condition, their clothing was similar to that of the other British sailors. No identification could be made, however, and they were listed as "unknown." According to Brown, the lumber for their coffins was donated by an Ocracoker who had been planning to build an outhouse. The two sailors were buried next to Cunningham and Craig.

Throughout the years, various individuals and organizations, both military and civilian, have cared for the British Cemetery. In recent years officials of the British government have attended an annual memorial service on May 11, the date the *Bedfordshire* was sunk. New tombstones have also been acquired, replacing the old crosses that originally marked the graves.

A few months after Cunningham's death, his son, Tom, was born. A few Ocracokers, especially Fannie Pearl Fulcher, have communicated with Cunningham's widow, Barbara. Fannie Pearl has also visited the Cunninghams several times, carrying news of the special care and attention that the graves receive.

When Elsie Garrish visited Barbara Cunningham a few years ago, she asked her if she ever wanted to visit Ocracoke. According to Elsie, Barbara's reply was, "I won't say that I'll never go there. But if I did it would be like opening old wounds."

As U-boat attacks continued in the shipping lanes off Ocracoke, the military presence within the village also began to increase. The old lifesaving station, along with the new Coast Guard Station which had recently been completed, filled with new men. One of these new faces was Theodore Mutro, who came to the island in January 1942. "When I first came here," he recalled, "we were picked up at Hatteras Inlet and driven down the beach to the village. I didn't know anything about the place. I didn't even know it was an island. When we got in the village I asked the driver where the heart of town was. He told me we were on the main drag. It looked like a pretty desolate place. I was from the city."

As a third-class petty officer at the Ocracoke Coast Guard Station, most of Mutro's duties, like those of other Coast Guardsmen, were confined to search and rescue. He recalls that they spent a lot of time training with the breeches buoy, blinker drills, and rowing practice.

When he first arrived, the Navy had not yet set up its section base. The station where he lived was designed to handle only twelve men, but as many as sixty men were crammed in there and many of them had to sleep on the floor.

One of Mutro's first rescues involved the dredge *LeHeigh*, which sunk in February 1942 near the entrance to Big Foot Slough Channel (only a few miles northwest of the village). The *LeHeigh* was attempting to dredge its way into the Creek, which needed to be dug out to accommodate Navy vessels that might be stationed there. All twelve crewmen aboard were rescued from the sinking dredge.

Mutro was involved in other memorable rescues, including the *Anna B. Heidritter*, a four-masted schooner captained by a sixty-three-year-old man, who was the youngest man on the ship, and the *Empire Gem*, at that time the world's largest tanker. The rescues were made in a thirty-foot boat that sometimes went offshore as far as thirty miles. "At first," said Mutro, "we had a little problem getting equipment for the boats. I even had to take my own shotgun. I never did see a sub. They were out there, though. I've heard of 'em surfacing near here to recharge their batteries. One also surfaced and sank a mine sweeper by opening up on her with the deck guns."

The constant threat of U-boat attacks sometimes had a serious effect on the crews of ships that continued to sail in the shipping lanes. Mutro recalled one incident where he had to go off to the merchant vessel *James Parker, Jr.* to pick up the bodies of three men who had committed suicide by drinking denatured alcohol.

By the time construction began on the Navy's Ocracoke section base in June 1942, the U-boat action offshore was much diminished. Although the attacks continued, the number of ship sinkings had begun to decline after March 1942.

Early in the construction process for the section base, the Navy realized that "the primary purpose for its establishment had practically ceased to exist." This observation and others about the operations at Ocracoke were made in a recently declassified document found in the Navy Department Library. The original purpose for the base was also spelled out in the Navy document.

The establishment of an anchorage at Cape Hatteras, protected by a contact mine field, necessitated an additional base to handle the patrol craft assigned to control and protect shipping using this anchorage. Such a base was authorized by the secretary of the Navy on May 13, 1942, just before the mine field was laid. The site of the Coast Guard Lifeboat Station on the west end of Ocracoke Island (located on the Creek, six miles from sea via Ocracoke Inlet) was chosen as the best available location. Plans called for three piers of sufficient size to berth twelve vessels, 135 feet in length and facilities for fueling, supplying, provisioning, and effecting minor repairs to vessels based there. Major repairs requiring dry-docking were to be undertaken at Morehead City.

Construction on the base began in June. By the middle of September about 80 percent of the project had been completed, and gradually more Navy personnel were assigned there.

The anchorage and contact mine field at Cape Hatteras had been

*During World War II a Navy base was built near the present Coast Guard Station (pictured at upper left). The facilities included additional barracks alongside the Coast Guard Station; a hospital, administration offices, and barracks in the main complex (center of picture); a training field (lower right); and maintenance building (lower left). The four private homes located on the base were purchased from the original owners and used as part of the base. Along with most of the base, the private homes were also torn down after the war. The former owners bought or built homes elsewhere. (Courtesy of Lanie Boyette Wynn, the Boyette House)*

abandoned by the time the Ocracoke base was commissioned on October 9. Although this had been the primary reason for establishing the base, the abandonment of the operations at Hatteras did not prevent the base from operating.

Since the Creek was not deep enough to handle the Navy's patrol boats, it was dredged and the spoil was used to fill several low areas in the village. Maurice Ballance remembers the dredging. As he now reflects back on it, he also remembers how the dredge spoils affected the island's ecosystem. "There were three basic spoil areas. The first one was called Mary Ann's Pond. It was located several hundred yards north of the Coast Guard Station. Most of the time it was more of a bay than a pond, but it did look like a pond sometimes when a thin sand ridge would build up at the mouth of it on the soundside.

"The pond ran southeast, up into the island some two or three hundred yards. Somewhere up in this area was another pond that was real muddy. I've always heard that a Confederate soldier got stuck in there and went right on down. I know a cow did one time.

"Anyway, they filled in Mary Ann's Pond. These two ponds were part of a depression that ran through the village right on to the back of the Methodist Church. On one edge of this spoils area was a ridge with some live oaks and red cedars on it. Some of the trees survived, but they still killed a lot of them.

"The second spoils area was out in front of the Island Inn. That whole area was mostly marshland. A small creek used to run through there right on out toward the beach. We called the creek 'Cockle Creek' and referred to the area around the mouth of it as 'The Gut.' There used to be two bridges there for people to walk across to the other side of the Creek.

"The actual body of water we call the Creek nowadays is about the same size, but the depth of it used to be anywhere from four to five feet. Because it was shallow, none of the bigger boats or ships could get in the harbor. This is why the Navy had to get it dredged. Your grandfather and some other men lost a ship one time during a bad storm because they had to keep her anchored out in the channel. They built her not far from your house. Anyway, she went to sea and nobody ever saw her again.

"Because the Creek was shallow and not many boats could get in or out, there was very little wave action. Therefore there was very little erosion until now.

"Around the time the Creek was dredged out, people didn't know the value of marshland—a lot still don't, or they don't care anyway. A war was going on and they had to dump the spoils somewhere. Of course the Navy got permission from different ones to dump, ones that needed the sand and so forth. While it was necessary to dig out the place, it was destructive. You see, anytime we'd have a storm, and especially if the force of it had turned and came out of the northwest, bringing a surge of sound water over the island, natural creeks like that would channel some of the water over the island and out toward the beach. In other words, they'd serve to relieve the pressure built up by the surge. Also, oysters used to grow plentiful around the Gut. Some still do, but you can't eat them. They were always the best oysters, and different ones had their own personal bed. So they pumped the Gut full and that ruined the oysters.

"The third and final spoils area was over to the right as you enter the Creek from Pamlico Sound. This is one of the highest points in the village because they kept building it up and building it up. They didn't expect to have all that much left over to pump out."

When the Navy base was finally in full operation, the population of the island quickly doubled. The Navy provided most of their own services, including three power plants, commissary, officer's club, medical facilities, and transportation. They also built the island's first road, which led from the base, through the village, and on into the present Oyster Creek and Jackson Dunes developments, where ammunition was stored. This area is still called the "ammunition dump" by some Ocracokers.

The Navy began beefing up security measures. "They didn't tell us anything," said Uriah Garrish, who continued to fish during the war. "They didn't want you to go on the beach, especially at night. They patrolled there and I reckon you could be mistaken for some Germans. Different ones around here always told me that some Germans landed here in rubber life rafts. We kept right on fishing down at the camps like we always did." According to other rumors German spies lived on the island before and during the war, from which they studied the channels, buoys, and markers off Ocracoke.

Other security practices included instituting regular blackouts at night; painting the top part of car lights black; and covering windows with dark green shades so residents could continue burning lights at night.

Many Navy personnel considered the Ocracoke section base a difficult assignment. As the following excerpt from a report addressing this issue indicates, there were perhaps reasons for this charge. "It is realized that much of the melancholy moaning about duty off this base comes from a deep distaste for Ocracoke in the minds of the men of the ships that call here, which may have some effect on their opinion concerning the practicability of the port. This sentiment seems to be universal and is due to the isolated position of the base, the poverty of entertainment of any kind, no liquor, and a lack of supply of the ladies of negotiable affections sought by sailors."

Realizing the loneliness of the Ocracoke section base assignment, some Ocracokers opened their homes to Navy personnel. Sometimes the families of Navy men came to the island to visit, and they roomed with island families. One officer and his wife occasionally stayed with my grandmother. Since his mother and father had died while he was young, he grew attached to my grandmother and eventually came to call her "Ma."

Like Theodore Mutro, other Navy and Coast Guard personnel married and settled at Ocracoke. These matches continue as some of the Coast Guardsmen from the present station meet and marry Ocracoke girls.

The Navy's operations at Ocracoke were maintained as a section base until January 16, 1944. The facility was then developed into an Amphibious Training Base, which was involved in "training personnel in the use of new secret equipment," and finally into a Combat Information Center in 1945. Shortly after the war, most of the base was torn down. Much of the lumber was scavenged by Ocracokers who considered the property abandoned.

While the Navy left Ocracoke after World War II, the Coast Guard has continued its mission of search-and-rescue operations. The station is now manned by a crew of approximately twenty-two.

When the Navy abandoned Ocracoke at the end of World War II, it left behind the beginnings of a road system that would be critical to Ocracoke as it changed from a small fishing village to the more tourist-oriented community of the present. The island's first piece of road was the "Ammunition Dump Road," as it is known locally, which led from the base, near the present Coast Guard Station, to the northernmost part of the village. The Navy used it to transport ammunition to and from storage facilities located near the present-day Jackson Dunes and Oyster Creek developments.

Shortly after the road was constructed, Ocracokers began to see the advantages of being able to move around the village without getting stuck in the sand. By 1950 another two miles of paved road was under construction. Since there was no town government, a committee of residents led this effort. The committee carried the community's concerns to the state, citing, for example, the needs of children for safe, dry routes to school and fishermen for better access to their boats.

The 17,600 bags of cement for the new piece of road were shipped from Norfolk on two of Ocracoke's freight boats, which traveled fourteen round trips, or a total of 3,360 miles. Due to a shortage of cement, the boats were loaded as the hot cement came out of the kilns, eventually causing one of the vessels to open at the seams during passage. Because the cost of shipping material to mix with the cement was too great, the contractor used a mixture of beach sand and shells.

During the road's construction, approximately forty cars were in use on the island. Though the number increased after the road was completed in September 1950, it didn't match the increase in bicycles. Ocracoke kids were quick to take advantage of the newly paved segment that led to the school. Those who did not have a bicycle when the road was finished that fall got one for Christmas.

Eventually a 6.8-mile section of highway from the present Ocracoke Campground to an area within two and a half miles of the Hatteras ferry landing was completed. The missing links between the village and the campground and the last section south of the ferry, however, would take a few more years.

One of my earliest childhood memories is associated with the inconvenience of these missing links. We used to take Sunday drives, traveling from the village to the beginning of the pavement on old Air Force landing mats, then driving on the new pavement until we reached the area a few miles south of the ferry. Sometimes we would attempt the rest of the trip to the ferry, but more often than not we'd stop and turn around.

Perhaps the sharpest image I have of those rides is the large number of nesting birds on the sand dunes that once stood tall, grassy, and several hundred feet seaward of the unpaved area. The ocean now threatens the highway itself along this same segment, and the dunes have long since disappeared.

The paving of the remaining sections of beach highway was aided by the organization of the All Seashore Highway Association, whose main purpose was to get a paved highway through the entire Cape Hatteras National Seashore. Stanley Wahab of Ocracoke served as the association's vice-president. By the end of 1963, the All Seashore Highway was completed, a new bridge at Oregon Inlet had been dedicated, and traffic began to increase along the Outer Banks.

Stanley Wahab's influence on the All Seashore Highway Association was but one of his many contributions to the modernization of Ocracoke. Born on Ocracoke in 1888, he attended the small school which was set up for the children of men stationed at the Cedar Hammock

Lifesaving Station (located near Hatteras Inlet). Stanley sailed on several boats before going to Goldey Commercial College at the age of eighteen.

After graduating from business college, he worked in Wilmington, Delaware, then returned to Ocracoke to teach school. A few years later he began work as a bookkeeper for the Newport News Shipbuilding Company and later became president of a chain of furniture stores before retiring to the island in the 1940s. But in all his years away from Ocracoke, he never lost his interest in improving life on the island.

In 1914 he built and operated the Ocean Wave, Ocracoke's first moving-picture show, and brought to the island the first automobile, a Hudson coach. In 1936 he built the first ice plant, which produced both saltwater and freshwater ice, and the first electric plant. He established a flying service in 1939, but it was discontinued during World War II. That same year he also built the Wahab Village Hotel (know today as Blackbeard's Lodge). One wing of the hotel was used as a roller skating rink, while another wing was converted into a movie theater. A dance hall called the Spanish Casino was also put into operation.

When the Carolina Telephone and Telegraph Company introduced long-distance commercial telephone service to the island in the early months of 1956, Stanley placed the first call from Ocracoke to State Utilities Commission Chairman Stanley Winborne. Before this service began, the only telephone on the island was located at the Coast Guard Station. On June 16 of the same year, the local exchange was also completed. On this first day of local service, more than 1,700 calls were placed on the eighty-eight telephones installed.

Stanley was driven by the belief that Ocracoke was located at a "strategic point on the coast," and he wanted it to become the "Bermuda of the USA." His widow, Myra Edwards Wahab, said if he were living today he would be pleased at the amount of progress that has taken place.

Along with the gradual road improvements and the introduction of

*Stanley Wahab (right) discusses promotional literature for Ocracoke dur-*
*ing a meeting of the Ocracoke Civic Club. (Courtesy of Myra Wahab)*

other modern conveniences, efforts to upgrade ferry service was also
being made. Until the first car ferry was introduced in 1950, passengers, supplies, fuel, livestock, and even automobiles were transported
by freight boats.

One of the early freight boats was the *Annie*, captained by Cass

*Freight boats like this one also carried some of the island's first cars. (Courtesy of Danny Garrish)*

Williams. Others included the *Nellie* and the *Preston*, operated by Dave Summers Williams and his brother Phil, the *Relief*, run by Captain Isaac "Little Ike" O'Neal and his brother Walter, and the *Dryden*, whose operation was managed by Captain Ike O'Neal, Sid Tolson, and Jesse Garrish.

The last freight boat to serve Ocracoke was the *Bessie Virginia*, a 65-foot vessel that could take ninety tons of freight. Operated by Van Henry O'Neal and Powers Garrish, the *Bessie Virginia* made one round trip per week from Washington, North Carolina, at first taking passengers as well as freight, but in her later years taking only freight. While some freight was shipped to Ocracoke from Morehead City, Beaufort, and later Atlantic, most came from Washington.

In 1950 Frazier Peele of Hatteras introduced and ran the first car ferry between Hatteras and Ocracoke, replacing in part the dying freight boat trade. His bargelike vessel, which made three scheduled departures each day from each side—and sometimes made special trips for an extra charge—carried four cars at a cost of five dollars per car.

Better transportation on and off the island was still needed. Ocracokers complained of the need for better access to the county seat in

*The* Bessie Virginia, *operated by Van Henry O'Neal and Powers Garrish, was the last freight boat to serve Ocracoke. The sixty-five-foot vessel made one trip per week to Washington, North Carolina. (Courtesy of National Park Service, Cape Hatteras National Seashore)*

Swan Quarter. The three-hundred-mile trip took three days and re-quired one to pass through three county seats. This issue soon caught fire with the Ocracokers, and many supported moving Ocracoke into Dare County. The Dare County Board of Commissioners even issued a resolution welcoming the island. Efforts to make this move a reality failed, however.

Editorials in local newspapers began to appear in support of free ferry service to and from Ocracoke, arguing that Ocracoke residents were suffering under a kind of discrimination. Since Ocracokers were required to pay to get off the island, many people felt they were being denied free access to the "Good Roads State."

In August 1957 the state bought Frazier Peele's ferry service for $20,000. Peele continued as the ferry captain. A reconditioned boat with a loading ramp that lowered to the beach was sent from Oregon Inlet. The schedule consisted of four daily departures from both Hatteras and Ocracoke, including an early run from Hatteras at 7:30 A.M. and a late run from Ocracoke at 4:00 P.M.

Efforts to improve transportation along the Outer Banks continued even after free ferry service between Hatteras and Ocracoke was secured. The All Seashore Highway Association began to focus on establishing a ferry service at Ocracoke's south end so that motorists could travel north and south along the Outer Banks.

Ferry service for the south end of Ocracoke became a reality on March 1, 1960, when the *Sea Level*, a privately operated ferry owned by four brothers, Alfred, Dan, Leslie, and William Taylor, began running between Ocracoke and Cedar Island. The *Sea Level* was named in honor of the Taylor's hometown, Sea Level, North Carolina. The $350,000, all-steel vessel could carry twenty-two cars and 196 passengers. The fares were $6.50 for a car and driver, $2.50 for additional passengers, and $1.25 for children.

Before long the Taylors realized that their ferry venture would not make any money because the fares were not meeting expenses. In December 1960, only eight months after beginning the service, the Taylors made a plea to the Highway Commission to take over the ferry. Though refusing the Taylors' first request, the commission eventually agreed. The ferry tolls were maintained, however.

Within a few years after free ferry service was established at Hatteras Inlet, the National Park Service helped the state of North Carolina acquire several old landing crafts, which were put to use as ferries.

During the late 1960s and early 1970s, six new ferries were brought into operation by the state on the Hatteras run. Each of the six ferries, the *Herbert C. Bonner*, the *Lindsey Warren*, the *Ocracoke*, the *Conrad Wirth*, the *Alpheus Drinkwater*, and the *Bruce Etheridge*, is 110 feet long and equipped to carry twenty-two cars and 100 passengers.

The popularity of these ferries has now reached the point that departures are required every forty minutes and often every twenty minutes during the busy summer days.

Through all of 1988, 264,539 cars and 674,058 passengers traveled on the Hatteras ferries. The slowest month, not surprisingly, was January, with 5,357 cars and 9,937 passengers, and the busiest month was July, with 41,780 cars and 122,498 passengers. Future plans call for the gradual replacement of these six ferries with larger and faster vessels.

The *Pamlico* and the *Silver Lake*, two 160-foot-long ferries with a capacity of thirty cars and 300 passengers each, were added to the Cedar Island run in 1965. These two vessels operated along with the *Sea Level* until that boat was moved to the Fort Fisher run in 1983.

As the demand on the *Pamlico* and the *Silver Lake* began to increase, each of the vessels was cut in half and a sixty-foot section was added, increasing the length of each to 220 feet and carrying capacity to fifty cars and 500 passengers.

Like the Hatteras ferries, the Cedar Island runs have also seen gradual increases in traffic. During all of 1988, 87,239 cars and 209,247 passengers left Ocracoke on the *Pamlico* and *Silver Lake* ferries. In the busiest month, July, they carried 6,630 cars and 17,568 passengers.

In June 1977 a third ferry service was put into operation, between Ocracoke and Swan Quarter, finally relieving Ocracokers of the three-hundred-mile round trip to their county seat. With a carrying capacity of thirty cars and 300 passengers, the 160-foot *Governor Edward Hyde* makes two daily departures from each side. Through all of 1988, 15,280 cars and 32,623 passengers traveled on the *Hyde*.

Sound-class vessels such as the *Hyde, Pamlico*, and *Silver Lake* have a crew of six, including a captain, quartermaster, chief engineer, an oiler, and two deckhands. The captain must have a master's license, the chief engineer a chief engineer's license, and the oiler an oiler's ticket. The three other positions must be filled by two crew members who possess an able-bodied seaman's ticket and one who holds an "ordinary" seaman's ticket. An able-bodied seaman usually serves as the quartermaster.

While licenses are required on the sound-class vessels because they are toll ferries and of heavier tonnage, the Hatteras ferries, which are free ferries, do not require licenses. They also carry fewer crew members: the usual crew of four includes a captain, engineer, and two deckhands. Vessels that charge passengers, including charter boats, and vessels with a total weight over two hundred tons must have a licensed captain. For this latter reason, many vessels, including the six Hatteras ferries, are built just under two hundred tons.

To improve the qualifications of its ferry crews, especially the crews on the Hatteras ferries, the ferry division has instituted a new licensing program. As part of this new licensing program, Rudy Austin managed to acquire his master's license, even though he had served as a captain on one of the Hatteras ferries for almost thirteen years.

Like many Ocracokers, Rudy has made a career with the ferry division. He graduated from high school in 1961, spent four years in the Air Force, worked with an electrical company for another four years, and eventually moved back to Ocracoke to begin working for the ferry division in 1970. He worked as a deckhand for six months, an engineer for four years, and then became a captain in 1974.

Most of Rudy's career has been spent on the night run, a shift that begins at five o'clock in the afternoon and ends at five the next morning. Most ferry division employees work an eighty-hour week, then have the next week off.

During his many years with the ferry division, Rudy has seen ferry service and facilities grow to accommodate the increasing traffic along the Outer Banks. "The schedules have adapted to the traffic flow," he explained. "We also have more modern, up-to-date equipment, newer boats being brought on line, and better shore facilities.

"We're seeing our tourist season get longer than the usual three months of summer. The summer schedule now extends on up to November.

"The kinds of vehicles are also changing. The cars have gotten smaller. This happened after the gas crisis in the 1970s. During that time there were few campers; now there are more. We are also hauling more tour buses and bigger trucks. Business is growing at Ocracoke."

Another Ocracoker, Harry F. O'Neal, has also made a career with the ferry division. Like many others, however, he spent much of his career in the Coast Guard before beginning a second career on the ferries.

After spending three years in the Army and eighteen years in the Coast Guard, Harry F. eventually moved back to Ocracoke and began working on the *Hyde*. Part of his Coast Guard years was spent as chief of the Ocracoke Coast Guard Station. Six of his ten brothers also have Coast Guard experience. One of these, Carlton Boyd O'Neal, is a captain on the Cedar Island ferries. Harry F. received his master's license in 1978, eventually becoming captain of the *Hyde*.

While an average day on one of the ferries is usually routine, with the ferry following basically the same course, there are times when the experience and judgment of the captain are especially needed. Whether or not the vessel even leaves port is at the discretion of the captain.

Weather conditions along the Outer Banks can change rapidly. The sound-class vessels can often run during gales, depending on the wind's direction. Winds that blow broadside against the vessel are the more threatening. "If we've got a forty-mile-an-hour northeast wind," explains Harry F., "it makes it really rough on the Swan Quarter run because the seas are hitting you broadside. It also depends on how long the wind has been blowing. A northeaster that has been blowing strong for a couple of days will kick up the seas.

"During a northwester or a southeaster you can take more wind. I have been out in Pamlico Sound during a sixty-five-mile-an-hour wind.

"We don't leave shore sometimes when it's foggy because there's always the chance of running over a smaller boat out there. You can't stop this ferry as fast as you can a smaller boat. The radar helps, but it can't always pick up the smaller boats."

The Hatteras ferries can run in up to a fifty-mile-per-hour wind. Like the sound-class ferries, however, a lot depends on how long the wind has been blowing and from what direction. During periods of strong winds which also build up higher than normal tides, the ferries sometimes can't get up under the ramps to unload. Snow or ice can also present hazardous conditions on deck for cars and passengers.

Ferry captains take their jobs very seriously, and while always cautious, they realize the need to keep traffic flowing to and from the island. There are times, however, when people have to wait. "If you're traveling anywhere today," said Rudy Austin, "you're going to have to wait. That includes airplanes, buses, trains, and toll booths. This is especially true when you're dealing with the elements of nature."

Improved roads and ferry service also aided Ocracoke's mail delivery. While passengers could come and go at their own pace, those responsible for handling the island's mail were often confronted with problems of "moving today's mail today." One Ocracoker who is quite familiar with these problems is Elizabeth Howard, a former postmaster. "If there's one thing I know," she said, "it's the history of the post office here on Ocracoke. I guess we've always had a rather peculiar way of getting mail to and from due to the place being an island and the need to rely on boats and sometimes planes for transport.

"Throughout the years, mail got here one way or another, but the first actual postmaster that I know of was a man named John McWilliams. The post office and boxes were usually kept in one of the several general stores on the island. After John McWilliams there was Ed Farrow, Billy Howard, and finally Mr. Tommy Howard, who was my father-in-law. He had a little place just for a post office down on the Creekside not far from the Island Inn.

"In his younger years in the post office, and I believe he was active in the postal service some forty years, he used to pole a boat all the way up to Avon and pick up the mail. Sometimes he'd carry passengers, but he could only go about once per week. It was a distance of about thirty miles.

"When Mr. Tommy retired, I took over and the mailboxes were

moved to my father's old store. Actually, there were mailboxes there before, but we used to keep medicine and such things as that in them. I believe there were some 125 boxes.

"I remember the first year being extremely rough on me. I had it all to do myself and just about couldn't do the work. I'd work from about four o'clock in the morning till around ten at night. At the time a construction company was here on the island building the Navy base, plus there were numbers of Coast Guard and Navy men coming in after the base was completed. In addition to handling all the local mail, I had to handle their business too. Many nights I'd go home and cry I'd be so tired.

"Finally an inspector came down and I told him that I just couldn't carry on like this. The work was increasing all the time and it was just too much for one person. He said that anybody could quit, but that it took a man to carry on. I told him that I was not a man and that man nor woman could handle what was being expected of me. He finally realized my situation and gave me a clerk for eight hours a day under unusual circumstances. They usually wouldn't assign a clerk to a place this small.

"Ocracoke was a busy place during World War II. Just about the whole time that the Navy base was in operation we also had Sunday mail. During this time, I had to leave the island for a couple of days, and a woman worked for me while I was gone. She lasted one day before she quit. She said it was the hardest work she knew of and that she just couldn't continue another day.

"The clerk helped out with the main business hours, but I had to pull the mail bags around, keep the place clean, and do other non-paperwork things. I would have to get up at four o'clock in the morning to get the mail ready to go out. The boat left at five o'clock. We had mail to come from Hatteras as well as Atlantic, North Carolina.

"The first mailboat service was actually from Morehead City and was runned by two men called Mr. Gus and Mr. Pinter. This was before I ever got into the postal service. They had two boats. One would leave Morehead City early in the morning and the other would leave from Ocracoke at the same time. In addition to the mail, they also carried passengers and freight.

"In the late twenties the mailboat service shifted to Atlantic, but they only used one boat. Captain Will Willis and his son Clyde and later Wilbur Nelson ran this boat. They would bring the mail in from Atlantic around four o'clock in the evening and depart the next morning around five. They could only make one trip per day because of the distance, the speed of the boat, and several stops they had to make along the way. One of these was Portsmouth Island. Every afternoon, Henry Piggot from Portsmouth would be waiting for them in his little skiff to pick up the mail from the boat and carry it to the island.

"I guess there were times when the mail didn't go because of the weather. Elmo Fulcher and George O'Neal, who ran the boat after Wilbur Nelson, were held up only three days during the 1944 hurricane. The boat was washed up there by the Island Inn, and it took them a while to get it off. Also, there was so much debris floating in the water that they probably couldn't have runned anyway.

"The postmaster had the responsibility to get the mail on its way, and I always took the message on the envelopes, 'Move Today's Mail Today,' seriously. I even had it flown out of here several times. I tried to get some sort of permanent air service set up, but they wouldn't agree to it."

To know Elizabeth Howard is to understand how she managed to survive the demands and long hours of hard work required of a postmaster. Her determination and endurance began at an early age. "I was a bad girl when I was growing up," she recalled. "You see, I grew up around my father's store, and after I got a little older I would go down in the morning and help him. I'd also help him evenings after I started going to school. Most of the time there'd be a group of men outside on the road pitching rings. I used to get out there and pitch right with them. I wanted to do everything they did. They all loved me, but they'd tease me and that made me sassy.

"My father made a fair living from the store. Before this he was in the old lifesaving service. He was stationed around different inlets like Hatteras and Ocracoke. He used to patrol the beach on an old retired racing horse called Old Bill. He loved doing this, but got out when the Coast Guard took over because he didn't like the restrictions. He wanted to be free.

"Before he got out of the lifesaving station, he had already set up the little store. When I got out of school, I had considered going somewhere off the island to find work, but my mother needed me at home to help with the store. Since my father had cancer, I decided it was best for me to return home and try to manage the store.

"The whole business was then dumped into my lap. I stuck it out for a while, but there was no money in it. People just did not have it to spend. This all took place close to the Depression.

"About this time there was a job opening in the post office. I decided to take a correspondence course in fourth-class postmaster. After passing the course and the civil service exam, I got the job."

Not long after she began working for the post office, Elizabeth got married to Wahab Howard, also an Ocracoker. Wahab was employed as manager of the Ocracoke Electric Power and Light Company. During World War II he joined the Navy and was stationed on the island as chief electrician of the Navy base. "I continued to work," said Elizabeth, "even though most married women stayed in the home. There was a housing problem with all the servicemen around, so we rented our house and I stayed with my mother. She also helped take care of our only child while I worked. My daughter was born the day after Christmas. I even worked that Christmas day, but had to take several months leave when she was born."

According to Elizabeth, the first "real" post office was built at Ocracoke in 1952 and was located near the present one. Behind it was a dock where the mailboat tied up. After Elmo Fulcher and George O'Neal stopped running the boat, Ansley O'Neal received the contract, continuing the service until it became obsolete in 1964. By then most of the mail was coming from Hatteras, and the amount of

*Elizabeth Howard, postmaster at Ocracoke for many years, hands the daily mail bags to Charlie McWilliams, who drove the mail to Hatteras. (Courtesy of Elizabeth Howard)*

business had increased to the point that Elizabeth had three clerks working with her. Due to this increase and the need for a better facility, a new brick post office was built in 1968 and is still in operation today.

I can just barely remember when the forty-two-foot mailboat *Aleta* used to bring mail to Ocracoke. My father used to run with some of the captains and fill in for them when they had to be gone. I guess I've watched it many times pull up to the dock in front of our house and

*The mailboat docks along the edge of the Creek before a gathering of Ocracoke residents, most of whom were there every day to greet the vessel's arrival. (Courtesy of Margueritte Boos)*

unload passengers and mail. It would leave the island around 6:15 A.M., arrive in Atlantic three and a half hours later, leave Atlantic at 1:00 P.M., and arrive back at Ocracoke at 4:30 or 5:00 P.M.

I can also remember when Charlie McWilliams used to deliver mail from Hatteras. His truck, along with any passengers, would leave Ocracoke at 5:30 every morning. The trip to the Hatteras Inlet Coast Guard Station would take him about thirty minutes, sometimes longer if the tide was high. This was before the road was paved, and he had to travel on the beach. When he reached the inlet, he would then take the forty-two-foot cabin boat *Miss Hatteras* to Hatteras Village. The return trip began at 12:30 P.M. from Hatteras. "Charlie Mac," as he was called, hauled Ocracoke's mail from 1949 until the early 1970s.

Although the new modern brick post office and small mailbus that comes in every day from Manteo don't compete with the old wooden structure and mailboat in island "flavor," something of the old excitement generated by the mail delivery still remains. "The post office has always been something of a gathering place," said Elizabeth. "When the mailboat used to come in, everybody that could get down there, and who had the time, would show up. They were anxious to see who came, to see if they had gotten any mail, and to see their friends and relatives who would also be there.

"Some people would get there well before four o'clock. While they were anxious for the boat to get there, they usually didn't seem to mind killing the time talking to other people and keeping up with what was going on around the island. Pretty much the same thing goes on today. I guess the post office was more important than just to handle mail. It became a place where old friends meet and greet."

Throughout the history of Ocracoke, the tourist trade, though by no means as developed as it is today, has furnished a livelihood for many residents. Even during the early years, when piloting and shipping provided the main employment, some residents recognized and took advantage of the need to accommodate those who came to the island to enjoy Ocracoke's fine natural resources. In addition to tourism, fishing and hunting, both commercial and sport, have played important roles.

Even before the first Europeans arrived on the Outer Banks, coastal Indians were drawn to the fresh sea air, quantities of seafood, and isolation that Ocracoke offered. During the warmer months, various tribes paddled their canoes to the Outer Banks to spend time collecting and feasting on seafood and to get away from swarms of insects which often plagued their mainland villages.

Due to its isolation, Ocracoke was also a favorite retreat for pirates, particularly Blackbeard, and even they needed a rest from their notorious activities.

Although never an industrial site, Ocracoke did have a clam factory during the late 1800s and early 1900s. J. H. Doxsee of Long Island established the Doxsee Clam Factory on Windmill Point near the entrance to the Creek. Clams were brought to the factory from as far away as Hatteras and Morehead City. They were processed as clam chowder, clam juice, and whole clams. The whole operation lasted about twenty years.

*The Doxsee Clam Factory, which operated at Ocracoke between the late 1800s and early 1900s, was located along the southwest side of the Creek. In addition to the factory (left), a boardinghouse and hunting lodge (right) were also part of the complex. (Courtesy of Larry Williams)*

One Ocracoker who worked in the Doxsee Clam Factory was "Miss" Lillian Jackson. A few years before she died she explained to me how they processed the clams. "Let's see, yes, I did work in the ole factory. I remember just barely when they opened the thing up. I went to work down there only three or four years 'fore they closed down. You see, the ole factory set over there on that point where the ferry comes in the ditch.

"I was with some of 'em that picked the clams out of the shell after they had been steamed and dumped on this table. They had two men to load these big galvanized baskets with clams. The baskets had holes in 'em, but they weren't big enough for the clams to drop through. I believe they had two baskets and they would hold about seven bushels apiece. It took a strong person to handle 'em.

"After they loaded the baskets, they'd run 'em through this big ovenlike thing that steamed 'em. This fellar called Bennett and my husband, Wilson, did the dumping. Some of us did the picking then. You'd throw the shells out a window they had for us near the table. Sometimes ole Doxsee would go around and look out of each window to see if anybody had thrown away any of the clams. If you did, he'd throw 'em back through the window.

"We'd put the clams in a wooden box. Two used to pick for a box. Then we'd dump the box in a bigger tub where some of the other ones would take and wash 'em. You see, they'd wash 'em in two waters. Your Grandmommie Brittie used to be one of the ones to do this. After they'd wash 'em, they had different ones that would pack the clams. Some would put the juice in the cans and other ones would put the clams in. Then this other fellar, a Mr. Howard, would fix the lids on. I believe after he did this they even cooked 'em some more. One thing about it, they must of been good and done by the time they got through with 'em.

"They'd ship 'em different places, you see. The people around here and different places would provide the clams for 'em. I reckon they went out of business in 1920. They moved out and went to Sea Level and then down to Florida."

In addition to the buildings of the clam factory itself, there were other buildings used as a hunting lodge and boardinghouse. According to Miss Lillian, dances were also held there. "They used to have a place down there for people to dance. I went to it one time, but not while I was single. Wouldn't do that. Wilson carried me after me and him was married."

Most of Ocracoke's early tourists stayed in boardinghouses such as the one provided by the Doxsees. One of the earliest hotels, however, was the Ocracoke Hotel, which was built in 1885 by a group of mainland businessmen who wanted a place for their families to vacation. The hotel was located near the present Coast Guard Station and was shaped like a cross, with the head fronting Pamlico Sound.

The opening season for the forty-room hotel was so successful that eight rooms were added upstairs and the dining room downstairs was enlarged. It had its best season in 1889.

*The steamer* Hatteras *leaves Washington, North Carolina. This vessel sometimes carried passengers to Ocracoke during the late 1800s and early 1900s. (Courtesy of North Carolina Division of Archives and History)*

Many of the people visiting the Ocracoke Hotel were from Washington, North Carolina, and some were from New Bern. To accommodate them, two steamers, the *Ocracoke* and *Hatteras*, ran regular schedules from both Washington and New Bern.

The hotel's first proprietor was Mose Fowler. A few years later two Spencer brothers operated it. In 1899, George Credle of the Hyde County mainland and his brother Griff Credle of New Bern owned the hotel.

The structure suffered much damage during the hurricane of August 1899, one of Ocracoke's worst. As twenty-five guests huddled in the dining room during the peak of the storm, the roof of the upstairs veranda gave in. Soon after this, though, the wind and water started to drop. Some guests attributed this near miraculous abatement of the storm as the answer to the fervent prayers of one of their number.

The Ocracoke Hotel was destroyed in the spring of 1900. George Credle was cooking a goose and left the pot boiling on the top of a Wilson heater while he went to get some pepper. While he was out, the pot boiled over, starting a fire. The structure was a complete loss.

One Ocracoker who worked at the "old hotel" was "Miss" Sara Ellen Gaskill. A few years before she died (at the age of 104) she told me about her experiences there. "My father was the caretaker for the old hotel one time. He also cooked, and I would help clean the rooms. He stayed there sometimes during the winter when it was closed.

"The old hotel was filled up most of the time during the summer. The rooms were plain. They had a bed, chair, washstand. That was about all. The people ate in the dining room. They ate what was put on the table, mostly seafood.

"There was a horse and cart that would carry people to the beach. They would be dressed up in their pretty bathing suits.

"I got paid three dollars a week. The people tipped me sometimes. They were nice people, money people. I was working at the ole clam factory when the hotel burnt down. I was only nineteen years old."

Around the time that the Ocracoke Hotel burned, another hotel, referred to as the Gus Taylor Hotel or the Taylor House, was in operation. The proprietors were Steve and Augusta Taylor. He was from Washington, North Carolina, and Augusta, or "Gus," was from Ocracoke.

In 1913 the Taylors sold their hotel to Bill Gaskill of Ocracoke. After making some improvements, he reopened and named it the Pamlico Inn. Before he got into the hotel business, Gaskill made part of his living market hunting ducks and geese as well as serving as a hunting and fishing guide.

His son, Thurston Gaskill, has spent most of his life as a hunting and fishing guide as well. Some of Thurston's fondest boyhood memories center around the Pamlico Inn. "My father made perhaps his biggest move when he bought the ole Gus Taylor Hotel. He had to do some work on it, but eventually he opened for business. It had about twenty-five rooms and a central dining room where everybody ate. The rooms were nothing fancy. They were simply furnished with a bed, table, couple of chairs, stuff like that. The dining room could seat about forty people who all ate pretty much the same time if they wanted anything to eat. My mother fixed all the desserts, while some

*Two guests of the Pamlico Inn hold their catch of the day. Captain Bill Gaskill ran the inn for about thirty years. Ten years later it was destroyed beyond repair by the 1944 hurricane. (Courtesy of Thurston Gaskill)*

other local women and men did the main cooking. It was good wholesome food. They might have fish one day, clams the next, or any of a number of seafood dishes.

"We had the best class of people anywhere to stay at the Pamlico Inn. Most of them were from Eastern North Carolina, but a few did come from Virginia and even farther up north. They'd either take the mailboat out of Morehead City or come on the old freight boat from Washington. It was supposed to have been just a splendid trip to arrive on the old *Annie Wahab* from Washington. She was a two-mast schooner run by Captain Cass Williams. She only took about one trip per week. Sometimes it would take much longer than others because they would get becalmed.

"To serve these two boats, my father built a dock from the inn all the way out to the edge of the channel. In those days the Creek was too shallow for bigger boats. People would hop off the boat and be able to walk right up to the hotel. Someone could spend a whole week at the inn for fifteen dollars, and that included room and board.

"I was thirteen years old when my father sent me out with my first fishing party. He also had a guide service set up at the inn. Anyway, I remember going out in a twenty-five-foot, flat-bottomed boat that had a three-horsepower Palmer engine in it. I would carry people in the channels and sloughs only a few miles from shore. We only got about five dollars per day for a party. In the modern times I get around one hundred dollars per day and just about can't live on that."

An explosion and fire destroyed the fuel tanks and dock at the Pamlico Inn during the early 1930s. A few years later, in 1935, Bill Gaskill died. His wife and son David ran the inn until it was damaged beyond repair by the hurricane of 1944. "At about the time the inn was destroyed," recalled Thurston, "I was in the Navy and couldn't help out too much. After I got out of the Navy, I started to build up my own fishing and hunting guide business. I also bought the *Southwind*. She was over thirty years old, but I still used her to carry fishing parties out in the inlet and channels of Pamlico Sound.

"I have met some of the finest people in the world in this business. I've also found that it's been a pleasure to serve no less than 98 percent of them. Some of my customers have been coming back for forty years.

"When I think about it, I guess I'm just part of the island machinery for serving tourists. People come down here to hunt and fish, that's where I come in. When they come down here, they've got to have a place to stay and eat, and that's where the motels and restaurants make their money. We each depend on the other.

"I often think about the old Pamlico Inn, and that if a place such as that were in operation today here on Ocracoke it would probably be a big success. I also think that people would really like the idea of a common dining room as well as a central lounge. It would be nice to have a place where people could get together and talk about their experiences of the day, of the big one that got away, the goose they missed, and so forth."

Other Ocracokers gradually began to realize the economic advan-

*When he was twenty years old, Charlie Williams converted this Model T into a flat-bed truck and used it to take fishermen to the beach for surf fishing. (Courtesy of Charlie Williams)*

tages of tourism. Charlie and James Williams, two elderly brothers who rent cottages near the lighthouse, got a taste of the business when they were growing up in the 1920s. They used to help their father when he guided hunting and fishing parties. Eventually some of the regular parties became interested in having a place to stay, and this led to the cottages. "When we were growing up," recalled Charlie, "Papa and us had this camp down below by Molasses Creek. We used to take hunters and fishing parties out. Boy I loved doing this stuff. I wanted to stay in the sound all the time. I even had me a little fish house along the shore and Papa had built me a little skiff about twelve feet long.

"One summer this fellar said he'd like to come down to hunt and stay part of the winter with us. We told him he could, but I didn't expect to see him. Come that winter and he showed up. He had got Frazier Peele from Hatteras to lash two flat-bottomed skiffs together to carry his ole six standard Buick across Hatteras Inlet. Well, keeping with my word, I packed an ole featherbed mattress and different stuff I thought I'd need and set out for the camp.

"We hunted down there for nearly two months. It was a mild winter and we'd hunt on the bad days and fish off the beach during the good ones. We caught nineteen channel bass the week before Christmas. I believe it was during the winter of 1929 and 1930. The fellar's name was Theodore Dewey, some of ole Admiral Dewey's relatives.

"We carried hunting and fishing parties before and after World War II. This fellar Dewey had the idea about coming down and staying with us for periods of time, and I reckon other parties begin to get the same idea. They'd usually stay at the Pamlico Inn. So, after the war was over, I decided to fix 'em a little place to sleep and store their stuff, and James's wife would do the cooking for 'em. Before long they tuned up for me to fix 'em a place to do their own cooking. I eventually got around to this and made some other changes to make the places more comfortable.

"I started losing my eyesight in 1950 and couldn't fish and hunt like I had been doing. I figured that I'd better fix the two cottages so they'd rent year around. When I first started, I was just renting to hunters and fishermen, but this was mainly in the fall and winter. After the cottages were fixed up, I started renting them in the summer also. This was more income and I needed it because I really couldn't do much else, being blind.

"I can still see a little, mostly things real white or dark. I haven't let it stop me. I try to live as if I'm twenty years old and had twenty-twenty vision. I try to get out on the water as much as I can. Sometimes I go out fishing with my guests, and I tell them how to get around the shoals and stuff.

"When James moved back home for good, he started into the fishing business again. We were one of the first ones around here that started the surf fishing. James had an old truck that we used to carry people to the beach in. These fellars that wrote for the sport's section of the *Winston-Salem Journal* used to come down and go with us. I remember one night there were three of them and they caught sixty-two channel bass off the beach. We also carried Len Dole, who used to play the part of 'Mr. District Attorney' on the radio.

"I think we had a different class of people to come down and stay with us back then. They were the sportin' class. They weren't afraid to spend money either. Nothing for 'em to give you a twenty-dollar tip, and of course that was good money in those days.

"We now have people to come down from all over the country and even overseas. One thing that we like is that they talk to us and tell us about the rest of the world. A lot of our people have been coming back over the years.

"I got into renting these cottages because I had to do something here. I just didn't want to leave Ocracoke. James he left and worked up in New Jersey for a while. I think he sort of liked it, but not for me." There were periods in Ocracoke's history when jobs were scarce, and many Ocracokers, like James Williams, had to leave home to work elsewhere. The most recent period of migration occurred before tourism developed into the major industry it is today, or roughly between the end of World War II and the 1970s.

"I've never lived anywhere else but here," continued Charlie. "I've been through many hard times here and done without a lot of things that I might have had if I'd left and worked somewhere else, but I just didn't want to leave. I've never made a dollar away from Ocracoke, and I don't regret it either."

Ocracoke men returning home from World War II and the Korean War found economic opportunities lacking, especially opportunities to support their new families. This situation prompted them to leave home once again to search for work. Many men, including my father, went to the large port cities of the North to work on dredges and other ships.

My father worked for twenty-five years on a 476-foot Army Corps of Engineers sea-going hopper dredge. The *Goethals* dredged the channels and harbors of the major port cities along the East and Gulf coasts. Six months before he retired (the *Goethals* was also to be decommissioned after forty-four years of service), I spent Christmas with him aboard the ship, which was tied up in New York City for the holidays.

A skeleton crew was keeping watch over the vessel. One of these men was Joffre Bryant, who had grown up on Ocracoke as part of the island's only black family. His sisters and brother, Mildred, Musa, and Julius Bryant, were still living there.

Sitting in my father's cabin that first evening of my visit, with the sounds of the Hudson River lapping the vessel and continuous clangings throughout the whole ship, Joffre, my father, and I talked about home. "I haven't been home in twenty years," said Joffre. "I do miss it occasionally. I fished, crabbed, and oystered like the rest when I was there. I also worked in one of the stores on the island and ran on a freight boat to Washington.

"I never did want to go back. You stay away so long that you tend to forget it. You get adjusted to a different way of life. I don't know most of the people there now."

Although my father offered on many occasions to take Joffre home with him, he never accepted. My father came home as often as he could, sometimes driving the eleven-hour trip from New York just for a weekend with us.

On my last day in New York, my father and I were standing on the deck of the Staten Island Ferry, looking over at Manhattan, saying little but obviously thinking of home. Finally he said, "I wouldn't trade Ocracoke for all of it, money and all."

Much growth and development has taken place at Ocracoke since the early days of the few cottages, boardinghouses, and hotels. Of the approximately 600 dwelling units in the village in 1987, about half were cottages or second homes. There were also about 250 motel rooms available for rent.

The construction of the island's first central water system in 1977 made possible a safe, dependable source of water for more motels, restaurants, and cottages. The building boom set off by the introduction of the water system continues today, and this has provided more jobs for local tradesmen.

It is said throughout the village that anyone who wants a job today can have one. Since there are more economic opportunities available than ever before, fewer Ocracokers are having to leave the island to work elsewhere to support their families.

Ronnie O'Neal has made a living for himself and his family by adapting to Ocracoke's growing tourist economy. His decision to get into the charter boat business came after he realized the need for more Ocracokers to take advantage of tourism.

After graduating from Ocracoke School in 1968, he attended college three years before moving back to the island to fish commercially. In 1982 he began converting his 33-foot boat, the *Miss Kathleen*, to accommodate sport fishermen. "That first year I felt a little uncomfortable. I had worked around the public some as a park service lifeguard, but in the beginning I kept wondering what people would think of me, my boat, and what would happen if I didn't catch a lot of fish.

"When I started fishing commercially, I just didn't like to see so many people coming down here. I soon learned after I got into taking fishing parties that ninety-nine percent of the people were coming to Ocracoke for the good fishing and quaintness of the island. Most of 'em want to leave Ocracoke like it is."

His charter boat season runs from the beginning of May to the end of November. During the winter and much of the spring, he continues to fish commercially, and even sets some gill nets during the summer. "I keep nets out during the summer to catch fish for restaurants and to get bait for my parties. I'll get up around 4:30 in the morning, go out and fish my nets, clean most of 'em, then get ready for a party that leaves at 7:30."

Although he has had several mates to help him, he prefers to go alone. "I'm particular about fishing, the way I put the bait on, stuff like that. You've got to study it and be scientific." He plans to start training his son Ryan, who will one day be his full-time mate.

Captain Thurston Gaskill, who ran a fishing and hunting guide business for seventy years, has had a big influence on Ronnie. "My advice to all fishing and hunting guides," explains Thurston, "is to treat all people the same, whether rich, middle class, or poor. There's a limit to how much you can charge people. Be honest with them and give them your best service."

"Thurston has helped me out a lot," said Ronnie. "Somebody like him, who's fished as long as he has, sees and understands things that you or me would miss.

"He'll call me up and tell me something, then he'll say 'Next time I see you I'll give you another tip.' He asked me one day, 'Ronnie, do you think you'll be taking parties for seventy years like I have?' I looked at him and laughed and said I'd be lucky to be alive at seventy."

As I walked onto the deck of the *Governor Edward Hyde* ferry, which would leave the Hyde County mainland for Ocracoke at four o'clock in the afternoon, the events and issues of the day were still much in my mind. Along with the other four Hyde County commissioners, I had listened to complaints and concerns throughout the day from various groups and individuals. The two-and-three-quarter-hour ferry ride back to the island would provide a much-needed time to rethink these issues.

I was elected to the Hyde County Board of Commissioners on November 6, 1984, replacing Irvin Garrish, Ocracoke's first board member, who for health reasons had decided not to run again. Irvin had made history in 1980 by defeating a mainland opponent. With Irvin's election, Ocracoke finally had a voice on the board, ending what Stanley Wahab once called "taxation without representation."

At the time of his election, the county had three commissioners who were elected by all voters in the county. It had been difficult for an Ocracoke resident to compete against a mainland opponent be-cause approximately 5,200 of the county's total population of 6,000 lived on the mainland. Irvin had had to muster enough mainland support to win the election.

Soon after the 1980 election, however, the three commissioners decided that each of the five townships in the county—Currituck, Fairfield, Lake Landing, Ocracoke, and Swan Quarter—should have its own commissioner, with each commissioner living in the district he or she seeks to represent.

By the time the ferry eased away from the ramp, the southwest wind had increased to twenty knots and white caps were springing up further from shore. Although a thunderstorm loomed far in the south, the chances for badly needed rain still weren't promising.

Hyde County is mostly farmland, but while farmland decreased in value and other mainland properties increased an average of only 30 percent, the value of Ocracoke property skyrocketed by an average of 300 percent between the 1979 and 1987 revaluations. Some properties on the island went up in value as much as 1,000 percent.

No issue has awakened Ocracokers more than the sudden increase in property taxes. As a result of the revaluation, many residents are paying two, three, and four times as much in property taxes as they used to. Attempts to find some avenue of relief, especially for our elderly on fixed incomes, have proven unsuccessful. State law requires property to be valued at "fair market value," which is what a willing seller and buyer can agree upon.

Residents are concerned that more and more property will fall into the hands of those able to pay the high prices, leaving out of the picture many of our youth whose families have been rooted here for many years and who want to continue living at Ocracoke themselves.

To help pay for increased taxes and other growing expenses, more and more residents are holding second, third, and even fourth jobs. It's not uncommon to see someone who's a full-time employee with the state or federal government working additional jobs. Sources for extra work include sport or commercial fishing and any of a number of jobs related to the tourist industry.

As we left the Hyde County mainland behind, the wind breezed stronger and the sky darkened. Of the nine cars on the ferry, six were from North Carolina (three from Ocracoke), two from Ohio, and one from Massachusetts. Sitting near me in the passenger lounge were Keith and Kathy Cutler, a young Ocracoke couple who had recently married and were returning to the island from their honeymoon.

Ocracokers often ask, "How's this younger crowd going to be able to live around here?" But some of the same people also add, "They would be able to if their parents and grandparents hadn't sold their land up from 'em." Though life-long residents lament the increasing ownership of Ocracoke property by "off-islanders," they continue to sell to them when the price is right. We were once naive enough to believe that an Ocracoker would sell to another Ocracoker just to keep the land "in the family," but a frequent complaint among the older residents themselves today is that another Ocracoker would rather sell to an "outsider," even while muttering about "that crowd moving in here, buying up the land, and wanting to make the island like the place they left."

Sullivan Garrish once said, "Uriah, you and me have spent our time here. We've seen the best of it. It's the younger ones that are gonna have it hard."

To Captain Thurston Gaskill, however, the future looks brighter. "There are more jobs available today for young people than ever before."

"Young people are going to have to be creative," said Philip Howard, who moved to Ocracoke in 1971 to open a craft shop. "They are going to have to create their own jobs."

At the end of my first year as a teacher at Ocracoke School, I was asked to give the commencement address to the ten seniors of the class of 1983, to give the perspective of someone who had left the island and returned to make his living. I told them that they were entering into the most complicated period in the history of the island and that they would likely find no easy answers for the problems they would encounter.

In earlier times, I said, it was possible to believe that things would work out, that jobs were available for those who wanted to work, and that eventually one could buy some land and a house and settle down. Today, though, it was necessary to plan for the future. And I told them that, to endure, Ocracoke needed their effort and creativity.

I entered the pilot house to visit with the ferry crew, most of whom are Ocracokers. Little was said at first because lightning had been spotted in the southwest and the captain had turned on the radar. The wind breezed stronger and the seas built as the thunderstorm approached. The ferry rolled and shook as she pounded down on the waves. A crew member said, "I've had as much as thirty degrees right rudder on her."

As the mainland disappeared in the haze behind us, the wind reached its peak. There was still no sign of rain, nor had any fallen on Ocracoke, according to radio contact from the port captain there. A trawler approached on our port side with its outriggers spread for balance in the heavy seas. As it passed, the ferry crew identified her as the *Restless Lady*. It was the only fishing boat in sight. A slice of sunlight broke through the clouds to shine on the boat, illuminating the white paint.

As the squall passed and we approached Ocracoke, the wind fell considerably. We spotted a dozen trawlers lying at anchor near the island, waiting for darkness so they could drag for shrimp.

Leaving the pilot house, I descended to the deck where several tourists were standing on the bow feeding the seagulls. As the ferry sliced through Big Foot Slough Channel, I tried to imagine for a moment how I would feel if this were my first trip back to the island after a long time away. Perhaps even one of the tourists near me was experiencing such a return.

Like others who do return after a long absence, I would probably be most concerned about the changes within the village. I would wonder what open spaces had now been developed, what former residences had been torn down or converted to businesses, and which Ocracokers had moved or passed away.

Over the past few years, more and more of our regular tourists have been lamenting the changes that have taken place. Most are expressing serious concern that the island is becoming too much like the rest of the North Carolina coast. A few have vowed never to return; they would rather remember the place as they once knew it.

*In the foreground an old wooden boat lies rotting along the edge of the Creek as the* Governor Edward Hyde *ferry pulls into the dock.*

As my eye scanned the shore of the village from one end to the other, I tried to recall "how it used to be." Like others, I wished some things had not changed, but I have learned to accept and even welcome other changes.

More growth and development has taken place at Ocracoke in recent years than any other period in the island's history. Between 1970 and 1980 the number of year-round residents increased from 541 to 658, while the number of housing units increased from 305 to 471. By 1986 there were 562 housing units in the village, approximately half of which were cottages and summer homes, and 250 motel units.

Although the year-round population of Ocracoke has grown slowly, the number of tourists visiting the island has increased dramatically. The growing popularity of the Cape Hatteras National Seashore, as well as improved roads and ferry service, draws many people who are passing through Ocracoke as part of a tour of the Outer Banks. In the past, most tourists who came to Ocracoke came just to spend time on the island. Most old people associated with accommodating tourists decades ago agree that "we had the best class of people anywhere back then."

As more people visited the island, some of these managed to buy property, either as second homes or retirement homes. The people who move to Ocracoke to live permanently are as varied as the many tourists who come from all over the world. "Many people come to Ocracoke," observes Philip Howard, "to get away from things like a divorce, death in the family, and other problems. Because of this, many don't want to get involved in the community.

"If you don't want to be a part of this community you can certainly alienate yourself. There are people living here now who have lived here all their lives that I've almost never seen. You can be pretty much who you want to be here."

"When someone moves to Ocracoke," adds Al Scarborough, "you think more about why they are here. You feel some affinity for them. You have a feeling of responsibility, especially during times like hurricanes."

Although people have been moving to Ocracoke since the early 1700s, perhaps the largest influx occurred after the central water system was introduced in 1977. "Many of these people were well educated," said Howard, "and they jumped into leadership roles in the community. They didn't mind talking in front of crowds. The Ocra-cokers felt intimidated and backed off."

At the time of this influx, however, one resident observed that little activity was taking place in the civic club and other organizations. The new people in the community were not stepping in to take over anything. They had entered a "vacuum" into which they saw various community needs and wanted to do something about them.

Some Ocracokers, however, began to complain about people who appeared to be "moving in, taking over, trying to change things to resemble places they had left." "Although some things challenged have been good for Ocracoke," said Howard, "it helps to get to know a community before you get so involved. Those who come here and accept people for who they are, are more likely to be accepted."

Adds Dave Frum, "I think that you have to spend a year at Ocracoke just listening before you start inflicting."

According to most Ocracokers, people who move in and respect the place and its people, who try to "live with us rather than make us live like them," come to be accepted as Ocracokers. "I've heard some people say," recalls Elizabeth Howard, "that if you're not born an Ocracoker you'll never be one. I don't feel that way about it. Many people that lived here when I was growing up were not born here. They came to be Ocracokers. I think that it's just something that those that move here sometimes feel."

Ellen Marie Cloud agrees with Elizabeth, adding, "Somebody who had lived here for a short period of time told me that no matter how hard they tried or how long they lived here, they felt they would never be accepted. I don't believe this. Mr. and Mrs. Ronthaler and Selma Spencer were not from here, but they certainly came to be accepted and well respected."

As Ocracoke became more popular as both a tourist resort and retirement community, it was inevitable that growth controls would be needed. Before we had such controls, development within the village was haphazard. Motels, restaurants, and other structures were jammed against property lines, and residents and tourists alike had to park along the sides of the road because businesses had neglected to provide enough parking spaces. A formal zoning ordinance was introduced in 1981, but property owners, who were given a chance to vote on the proposal, rejected it by a two-to-one margin.

A public hearing for another attempt to introduce a controlled growth ordinance was held in April 1986, before a crowd of approximately two hundred residents. Since no opposition to the ordinance was expressed at the meeting, our board of commissioners unani-

*An aerial view of Ocracoke Village from the late 1950s. (Courtesy of Margueritte Boos)*

mously adopted it several months later, giving the village its first development ordinance.

Unlike many zoning ordinances, the Ocracoke ordinance is intended to allow all uses, both commercial and residential, anywhere within the village. Most of the regulations deal with lot size, setback from property lines, a height limitation, and parking requirements. To answer complaints about the earlier proposed ordinance, every effort was made to keep the regulations to a minimum and to present them clearly.

Although most people identify the water system as the biggest change at Ocracoke in recent years, Philip Howard recognizes another, perhaps more significant impact. "The biggest change is in the number of people buying property here, not because they want to live here, but because they see it as a good investment. When you buy here because you want to live here, raise your kids, have a little business, then you have an investment in the community. If, on the other hand, you see Ocracoke as just another way to make money, then your whole attitude is different."

As the ferry turned into Teach's Hole Channel, I stared ashore toward Springer's Point and wondered what the future had in store for our village. We had come a long way since Blackbeard sailed the *Adventure* within these same waters. Our future was not clear, but our determination was. Elizabeth Howard once said that Ocracoke would never be destroyed. "If God had meant for this place to be destroyed, with all the storms we've had, he would have done it a long time ago."

I flew to Ocracoke for the first time in 1978. We were flying from Chapel Hill, coming across Pamlico Sound from the mainland. The Outer Banks appeared below us as a thin strip of sand separating the sea from the sound. Since I was sitting in the back seat, the pilot looked back at me and asked, "Is that it? Is that Ocracoke?" I must have taken about thirty seconds to respond, amazed at how fragile the island looked. How could it have survived for so long? I couldn't help wondering if the early settlers would have been so intent on moving there if they could have seen what I saw now. It must have taken a lot of determination for them to continue living here, and I reckon if we've been here this long, we'll be around for some time to come.

# Afterword

That Saturday afternoon in September was perfect for mullet-ing. Although Bobby and I had planned to go mulleting often during that summer, other things had kept getting in the way. Now, determined to make better use of the new net, we cast out after lunch that day, at first unsure of whether the tide was flowing or ebbing.

We had bought the net, lines, and other material the winter before, but putting it all together had taken much longer than we expected. We had worked on the net during late afternoons and on into the evenings, and we had talked a lot about the catches we would make during the coming summer. When the net was finally completed, though, it had lain unused in the skiff several weeks before we took the first mulleting trip.

We were finally prompted to get the net in the water because Uriah Garrish, who had taught us both about mulleting, had asked us repeatedly over the early part of the summer when we were going to "get her lined and get her in the water." Mulleting was still on his mind even though he was sick and confined to the house, unable to scan the shoals for mullets and participate in the catches that had so long sustained him and his brother Sullivan.

We had caught nothing on the late summer evening when we set the net for the first time. The tide was low and Bobby's five-year-old son, Mark, had been with us. We hadn't gone far from the village because our thoughts were still on unfinished responsibilities ashore.

Our big catch of the year, however, would take place on this Saturday afternoon under a clear blue sky and a light northeast wind. Leaving around noon, we decided to fish on Six Mile Hammock Reef, a place which held many memories of catches made with Uriah and Sullivan.

We had set the net twice and caught about seven hundred pounds. During the last set, which had taken place in an area of Six Mile Hammock Reef where Uriah and Sullivan had gone many times, Bobby, taking out a mullet while handling the lead line as I stood on the stern thwart and handled the cork line, said, "They'd like to be out here with us today."

"Yeah," I responded, saying nothing else but thinking of Uriah and Sullivan. After a long painful winter, Sullivan had died at his home on May 20, 1987. Uriah was never really the same without the brother he had communicated with almost every single day for most of their lives. After Sullivan's death he never got to go mulleting again and generally gave up any attempt to get back on the water.

Uriah's health had begun to decline throughout the year following Sullivan's death. By the summer of 1988 we all knew that his time was limited and that he probably wouldn't live to see the fall. After a visit to the hospital which confirmed his terminal illness, Uriah choose to spend his remaining days at home with his many family members and friends.

My last conversation with him was about recent catches of fish, a shift of wind to the northeast, and particularly mulleting and how Bobby and I were going to "put it to 'em" the next pretty Saturday we had.

When he died at his home on September 1, 1988, the last of the old mullet crew, whose core had consisted of him and his brother Sullivan, had passed on, leaving behind them new generations to live and work in the village spread under the lighthouse and water tower.

As we left Six Mile Hammock Reef that afternoon, our skiff almost loaded with mullets, Bobby called his wife, Donna, on the radio to see if there had been any power problems. As a lineman for the power company, he is more or less on call twenty-four hours a day.

We were pleased with our catch, and as we sped on toward the Creek, I looked back over my shoulder toward Six Mile Hammock Reef, then up at the clear blue sky, and I knew that if Uriah and Sullivan could see us now, they'd be smiling.

# Index